Achieving Sustainable Development

Achieving Sustainable Development considers sustainable development in all its dimensions – ecological, social, economic, and political. Instituting policies on wilderness preservation or pollution prevention alone is not enough to achieve sustainable development. We also have to think through the connections between poverty, gender issues, institutional organization, and decision-making and to address these issues in an integrated way. *Achieving Sustainable Development* does just that, bringing together the work of Canadian scientists and researchers in order to educate the concerned public and to influence key decisionmakers in government, industry, and non-government organizations. The book provides comprehensive, independent, and essential discussion about the actions required not only of various sectors of society but also of individual Canadians to meet the challenges of sustainable development.

Ann Dale is a senior associate of the Sustainable Development Research Institute and chair of the editorial board of its Sustainable Development Series. She is also co-founder of the Canadian Biodiversity Institute.

John B. Robinson is the director of the Sustainable Development Research Institute and a professor in the Department of Geography at the University of British Columbia. He is co-editor of *Managing Natural Resources in British Columbia: Markets, Regulations, and Sustainable Development* (UBC Press 1995) and editor of *Life in 2030: Exploring a Sustainable Future for Canada* (UBC Press 1996).

The Sustainability and the Environment series provides a comprehensive, independent, and critical evaluation of environmental and sustainability issues affecting Canada and the world today.

SUSTAINABILITY
AND THE
ENVIRONMENT

Edited by Ann Dale and John B. Robinson

Achieving Sustainable Development

A Project of the Sustainable Development Research Institute

UBCPress / Vancouver

Printed in Canada on acid-free paper ∞

ISBN 0-7748-0556-0
ISSN 1196-8575 (Sustainability and the Environment)

Canadian Cataloguing in Publication Data

Main entry under title:

Achieving Sustainable Development

   (Sustainability and the Environment, ISSN 1196-8575)
   Includes bibliographical references and index.
   ISBN 0-7748-0556-0

   1. Sustainable development – Canada. 2. Environmental policy – Canada. 3. Sustainable development – International cooperation. I. Dale, Ann, 1948- II. Robinson, John Bridger, 1953- III. Series.

HC120.E5A33 1996   333.7'2'0971   C96-910023-X

UBC Press gratefully acknowledges the ongoing support to its publishing program from the Canada Council, the Province of British Columbia Cultural Services Branch, and the Department of Communications of the Government of Canada.

UBC Press
University of British Columbia
6344 Memorial Road
Vancouver, BC V6T 1Z2
(604) 822-3259
Fax: 1-800-668-0821
E-mail: orders@ubcpress.ubc.ca

Contents

Figures and Tables

Tables

Foreword
Maurice Strong

We live in paradoxical times. At a time when our society is experiencing an information revolution, systemic gaps have developed in how we communicate with one another. These gaps in the timely transfer of knowledge between the academic, industrial, government, and non-government solitudes seriously affect our progress as a nation into the twenty-first century. Yet to move forward in any field requires knowledge about the issues at hand and demands that all stakeholders have a common understanding of the information, that gaps be identified and bridged, and that barriers to action be removed. In order to make a difference, this information must be relevant, timely, accurate, and noticed.

Gaps in our knowledge affect our capacity as a nation to respond to international obligations arising from the United Nations Conference on Environment and Development – the Earth Summit – and our commitments to *Agenda 21*. It is important that these gaps be corrected in order for us to contribute in a meaningful way to public policy decisions and actions leading to sustainable development. Accomplishing this goal will require extensive cooperation, information exchange, and knowledge sharing among all sectors of Canadian society.

In order to meet this need, the Sustainable Development Research Institute of the University of British Columbia plans to publish books in a sustainable development series. Our intention is to stimulate an exchange of information between academic communities, governments, non-government organizations, and industry. We hope to go far beyond simply presenting information by producing policy analysis and specific recommendations in each book. The series will provide comprehensive, independent, and critical discussion about the actions required of various sectors of society and individual Canadians to meet the challenges of sustainable development. As well, we hope to stimulate discussion and debate about existing paradigms and alternative ways of doing business and making decisions.

The goals of this series are threefold: to educate the concerned public about the necessary processes leading to sustainable development; to influence key decisionmakers in government, industry, and non-government organizations by disseminating leading-edge Canadian research; and to publicize Canadian achievements in sustainable development and highlight the work of Canadian scientists and researchers domestically and internationally.

The credibility of *Achieving Sustainable Development* and future volumes depends on their independence from single interests, including governments, private industry, and other groups seen as promoting their own agendas. Polling data consistently confirm that scientists and environmental organizations have the most credibility in explaining environmental issues. We therefore draw on the best Canadian researchers, scientists, and environmentalists as authors.

I am honoured to chair the advisory board for this ground-breaking series. I am assisted by representatives from the government, non-government, scientific, industrial, and public policy communities, which with the editorial board oversaw the conceptualization of the series. The role of the board is to provide strategic direction, to identify overarching issues, and, through its membership, to provide links to other key stakeholders. The editorial board includes the heads of all postsecondary sustainable development research institutes in Canada, as well as the heads of the five major environmental studies and teaching programs. Its role is to propose specific topics and to identify potential authors. The general series editors are responsible for overall coordination and for the accuracy and integrity of the research contributions. We are indebted to the authors of *Achieving Sustainable Development* for their continuing commitment to and enthusiasm for the project in spite of the inevitable delays that occur with any first effort of this sort.

By examining dominant paradigms in this and subsequent volumes, we hope to build common understanding about the nature of the lens through which we see and understand our world and our place on the planet. It is our hope that this series will influence leading decisionmakers by contributing to the production of more useful knowledge about how to achieve sustainable development.

Introduction

The origins of this volume, and the series it introduces, lie in a number of discussions we had in 1993 about four things. The first was the need to move from rhetoric to action in achieving sustainable development. Canada is, of course, internationally renowned for its contributions to global sustainable development, and in 1993 was basking in its leadership at the 1992 Earth Summit in Rio. In particular, Canadian officials were promoting the success of the 'Canadian way' of consensus-building on the basis of processes that were 'open, inclusive and transparent,' and, back home, of the *Green Plan* and the innovative provincial and national round tables.

Nevertheless, it seemed to us that most of this activity reflected the standard Canadian achievement of being very innovative and progressive on issues of process but much less so in integrating substance into process.

Second, it was clear to us that although more research was certainly needed on a whole host of topics, analysts and researchers knew enough about the causes and possible consequences of problems of unsustainability to support strong action in the policy arena. Furthermore, given the interlocutory and interactive effects of most sustainable development issues, incomplete knowledge and imprecise information were inherent to the problematique. Lack of knowledge and the need for further analysis and study were no longer valid reasons for lack of action in many areas.

Third, there was no regular vehicle for conveying the relevant information to the policy community or to interested Canadian citizens. While there was certainly no lack of research, analysis, opinion, and background information on sustainable development issues in Canada, much of it was not in an easily accessible form, nor one that spoke easily to policy issues. The Canadian research community in the sustainable development field was scattered among universities, NGOs, consulting firms, and government agencies, with no obvious means for bringing together relevant information about what could be done to address the problems of ecological and socio-economic unsustainability. There certainly existed no Canadian equivalent of the various publication series of the WorldWatch Institute or the World Resources Institute.

It seemed to us that the research and policy analysis community could make some contribution to these problems by initiating a series of regular publications that brought together the findings of this community in a form accessible to policymakers and the interested public, based on the premise that it was time to move from analysis to action. The focus would thus be deliberately prescriptive, with the goal not of simply describing the problems but of proposing some solutions. We envisaged a series that asked the best researchers and policy analysts in Canada to tell us what could be done to move from rhetoric to action in their field of knowledge.

Further discussion between ourselves and with members of the advisory board and editorial board that we established (see back of book) led us to the concept of a series, with each volume divided into four parts. The first part, called *Visions*, includes papers describing significant Canadian initiatives in articulating visions of some aspect of a sustainable society for Canada. The second, entitled *Connections*, represents an attempt to reach out beyond the field of sustainable development, as conventionally defined. In this section, we address topics, and include authors, from other fields, asking in each case for connections to be drawn to the field of sustainable development. In this way we hope to contribute to a broadening of the field. The third section, *Action*, is the heart of each volume. It contains papers on various sustainable development topics, always with the premise that we know enough to take action. Authors are encouraged to make concrete proposals for action. Finally, a section called *Assessing Progress* provides information on how we are doing and whether we are getting closer to or farther from our sustainable development goals.

The *Visions* section of *Achieving Sustainable Development* contains two papers, the first of which describes the results of one attempt to articulate the outlines of what a sustainable society might look like in Canada in the year 2030 if we made significant attempts to base our decisions and behaviour between now and then on principles of ecological and socio-political sustainability. (These results and the background to the project are described in more detail in a companion book to this one, published by UBC Press and entitled *Life in 2030: Exploring a Sustainable Society for Canada.*) The second paper, written by Barry Sadler, explores sustainability strategies as a policy tool for nations and communities to express their visions for a sustainable society and their means of achieving them. He describes national strategies for sustainable development from a number of countries, including the background to and some of the experiences of Canada's green planning initiatives at the federal, provincial, and local levels, including the innovative Projet de société.

The *Connections* section has one paper, by Ted Schrecker, on issues related to growth, competitiveness, poverty, and distribution. While we violated our goals for this section somewhat in that the author is no stranger to the sustainable development community, the issues he discusses, as he points out, have been rather neglected in the environmental and sustainable development discussion in Canada, as elsewhere in the North America. He argues forcefully that until these issues are faced head on, we are unlikely to make much headway in achieving sustainable development.

The *Action* section contains six papers. The first, by Ann Dale and Stuart Hill, addresses biodiversity issues in the context of decision-making for sustainable development. It suggests that meaningful solutions for biodiversity conservation will be found in the 'untidy' multi-stakeholder and interdisciplinary interface between the academic, public policy, and non-government communities. In the following chapter, Ray Côté and Thomas Plunkett suggest that the relatively new concept of industrial ecology has much to recommend it as a framework for policy decisions regarding industrial location and design. They identify the elements of a strategic framework for Canada and discuss preliminary findings of a current case study in a Nova Scotia industrial park. The paper leads naturally into George Francis and Sally Lerner's chapter on institutional transformation. There, the authors suggest that simply changing the substance of policy without also making fairly fundamental changes in the institutional context within which that policy is generated and implemented is unlikely to be successful, a point also made in some detail in *Managing Natural Resources in British Columbia* (UBC Press 1995).

Returning to some of the themes introduced by Ted Schrecker, Bonnie Kettel tackles the issues of poverty and sustainable development, arguing that gender bias in policy-making, in Canada as well as elsewhere, is a primary cause of both the increasing feminization of poverty and the international feminization of environmental degradation. Given the very strong gender-related dimensions to poverty, Bonnie Kettel's arguments overlap with those of Marilyn MacDonald, who turns the spotlight onto women's issues. Dr. MacDonald points out the big gap between the rhetoric of *Agenda 21* and the actual practice in Canada, one of the countries that might be expected to take an active lead in this, as in other areas of sustainable development. Finally, the focus moves north, and Fikret Berkes and Helen Fast describe some very similar problems as they apply to the aboriginal peoples of the Hudson Bay region, pointing out some possibilities for making better use of the socio-cultural resources and traditional environmental knowledge in aboriginal communities.

The final section, *Assessing Progress*, contains a chapter by Tony Hodge, who has been working on the issue of indicators of sustainability for the National Round Table and the federal State of the Environment office. Dr. Hodge argues that before producing quantitative indicators it is crucial to articulate their purpose and the role they will play. He proposes a conceptual framework for indicators, which we expect to guide our future chapters in this section of each volume.

If there is any common theme to the papers in this volume, other than the shared view that action now is both warranted and possible, it is that we need to consider sustainable development in all its dimensions, including a mix of ecological, social, economic, and political imperatives. Achieving sustainable development does not just mean instituting policies on wilderness preservation or pollution prevention. It also means thinking through the connections between poverty, gender issues, institutional organization, and decision-making, and it means taking actions that address all of these issues in an integrated way. The good news is that even though the issues are complex, indeed much more complex than was generally understood when these topics were seen as separate issues, there is nevertheless a solid basis in this country for immediate action. While understanding the full ramifications of all these dimensions of sustainable development will require ongoing research, this need not prevent us from taking steps in the meantime. It is our hope that the papers in this volume help to show us how we can begin to do this.

Visions

1
Life in 2030:
The Sustainable Society Project
John B. Robinson, Caroline Van Bers, and Deanna McLeod

Environmental problems pose important questions not only about scientific knowledge and technological change but also about the social and political organization of our society and how these affect and are affected by global change. As we move into the twenty-first century, sustainable and environmentally friendly patterns of socio-economic development and resource use are an essential priority for Canadians. One approach to sustainable development research is to construct and evaluate scenarios of future societies that function according to the goals of sustainability. To achieve such a vision of the future we need to ask in what ways each sector of society might change by 2030 if Canadians made a serious commitment to sustainability.

This chapter describes the results of a five-year project that attempted to answer that question and explored the prospects for developing a Canadian society that is sustainable environmentally, socially, economically, and politically. By creating a detailed scenario, or evolving picture, of what a sustainable society might look like, the Sustainable Society Project (SSP) traced the path of Canadian culture, institutions, and industry from the present to a more sustainable fictional future. Assumptions were made about how Canada might evolve from 1990 to 2030 in order to conform to certain sustainability principles and design guidelines. Forty years was considered sufficient time for the complete turnover of capital stocks, the generation of new structural relationships in the economy, and the development of new institutional relationships in the political system.

Computer simulation of these factors allowed investigators to comment on the feasibility and implications of this vision, providing a basis for the discussion of alternative futures. The technique used – called backcasting – does not involve prediction; instead, simulation of desired future conditions is used to review various possibilities and what the path would be to reach them.

Theoretical Approach

A sustainable society has socio-political as well as environmental and technological implications. The challenge in examining alternative futures is to analyze these implications in a way that integrates all dimensions. Moreover, the human and technological dimensions of a socio-economic system are dynamically interrelated; socio-political structures are reflected in technological and economic development and vice versa.

This project was based on the view that science and technology are deeply value laden and that the relationship between technology and social organization and the one between science and decision-making need to be closely examined. The result is an openly normative approach to the assessment of technology and social organization, an approach represented by the links we made between technological development, social change, and sustainability values and by the development of a method to express and evaluate different values and views of preferred futures. The purpose of the assessment was not to determine the right course of action, however, but to propose both a preferred alternative to current policy – which is explicitly grounded in a set of values – and a means by which others could propose and assess their own views and preferences.

The values forming the normative basis for the project are a version of those associated with the concepts of 'sustainable society' or 'sustainable development' (Brown 1981; Clark and Munn 1986). They imply a critical, or even radical, approach to technological and social development (Robinson et al. 1990). In order to assess the implications of these values and to implement the normative approach described above, it was necessary to use an analytical method that departs from the predictive and ostensibly value-free orientation typical of most studies of the future. The 'backcasting' technique of scenario analysis (Robinson 1988) employed involves defining goals, articulating them in terms of preferred future states of the system being analyzed, and then attempting to construct a path of technological and social development between the present and the desired end. The goal is to assess the feasibility and impact of normatively defined futures. In so doing, the analysis serves as a kind of consistency and feasibility check on values from which the normatively defined futures are constructed.

Project Method

The general approach of the project was to articulate sustainability values, to derive environmental-ecological and socio-economic design criteria based on these values, to develop a qualitative picture of Canada in 2030 consistent with these criteria, to construct a quantitative scenario in a modelling system intended to describe a path between 1990 and 2030, and to analyze the implications, feasibility, and implementation requirements of that scenario. The implications for longer term policies that would be associated with successful implementation of the project scenario, and changes in individual and organizational behaviour, are discussed in a book on the project (Robinson et al. 1996).

The computer software used for the SSP was designed to allow the simulation of alternative futures by modelling aspects of the Canadian socio-economic system. The Socio-Economic Resource Framework (SERF), developed at Statistics Canada, is based on the design approach to socio-economic modelling (Gault et al. 1987). It is intended to examine the physical feasibility of alternative policy goals over thirty-five to seventy years and is thus particularly suited for backcasting analyses.

The SERF model analyzed relationships and characteristics of over 1,700 multidimensional variables based on an extensive Statistics Canada database. This computer analysis described energy, labour, and material flows in four major sectors: demography; the various consumption sectors such as housing, education, health care, and consumer goods; natural resources; and manufacturing. Based on sustainability values and principles, smaller, more specific scenarios of individual subject areas were developed, and design criteria developed by the researchers were integrated into an overall scenario.

The computer model then added up and compared the activities and assumptions in all sectors, and identified discrepancies between supply and demand for labour, services, goods, and materials. Areas of social, economic, or physical unsustainability were identified by the computer and on the basis of these inconsistencies, the specific assumptions entered were re-evaluated in order to mitigate problems. The researchers had the computer repeat as many attempts at developing such scenarios as were required to produce a reasonably consistent picture that conformed to the project's initial design criteria and then assessed the feasibility, implications, and implementation requirements of that scenario. Meanwhile, the socio-political analysis involved investigation of the changing institutional relationships and political structures that might be expected to accompany the technological and economic developments described in the computer-generated output.

The simulation process was begun by the demography sub-model, which calculated future population levels based on the input assumptions made by researchers. These numbers were then used to drive a set of consumption calculators – housing, consumer durables, health care, education, transportation, offices, and so on – to determine the level and type of goods and services required. Each of these consumption calculators, of course, contained many additional input assumptions that determined the kind and quantity of goods and services required. The required goods were then 'produced' in the manufacturing calculator, which was constrained by the availability of resources from the five resource sector calculators: energy, mining, forestry, agriculture, and fishing, hunting, and trapping.

Based on the calculations and simulation, an integrated scenario of one alternative for life in 2030 was produced. The following discussion describes this scenario by outlining, from the perspective of 2030, the main changes that have occurred over the preceding forty years. These results are not predictions and no effort is made to address the likelihood of this scenario. Rather, the scenario represents a possible future, one that might result if Canada made a determined effort to become as sustainable as possible using the most environmentally benign technology either available or under development in 1990. The scenario described is deliberately abstracted from economic issues; the implicit assumption here is that all of what follows is economically viable, given factors such as the level of economic activity, a reduced work week, and reduced consumption.

The values, principles, and design criteria for a sustainable Canadian society that were developed at the beginning of the project can be summarized under these categories: basic value principles, key characteristics of sustainability, principles of environmental-ecological sustainability, and principles of socio-political sustainability derived from both environmental-ecological constraints and socio-political criteria. The basic value principles were as follows:

- The continued existence of the natural world is inherently good. The natural world and its component life forms, and the ability of the natural world to regenerate itself through its own natural evolution, have intrinsic value.
- Cultural sustainability depends on the ability of a society to claim the loyalty of its adherents through the propagation of a set of values that

are acceptable to the populace and through the provision of socio-political institutions that make the realization of those values possible.

The key characteristics of sustainability were as follows:

• Sustainability is a normative ethical principle. It has both necessary and desirable characteristics. Because opinions may differ over desirability, there is no single version of a sustainable society.
• Both environmental-ecological and socio-political sustainability are required for a sustainable society.
• No one can or wants to guarantee the persistence of any particular system. We want to preserve the capacity for the system to change. Thus sustainability is never achieved once and for all but only approached. It is a process, not a state. It will often be easier to identify unsustainability than sustainability.

The principles of environmental-ecological sustainability were as follows:

• Life support systems must be protected. This requires decontamination of air, water, and soil and reduction in waste flows.
• Biotic diversity must be protected and enhanced.
• The integrity of ecosystems must be maintained or enhanced through careful management of soils and nutrient cycles, and rehabilitative measures for badly degraded ecosystems must be developed and implemented.
• Preventive and adaptive strategies for responding to the threat of global change are needed.

The principles of socio-political sustainability derived from environmental-ecological constraints were as follows:

• The physical scale of human activity must be kept below the total carrying capacity of the planetary biosphere.
• We must recognize the environmental costs of human activities and develop methods to minimize energy and material use per unit of economic activity, reduce noxious emissions, and permit the decontamination and rehabilitation of degraded ecosystems.
• Socio-political and economic equity must be ensured in the transition to a more sustainable society.
• Environmental concerns need to be incorporated more directly and extensively into the political decision-making process, through such mechanisms as improved environmental assessment and an environmental bill of rights.
• Increased public involvement is needed in the development, interpretation, and implementation of sustainability concepts.

- Political activity must be linked more directly to actual environmental experience through allocation of political power to more environmentally meaningful jurisdictions and the promotion of greater local and regional self-reliance.

Finally, the principles of socio-political sustainability derived from socio-political criteria were as follows:

- A sustainable society requires an open, accessible political process that puts effective decision-making power at the level of government closest to the situation and lives of the people affected by a decision.
- All persons should have freedom from extreme want and from vulnerability to economic coercion as well as the positive ability to participate creatively and directly in the political and economic system.
- At least a minimum level of equality and social justice should exist, including equality of opportunity to realize one's full human potential, recourse to an open and just legal system, freedom from political repression, access to high quality education, effective access to information, and freedom of religion, speech, and assembly.

These principles were converted into scenario design criteria and used both to derive the quantitative inputs to the computer model and to evaluate the results of the computer analysis. The derivation of those principles and design criteria, and the Sustainable Society Project itself, are described in detail elsewhere (Robinson et al. 1996). Here we focus only on the results of the analysis. The analysis assumes that sustainability values and principles have become firmly rooted in Canadian society.

Life in 2030

Personal Consumption and Living Arrangements

In the year 2030, Canada is representative of many countries around the world that are aspiring to sustainability, and Canadian society is one of the leading examples of the type of cultural change required to ensure sustainability. Significant changes in consumption behaviour, industrial structure, economic activity, governance structures, and environmental policy have combined to produce a country quite different from what might have been expected in the last decade of the twentieth century.

The levels and types of personal consumption and living arrangements that have become popular form one area of change. Increasingly, people live in housing complexes that offer the opportunity for sharing appliances, vehicles, and some services such as laundry and, to some extent, meals. The increase in shared space in such 'co-housing' units has caused a steady rise in the number of dwellings more efficient in energy and materials. As well, landscaping of residential areas routinely relies on native vegetation, requiring almost no watering or chemicals and contributing to energy conservation by reducing the exposure of · houses to both heat and cold. Canadians in 2030 are finding it natural to stress wise use of resources, durability, self-reliance, conviviality, and non-material pleasures in their housing choices as elsewhere. Ease of maintenance, energy and water efficiency, good design, and quality of work are highly valued.

Increased recognition of the environmental and social costs of suburban commuter-style living (sewage treatment, road construction, land use losses, and resource use and disposal, for example), reinforced by the internalization of such costs in the price of single-family homes and of travel, have led to greater urban densification. As a result, suburban land has been reclaimed for new urban nodes and urban sprawl has almost come to a halt. No new suburbs are being created around major urban centres. Instead, the conversion of suburban housing tracts to denser co-housing and row housing with their own employment bases, urban amenities, and transit lines is well under way. About 25 per cent of Canadians live in rural areas and the rest in small urban centres – what used to be the suburbs. These centres are for the most part complete communities in terms of employment, services, residences, and so on.

In general, purchases of many types of consumer goods have declined because they are frequently rented or borrowed from neighbourhood centres, or shared among family and friends. Polls have recently revealed a strong sense of 'less is better' when it comes to individual ownership of non-essential products, though people are still interested in enjoying their use. Rental and shared use are seen as key to wise personal budgeting as well as to reducing energy consumption.

Appliances are now much more efficient than in 1990; half of the stoves and clothes dryers and two-thirds of the hot water heaters are powered by natural gas, and appliance durability and therefore average lifetime have also increased. Consumption of household furnishings such as furniture, floor coverings, and fixtures have decreased somewhat because people prefer dwellings that are easier and less expensive to maintain, and in general have become accustomed to smaller living spaces and increased use of common areas. Purchases of recreational equipment such as electronic video and audio equipment have remained at late twentieth-century levels. These changes reflect a growing preference for simplicity in recreation and sport. Consumer goods are routinely designed to use fewer materials and less packaging and to be recyclable when they no longer function. The decrease in dwelling size per person has also led to a decrease in the consumption of non-durable and semi-durable goods such as cleaning products, light bulbs, and much of the paraphernalia of householding. The increased durability of many of these items has also contributed to reduced consumer demand.

Greater concern about efficiency, durability, and related values has not come at the expense of basic material comforts. Canadian lifestyles continue to be the envy of much of the rest of the world. Moreover, the shift to a less wasteful ethic and style of life has brought with it significant advantages, ranging from better made, more durable goods to improved quality of life from a cleaner and less stressed physical environment. Perhaps most important, rethinking 'consumerist' patterns of life has led to a general interest in less material sources of satisfaction, including community activities and the informal economy. This in turn has helped to renew interest in questions of equity and distributive justice.

Communications

Technological change has not slowed in the sustainable society described here. The 'information revolution' of the late twentieth century has continued. One manifestation is the presence in all homes of what have come to be called 'superboxes.' These superboxes combine all of the telecommunications technologies of the late twentieth century in one unit. They serve as combined fax machines, telephones, video-phones, televisions, and personal computers, and have other functions as well. They have powerful interactive capabilities that allow users to transmit and receive information, news, literature, mail, and entertainment in video, text, and voice form. This in turn allows various forms of telecommuting and teleshopping, thus reducing the need to travel.

The Canadian media provide comprehensive coverage of sustainability concerns from the local to the global level. In response to public demand this year, there have been a number of television programs and newspaper series detailing the progress finally being made in the transfer of 'clean' technologies to less industrialized countries. Advertising support from forward-looking industries who have greened their products, processes, and labour relations is routine.

The communications industry is quite different from that of forty years ago, as attitudes have changed about how broadcasting technology should be used. Broadcasting activities have increased fourfold from the 1990 level and telephone usage has doubled in the same period, although increasingly it does not make sense to talk about these activities separately. Much control of broadcasting is at the community level, with links to news and information from around the world. The goals of publicly funded community broadcasting are to provide education, information about local activities, and networking with other communities and regions and to promote community development. As people take more active roles in controlling their workplaces, communities, and lives, the media and advertisers are seeking other ways to attract audiences. Canadian programs routinely portray sustainable lifestyles as the norm. Governments, industries, unions, and local community groups make use of television both nationally and locally, via cable-linked local channels, to present their concerns and to showcase sustainability success stories from which others can learn. Public libraries circulate videotapes, many produced by citizens' groups, on a variety of 'change for sustainability' topics. Citizen study circles are popular in most communities and make effective use of these information sources.

Labour Force and Participation Rates

With a fertility rate of 1.7, Canada's population stabilized at 30 million in 2000. The unemployment of the 1990s is mitigated to some extent by shared work, a shorter work week, and part-time work. The actual activity of those working and bartering in the unpaid and alternative sectors is also not represented in the unemployment figures.

While labour participation rates have remained high, the average work week in the formal economy is 27.5 hours per week. Canadians increasingly devote part of the working hours of the week to unpaid activities in the informal economy such as community service and childcare. The resultant loss of cash income is partly offset by an increased rate of female participation in the formal economy and by the growth of bartering and payment in kind for many household services. The trade-off between work (and income) and leisure is increasingly made in favour of increased leisure wherever possible. In 2030, people often continue working past the age of sixty-five as the mandatory retirement of the previous century was overturned by the Supreme Court of Canada in 2010. Elders are more involved in and more valued by the community than tended to be the case in urban 1990.

Increasingly people have work, often in small cooperative ventures, that provides a measure of personal satisfaction and is supportive of sustainability. The share of total employment in environmental restoration, research, communication, and education has grown, as has work in social planning and community consultancy. Competitive companies have long since introduced sabbatical leaves, employee decision-making, sustainability policy mission statements, and other practices to improve quality of working life and productivity.

The aim is to ensure a viable, balanced, productive, and self-reliant economy that provides the basic necessities of life for all through a guaranteed annual income (GAI). The GAI was established because the transition to a sustainable society necessarily involved major structural adjustment and it proved to be less costly and more efficient to collapse the income support programs of 1990. It has also been a more effective way of relieving the cycle of perpetual poverty that many unskilled trades workers and seasonal resource industry workers were vulnerable to in 1990.

Childcare patterns have also changed. A parent who stays at home for the first three years is now paid a childcare wage by the government, thereby saving money relative to the state costs of the infrastructure of universal childcare, which many parents still prefer in the first three years. The slightly lower labour force participation rates for both men and women of childbearing age as a result of the childcare wage also helps to keep unemployment figures down.

Education
Education for sustainability is now firmly entrenched in schools, colleges, and universities. Elementary and secondary schools are recognized as centres for developing sustainable society skills. All schools have adopted a 'green school' program, which teaches students how to implement methods by which their school can operate more sustainably. Interactions that foster critical discussion are encouraged and students are given the flexibility to experience both cooperative and self-directed learning relevant to their community and beyond. Beginning in their sixth year of school, students assist in community sustainability projects, in which they develop their organizational and social skills and become familiar with community issues. This component of the educational experience allows students to exchange information and values with a wide variety of cultural groups and age groups in the community.

Teaching methods emphasize a team approach, and each teacher may also have helpers who assist groups of students. Many individuals over the age of sixty-five volunteer to help, for example. There are generally high teacher-to-student ratios, so education is comparatively more labour intensive than it was forty years ago.

College and university students and graduates constitute more than three-quarters of the population. Since education at all levels is now designed to develop Canadians who can engage in informed societal and environmental decision-making, most people have a relatively clear understanding of the types of constraints on human activities required by the imperative to preserve the biosphere. Many people are engaged in lifelong education, so they move in and out of the formal and informal workforce to engage in learning experiences that they need in order to explore personal interests or simply to keep pace with the changing society.

Health
In the healthcare sector, the growing requirements of a rapidly aging population are offset in part by changes in healthcare delivery. Patients hospitalized for treatment of acute problems, for example, are now encouraged to recover at home when it is appropriate, as home care is generally believed to provide the best opportunity for the individual to recuperate successfully. The number of hospital employees per patient, other than doctors and nurses, has increased by 25 per cent between 1990 and 2030, and many of these people are engaged in a variety of home care services as well as some attendance on long-term hospital and hospice patients. In addition, many more visits are made to health professionals practising what was known in 1990 as 'alternative' medicine – massage therapists, chiropractors, naturopaths, and acupuncturists – leading to a significant shift in the composition of the healthcare professions.

The average number of visits to doctors' offices per age group is lower but because the population is aging and visits are now longer, a slight increase in the total number of doctors has been observed. The number of visits to hospitals by all age groups under sixty-five is down and the length of stay is up slightly, reflecting fewer but more serious visits. The reduction in hospital visits is attributed to more leisurely lifestyles and healthier environments, particularly reduced urban air pollution. More nutritious diets, including reduced meat consumption, have also contributed to less demand for medical services. Because people are healthier both mentally and physically the demand for prescription and non-prescription pharmaceutical products has decreased by 25 per cent across all age categories. Canada is almost tobacco free and overall alcohol consumption is declining.

Transportation

Canada's transportation sector in 2030 suits its bioregions. The trend toward complete communities means that people do not need to travel as much as they did in 1990 for work, shopping, and recreation. Green space connects business, residential, and recreational areas. People walk or cycle in and around the urban core. Efficient public transit is seen as a basic social necessity for all and is generally much more comfortable, frequent, and easy to use than in 1990. Long distance travel for recreation and business has decreased since 1990 because full-cost pricing of fuels makes such trips quite costly and more business is conducted electronically through video, telephone, and computer linkages.

In 2030, attitudes toward using automobiles are quite different from those of forty years ago. Seventy per cent of Canadian households have one small electric car, 10 per cent own two electric vehicles, and 20 per cent have no motorized vehicle. In 1990 about the same number of households had one car but the number of two- and three-car families was much higher. There are now two categories of private cars; about 80 per cent are small electric vehicles, ideally suited for urban driving, and the rest are larger (mid-size by 1990 standards), fuel-burning, efficient cars for longer trips. The small electric cars are made primarily of a durable, light-weight plastic. Half are powered by batteries charged from the electrical grid network; the other half are run by hydrogen fuel cells. Taxi transportation has increased 25 per cent since 1990, and taxis are relatively less expensive due to competition. Alcohol-fuelled motor buses account for 60 per cent of urban transit vehicles, electric-powered trolley cars and light rail transit for 15 per cent each, and heavier rail transit such as subways for 10 per cent. There has been a modest shift from air travel to rail and bus, as these latter modes have become more pleasant and efficient and people have more time.

Arts and Recreation

Community theatre and cinema groups are popular in 2030 and enable regions to share experiences through electronic exchange. The number of theatres and cinemas has increased by 15 per cent. Educational programs focusing on music, art, and other cultural services, such as those found in local museums, have doubled in the last forty years. The shorter average work week allows more participation in these leisure activities. Non-profit organizations staffed mostly by volunteers have increased substantially. The number of religious organizations has remained constant, though people explore paths to a meaningful spiritual life through an even greater variety of organizations. The recreational use of parks and playgrounds has increased by 50 per cent because more people have access to open natural areas and other green space within a short distance from their homes. Community trails within and around urban areas are popular for walking and cycling.

Recreation in 2030 is varied and much of it is community based. This is partly because of the high expense of travel but also because of increased involvement in one's own bioregion. There is, however, strong interest in exploring the culture and landscape of one's own and nearby regions, with simplicity and minimum expense. Thus small country inns, hostels, and restaurants have proliferated, as have picnic facilities. Luxury hotels have been largely replaced with inexpensive, comfortable accommodation though a few upscale hotels have been maintained. Domestic demand for such facilities declined steeply when tax-exempt business travel and entertainment stopped in 2002.

Economy

As a whole, the Canadian economy has continued its structural shift in the direction of more services relative to manufacturing and resource production. While the resource sectors have also changed significantly in composition, such a compositional shift has not occurred in the manufacturing sector to any great degree. Manufacturing industries have, however, become much more efficient in use of materials, energy, and labour over the last forty years. On average, labour requirements per unit output have continued their historical trend and decreased about 50 per cent; capital stock per unit of output has, on average, decreased 25 per cent. These changes reflect better efficiency in use of inputs, including increased automation.

The move toward agricultural sustainability began as people became more aware of the impact from conventional agriculture. The transition to more sustainable, mid-sized systems of farming was by no means rapid. A gradual alteration was recommended to allow farmers, farm economies, and agro-ecosystems to adjust. The introduction of, or return to, natural pest control techniques and nutrient cycling has eliminated dependency on the synthetic chemicals of the twentieth century, and the use of appropriate technology has replaced energy-intensive high technology in the farm system. Wind, solar, and biomass energy are the main sources of power for the farm. The use of appropriate land preparation techniques – tillage, irrigation, and nutrient management practices – has reduced soil erosion significantly and protects soil quality. The volume of wastes generated is kept to a minimum to reduce the impact on biotic systems. These systems are flexible; farm methods are adapted to local ecological conditions and on-farm inputs are substituted for external inputs to the greatest extent possible.

By 1995, Canada's inland stocks of native fish species and its east and west coast ocean commercial fish stock had been depleted to below regeneration capacity. An international agreement to prevent continued severe depletion of commercial fish stocks was reached in 1997. Similar agreements were reached for large inland lakes in the prairies and Northwest Territories, in part due to the emergence of aboriginal self-government. Beginning in 1993 on the east coast, commercial harvesting was reduced to allow fish stocks to regenerate. The establishment of ecosystem management strategies, especially in the Great Lakes, and a steady decline in the practice of stocking inland waters with introduced fish species allowed native species to re-establish themselves in aquatic ecosystems, although sport fishing had to be heavily restricted. In 2030, harvesting capacity still remains 10 per cent below the 1990 capacity. On average, stock capacity is 10 per cent lower but harvesting rates are more flexible than they were in 1990 to respond to ecological indicators.

In 2030, having acted upon the principle of sustainable forest yield, Canada is harvesting 50 per cent less forest than in 1990. Increased timber processing within Canada has reduced the number of raw logs exported and increased employment. New technology and stricter practices have made the forestry industry more environmentally benign. The labour required per unit of production overall in the forestry industry has increased by 30 per cent since 1990 because of the importance placed on rehabilitation and the return to selective cutting rather than clearcutting. As a result, capital expenses to harvest a tree are 25 per cent less than in 1990. Roundwood processing capacity has decreased. Pulp and paper production has decreased 50 per cent from 1990, initially because of recycling efforts in the 1990s and later, by 2015, because a large portion of the print media had been replaced by electronic media. Building waste is no longer automatically destined for the landfill since buildings are dismantled in a way that allows materials such as lumber to be reprocessed and reused. Large tracts of forest no longer supply a few large sawmills operating in northern Canada. Instead, smaller woodlots are managed sustainably throughout the country and supply more and smaller local mills. The lumber needs for retrofitting existing housing stock and new construction are supplied mostly from these local operations.

Mining processes have changed moderately since 1990, although employment has dropped 20 per cent in this sector because of lower capacity and higher productivity. The concept of cradle-to-grave responsibility has been incorporated into the planning and development of mining activities: from exploration to rehabilitation of mining sites and from use of materials to collection of used equipment and scrap metals for reuse or recycling. The infrastructure required for mining is different for gold, iron, base metals, asbestos, gypsum, salt, and sand and gravel from that of forty years ago. Labour productivity has steadily increased due to 'smart' technology and a managerial style that considers employee satisfaction and self-fulfilment.

By 2030, total energy use in Canada has dropped dramatically. Much of the fuel used in 2030 is more environmentally benign than the fuels used in 1990 and is produced using renewable energy sources. Specifically, petroleum use has dropped by 40 per cent, coal use by 50 per cent, and electrical demand by 37 per cent while the use of cleaner burning natural gas has remained nearly constant. In response, energy supply patterns have changed significantly. Increased efficiency in all sectors has substantially reduced energy use per unit activity, and internalization of environmental costs into energy prices has caused a move away from non-renewable forms of energy, such as oil, gas, and coal, to several renewable sources of energy. With continuing technological advances, these became economically competitive with conventional sources by the turn of the century. These two changes have caused a decline in conventional energy sources and the emergence of strong new industries that either produce new, renewable forms of energy or sell energy efficiency services.

Two new industries in particular are connected with the new energy sources. First, a biomass-based alcohol fuel industry has arisen. The industry has two sources of feedstock: efficient use of forest and mill wastes, crop residues, and municipal wastes; and high-yield plantations of hybrid poplars grown entirely on abandoned farmland and unimproved land. These plantations represent an agricultural use of forest resources, growing crops of trees and harvesting them on an eight- to ten-year rotation.

Second, advances in the 1990s in thin-film technologies led to significant reductions in the cost of electricity from photovoltaic cells, which became fully competitive with utility electricity production from other sources just after 2000. This in turn opened the door to the economic production of hydrogen fuel from electrolysis on a large scale.

Cost-effective electricity and hydrogen from solar energy became available as battery and hydrogen storage technologies improved. Advances in wind turbine design over the last several decades of the last century have also continued into the new century, lowering costs and increasing reliability of wind power systems.

Governance

Far from being a static sustainable political culture, Canada in 2030 is a country of creative tension, with an informed and politically active public determined to maintain a balance between private initiative and environmental requirements. Increased participatory democracy is reflected in political decision-making in 2030. Canada is now organized somewhat differently with respect to political jurisdiction. Pressure for recognition of cultural and aboriginal differences, combined with a push to more localized and decentralized decision-making, has devolved powers to the various regions of Canada. Nevertheless, environmental concerns have provoked greater recognition of the need for coordinated strategies and strong common standards on issues like greenhouse gas emissions, use of toxic chemicals, waste management, and the sustainability of resource development.

Detailed political management of cultural and environmental matters is even more decentralized than it was in 1990 but the common legal framework of environmental and cultural rights is stronger. Increasingly, management responsibility devolves beyond the provincial level to smaller regions and communities. An innovative form of contract system has been developed whereby larger political units expressly delegate management power to smaller jurisdictions in return for legally binding agreements on basic environmental and cultural rights and responsibilities at the individual and community levels. This allows Canadian citizens to involve themselves more directly in political issues related to environmental management and cultural development, at smaller levels of jurisdiction that are better attuned to immediate ecological experience and boundaries.

To establish binding agreements requires definition of basic environmental and cultural rights and responsibilities. A process of public consultation at the national level, linked to international negotiations, has been established through which environmental strategies, programs, and goals can be proposed, debated, and decided upon. Such targets then become the basis of the agreements with lower levels of jurisdiction in exchange for delegation of cultural and environmental management authority. This process has been the primary means to integrate environmental decision-making into economic and social decision-making at the national level, a development intimately connected with changes in the legal and economic context of decision-making.

Increasingly, national politics is limited to the collection and disbursement of government revenue; the macro-economic management of the economy; the management of international relations; and the development of common national standards, rights, and responsibilities in the economic, environmental, health, and cultural spheres. Detailed management of resources is increasingly left to lower levels of jurisdiction or to the marketplace. Although this management is constrained by the agreements and standards mentioned above, it represents a real increase in local authority since the responsibility for determining how to meet the standards and targets has led to a burst of creative policy-making and entrepreneurship at the local level.

The widespread implementation of effluent charges designed to internalize the impact of pollution has increased prices for many goods and services, although revenues generated by the charges have offset tax revenue requirements to some extent. The political will to enact such measures was encouraged by public recognition that incurring such costs in the present was necessary to avoid even greater environmental costs in the future.

The changes described here have been accommodated without major reorganization of national and provincial politics. Canada is still a parliamentary democracy, but parties are now elected through proportional representation at both the federal and provincial levels, and the authority of the provinces has declined relative to smaller jurisdictions. In contrast to western Europe in the 1990s, green politics has tended to be internalized within the existing parties. The political spectrum as a whole, however, has shifted toward a conscious recognition of the need to respect certain environmental limits and to incorporate new approaches to economic and social decision-making. The main differences among parties concern ways to respect these limits and implement these approaches, ranging from the more market-based and biophysically oriented policies of the Progressive Conservationists to the more community-based and socially oriented proposals of the Green Democratic Party.

More change is visible at regional and local levels as increased decentralization and binding agreements have both given more power to and placed more constraints on the political process. Innovative approaches to monitoring and enforcing national and provincial standards, often based more on local involvement and political, legal, and economic incentives than on top-down regulation, have provided the impetus to behave in a more environmentally benign and culturally sustainable manner. As already demonstrated before 1990 at the provincial level, the devolution of powers to communities has led to more intercommunity bargaining, as each community attempts to balance its resources and capabilities in relation to other communities.

By 2030 the legal system has become an important means of aiding the transition to a sustainable society in Canada. There now exists a powerful, constitutionally entrenched environmental bill of rights, which guarantees each citizen the right to a healthy environment and requires the government to ensure its continuation through targets, standards, and regulations. The bill is a major legal enforcement tool for national, provincial, and local governments. It also provides the legal basis for citizen action by providing the right to sue public bodies if standards are not met. Fewer common-law restrictions on standing and class action suits mean that the threat of citizen action cannot be ignored by industry or government. A number of judgments in both lower courts and the Supreme Court of Canada have considered definitions of the terms 'sustainability' and 'healthy environment.'

Conclusion

The sustainable society scenario described in this chapter represents a very different future for Canada from the one that would result from an extension of current trends. It shows a future in which significant changes have moved Canada in the direction of sustainable society values and principles. Of course, not all these changes would be considered desirable, even by those who might agree with the values behind them. The intent of the Sustainable Society Project was not to describe the best or most sustainable future for Canada but to provide a detailed picture of one possible sustainable society scenario consistent with an explicit set of values, technologically feasible, and internally consistent with respect to social change and the flows of labour, materials, and energy. To our knowledge, no other such detailed scenario has been prepared for any country, and it is our belief that if we want to achieve any version of a sustainable society we need alternatives to conventional business-as-usual views of the future.

The Sustainable Society Project was an attempt to tie together some of the diverse threads of the environmental arguments that have developed from the conserver society tradition in Canada. In so doing, it applied a set of methodological approaches and principles that have emerged out of the same tradition. It was, in fact, the perceived need to develop methods of examining unconventional futures that led environmentalists and soft energy analysts to develop backcasting approaches and Statistics Canada researchers to develop the SERF modelling system used in our analysis. The Sustainable Society Project combined these methodological and substantive approaches in an integrated analysis. The results tell us something about the physical consistency and socio-economic dimensions of one particular scenario or storyline of a sustainable society in Canada. Important questions remain about how to incorporate biophysical and macro-economic relationships into such an analysis and how to devise more accessible modelling tools that lend themselves better to interactive learning with various audiences.

It is clear that this project can provide only a preliminary assessment of the feasibility and impact of a sustainable future for Canada. In the process, however, it can contribute to the ongoing debate about such futures. Of course, no futures analysis of the type proposed here can be definitive or exhaustive. At best it can reveal the rough outlines of a desirable future and suggest that such a future seems feasible and therefore worth striving for. This does not mean that the analysis, and analysts, have no role in the political debate about desirable futures. It does mean, however, that futures analysis should not be substituted for decision-making. The role of futures study is to explore possible futures and to indicate their apparent feasibility and implications. The rest must be left, as it should be, to the political process.

References

Brown, L. 1981. *Building a Sustainable Society*. New York: Norton

Clark, W., and R.E. Munn, eds. 1986. *Ecologically Sustainable Development of the Biosphere*. New York: Cambridge University Press

Gault, F., K.E. Hamilton, R.B. Hoffman, and B.C. McInnis. 1987. The Design Approach to Socio-Economic Forecasting. *Futures* 19 (1):3-25

Robinson, J.B. 1988. Unlearning and Backcasting: Rethinking Some of the Questions We Ask about the Future. *Technological Forecasting and Social Change* 33 (4):325-38

Robinson, J.B., G. Francis, R. Legge, and S. Lerner. 1990. Defining a Sustainable Society: Values, Principles and Definitions. *Alternatives: Perspectives on Society, Technology and Environment* 17, 2 (August):36-46. Sustainable Society Project, Working paper no. 1, University of Waterloo, Ontario

Further Reading

Sustainable Society Project Working Papers

Biggs, D. 1993. Exploring a Future Sustainable Energy Scenario for Canada between 1990 and 2030. May. Sustainable Society Project, Working paper no. 6, University of Waterloo, Ontario

Biggs, D., D. McFarlane, L. Kalbfleisch, C. Van Bers, S. Lerner, and J. Robinson. 1992. Canada in 2030: The Sustainability Scenario. October. Sustainable Society Project, Working paper no. 5, University of Waterloo, Ontario

Lerner, S. 1991. Socio-Political Design Criteria for a Sustainable Canadian Society. Sustainable Society Project, Working paper no. 3, University of Waterloo, Ontario

McFarlane, D. 1993. Health Care in Transition: Working Our Way towards a Healthier Future Canadian Society in 2030. October. Sustainable Society Project, Working paper no. 8, University of Waterloo, Ontario

Robinson, J.B., G. Francis, R. Legge, and S. Lerner. 1990. Defining a Sustainable Society: Values, Principles and Definitions. *Alternatives: Perspectives on Society, Technology and Environment* 17, 2 (August):36-46. Sustainable Society Project, Working paper no. 1, University of Waterloo, Ontario

Robinson, J.B., G. Francis, and S. Lerner. 1990. Canada as a Sustainable Society: Environmental and Socio-Political Dimensions. July. Sustainable Society Project, Working paper no. 4, University of Waterloo, Ontario

Slocombe, D.S., and C. Van Bers. 1992. Ecological Design Criteria for a Sustainable Canadian Society. *The Environmentalist* 12 (4):243-54. Sustainable Society Project, Working paper no. 2, University of Waterloo, Ontario

Van Bers, C., and J.B. Robinson. 1993. Farming in 2031: A Scenario of Sustainable Agriculture in Canada. *Journal of Sustainable Agriculture* 4 (1):41-65. Sustainable Society Project, Working paper no. 7, University of Waterloo, Ontario

Other Sources

Robinson, J.B. Forthcoming. Exploring a Sustainable Future for Canada. In *Global Environmental Risk*, edited by J. Kasperson and R. Kasperson. Tokyo: UNU Press

Robinson, J.B., and C. Van Bers. 1991. Exploring a Sustainable Future for Canada: The Next Step in the Conserver Society Discussion. In *Studies for the 21st Century: Proceedings of the Second International Meeting on 21st Century Studies, Washington, DC, July 17-21 1989*. Vol. 2, *National Studies – America*, edited by M. Garrett, G. Barney, J. Hommel, and K. Barney. Paris: UNESCO

Robinson, J.B., et al. 1996. *Life in 2030: Exploring a Sustainable Future for Canada.* Vancouver: UBC Press

2
Sustainability Strategies and Green Planning: Recent Canadian and International Experience
Barry Sadler

The closing years of the twentieth century are a hinge of history and perhaps its end, although not in the way envisaged by Fukuyama (1992). In his essay on the end of history, Fukuyama charts the triumph of capitalism and democracy as the only viable system of political economy. Yet the path toward economic modernity, to use Fukuyama's words, is also one of 'accumulation without end.' The course of progress, which brings enormous benefits, at least to some, carries fundamental contradictions in a greenhouse world of ozone windows and vanishing species. Sustainability is the defining theme of our time, and the question of how to achieve it became of pressing enough importance for 120 heads of state and several thousand other people to attend the 1992 United Nations Conference on Environment and Development (UNCED) at Rio de Janeiro.

All roads of sustainability thinking run through Rio, whether referentially, deferentially, or dismissively in relation to its activities and results. Whatever view is taken of the Earth Summit, it represents an international consensus on steps and measures for moving toward sustainable development. Integrated environment and development decision-making is a major theme of *Agenda 21*, the multifaceted program of global action adopted at UNCED. The agenda identifies preparation of national sustainable development strategies (NSDSs) and plans as a priority for countries and international organizations. Yet translating words into concrete policy and action will test the mettle of most countries, and Canada is no exception.

In this chapter, a critical review is undertaken of Canadian and international experience with sustainability strategies and related initiatives. An assessment is made of recent progress and problems on this front with a view to identifying the prospects for developing more effective approaches to green planning. The discussion is organized into four parts: the rationale for and approaches to green planning; international trends and case examples of the preparation of NSDSs; equivalent activities in Canada at all levels of government; and lessons and recommendations for moving ahead.

Green Planning and the Sustainability Agenda

Green planning is a shorthand description for the preparation of sustainability strategies and equivalent processes. These initiatives are a relatively new addition to the public policy tool kit, although they reflect a long planning tradition. In Canada, the tradition dates back at least as far as the Commission on Conservation, established in 1909, and the reports of Thomas Adams, which Richardson (1989) notes would not be out of place in the current sustainability debate. Today, sectoral and spatial planning systems are institutionalized at all levels of government in Canada. Many of these are or could become important processes for promoting components of sustainable development. Regional land use planning, resource management, and environmental impact assessment (EIA) are leading examples. Yet these processes are limited in their scope of application and often fall short of realizing their potential because of the absence of an integrated policy context (Sadler 1985, 1990, 1994).

As their name implies, sustainability strategies are meant to provide such a framework by linking together economic, environmental, and social objectives previously pursued separately by government agencies. This integrative approach is urgently needed to focus the sustainability agenda and is enormously difficult to accomplish in practice. Sustainable development has become a deceptively familiar term. There is general agreement on broad definitions and principles of sustainable development, for example, as introduced by the World Commission on Environment and Development (WCED 1987). Nevertheless, sustainability concepts continue to elude precise specification despite a major effort by policy analysts and others to nail them down. Often, the Brundtland version of sustainable development proves to be what Colby (1990) calls a 'pseudo-political consensus': it tends to break down quickly along conventional lines when specific policy issues are at stake or when strategies and action plans are drafted.

Sustainability Revisited: A Prologue to Planning

Seven considerations are outlined here as a prologue to and rationale for green planning.

First, consider why action is necessary. Nothing less than the future of the planet hangs in the balance. Human activity and numbers are altering natural systems and processes on a global scale and at unprecedented rates. Well-documented effects include loss of biological and cultural diversity, thinning of stratospheric ozone, climate change, and acid rain. In many regions of the world, cumulative deterioration of the resource base is resulting in social and economic instability. The fundamental concern is that we are transgressing, perhaps irreversibly, critical thresholds, and threatening the very habitability of the earth (Brown et al. 1987, 1994).

Second, consider the source of these threats. Environmental deterioration is rooted in exponential population and economic growth. It is the cost of production and overconsumption in industrial countries and the price of poverty and overpopulation in much of the developing world. So-called 'throughput growth,' the accelerating transformation of natural resources into waste residuals, presents an increasing problem in a crowded world where ecological limits loom (Daly and Cobb 1989). Yet radically changing the course of our development trajectory, now widely called for, remains out of the question as long as political priority is given to economic growth, whether to meet rising expectations or to feed new mouths, or both. These contradictions carry profound consequences in a world where the population is expected to double during the next forty years and where it is estimated that 40 per cent of net primary production on land is already appropriated by human activity (Ehrlich and Ehrlich 1990).

Third, consider just how much has changed and in how little time in Canada. At Confederation the western interior was still largely wilderness, with countless free-roaming buffalo herds. Now, only remnants survive in national parks (Ogilvie 1979). Until quite recently, the Arctic was remote and pristine; today, it is said to be at an environmental crossroads, with toxic contaminants accumulating in food chains and in the tissue of marine animals on which indigenous peoples still rely for 'country food' (Pfirman, Crane, and deFur 1993). Despite current growth and prosperity, or perhaps because of it, the economic, environmental, and social aspects of sustainability are reportedly on 'a collision course' in British Columbia, and many of the most productive areas continue to deteriorate (BCRTEE 1992).

Fourth, consider that we live in a greenhouse world. This term is used both as a climatic reality and as a metaphor of global interdependence (Elkington 1992). On both counts, sustainability is dependent on the weakest link in the ecological-economic chain. A 'common future,' as described by the WCED (1987), means just that: there is no escape from the global cycles and processes that link the atmosphere and oceans and regulate the earth's climate and life support systems. Nor will a lifeboat ethic work in the face of the future tidal waves of people it is predicted will flee poverty or environmental breakdown (MacNeill, Winsemius, and Yakushiji 1991). In this context, tackling the pressing issues of world poverty is a matter of self-interest as well as an humanitarian obligation; the tests of intergenerational and intragenerational equity coincide (Sadler 1995).

Fifth, consider the risks of continuing down the present path of development. This represents nothing less than a biological, physical, and chemical experiment on planetary systems and processes (Schneider 1989), a calculated gamble in which the stakes are high. Of course, people interpret the risks differently depending on their values, interests, and world views. Accordingly, it may help to illustrate the consequences of alternative responses to the present situation. Table 2.1 and Figures 2.1 and 2.2 identify the differing pay-offs associated with switching from 'business as usual' to precautionary policies and shows how risk varies according to whether ecocentric pessimists or technocentric optimists are right or wrong in their evaluations about the true state of the world (see Costanza 1989).

Sixth, consider the implications for future generations, for our children and theirs, if the more pessimistic risk scenarios in Table 2.1 come to pass. The Brundtland test of sustainability is intergenerational equity: passing on to the next generation a resource endowment at least equivalent to the one we inherited from the previous generation. By many counts – an increasing preponderance of degraded lands, contaminated waters, acidified soils, extinct species, threatened ecosystems, and the future threat of massive movements of impoverished people and consequent social, economic, and political instability – we are failing this test, nationally and internationally. For the first time, young people in Canada have lower economic expectations than their parents. Theirs is a mortgaged future, a bequest threatened by fiscal and ecological deficits (Sadler 1995).

Last, consider how a sustainable future might be secured. It involves the reconciliation of three 'pillars of sustainability': (1) living within global biophysical carrying capacity; (2) providing a decent living standard for all people; and (3) ensuring a reasonable measure of distributional fairness in access to resources and their economic benefits

Table 2.1

Pay-off matrix for business as usual versus transitional policy options based on the worst possible case

Policy option	State of the world		Corresponding world view
	Optimistic view (borne out)	Pessimistic view (borne out)	
Development as usual	High pay-off (maximum economic benefits)	Disaster (irreversible environmental damage)	Technocentric: hope for the best; scientific and technocentric fixes will circumvent environmental limits (Figure 2.1)
Transition to sustainability	Moderate pay-off (economic gain unnecessarily forgone)	Tolerable pay-off	Ecocentric: expect the unexpected and prepare for the worst; impact of throughput growth is transgressing critical thresholds (Figure 2.1)

Note: In the jargon of game theory, we should choose the 'maximin' strategy if we are unsure of the outcome. Here this would mean opting for a prudent or precautionary policy. The 'transition to sustainability' is preferable because the worst possible result (tolerable) is better than the worst pay-off under 'development as usual' (disaster). Moreover, as Figure 2.2 shows, we may be able to achieve far more than tolerability with a new, more sustainable development pathway; for example, per capita income could increase with a shift in emphasis from qualitative to quantitative forms of production (i.e., accelerating the transition from smokestack to microchip economy).

Source: Adapted from Costanza (1989, 4)

Figure 2.1

'Throughput' economic growth and carrying capacity (CC)

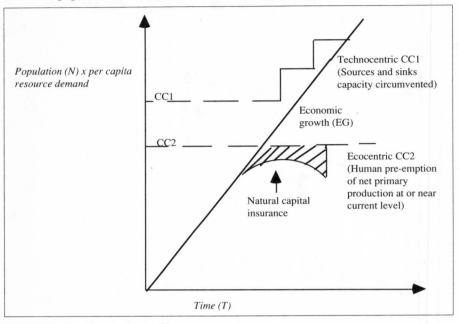

Source: Adapted from Sadler (1995)

(Robinson 1994). To these ends, sustainability will require significant changes in public policy and governance, in the structure of the economy (essentially moving away from 'throughput growth'), and in personal attitudes and values that ultimately circumscribe the 'politics of consumption' (Sadler 1992a). A true sustainability strategy should address the ecological, economic, and ethical imperatives above on each of these levels and take account of their global dimensions. This prologue provides a normative perspective from which to review trends and developments in strategy-making and to gauge progress. Less restrictive, empirical criteria are introduced below, consistent with the political-institutional realities under which planning operates.

Strategy Aims and Approaches
The macro-issues of population and economic growth and resource and environmental deterioration, referred to above, cannot be dealt with by traditional sectoral policy and planning frameworks and piecemeal reactive controls. Strategic approaches, by definition, recognize the need

Figure 2.2

Sustainable economic development and carrying capacity

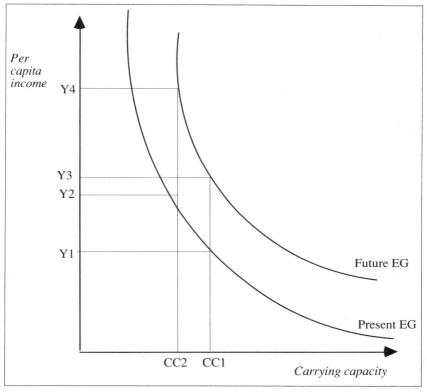

Source: Adapted from Sadler (1995)

to develop a broader, forward-looking perspective and to address in an integrated way issues that apply across sectors (INGP 1994a). A national strategy or plan is the generic term used to describe the framework and processes for giving the highest level of policy force and expression to sustainable development. National sustainable development strategies, simply stated, are guides to and catalysts for a country's efforts to secure a common future.

In the first instance, this often involves integrating environmental considerations into national social and economic development policy-making. Nearly one hundred countries are reported to have embarked on NSDSs along these lines (Carew-Reid 1993). There are also numerous local, regional, and thematic variants. As a collective, societal goal, sustainable development requires thinking globally, planning bioregionally, and acting locally, and using different strategies at each level. The main planning models used to prepare national strategies are listed in Figure 2.3. Early versions include national conservation strategies, national environmental action plans, and other green plans. Each not only has its own aims and approaches but also has principles and procedures that reflect their policy and institutional basis.

Figure 2.3

Examples of national sustainable development strategies and equivalent plans and reports

- National conservation strategies: based on the *World Conservation Strategy* (IUCN, WWF, and UNEP 1980), widely applied by industrial and developing countries
- National environmental action plans: required by the World Bank as a condition for investment and donor assistance to developing countries
- National tropical forestry action plans: multisectoral forest policy and management programs promoted by the UN Food and Agricultural Organization (FAO)
- National reports on sustainable development: descriptive overviews of policy and institutional trends and initiatives produced for UNCED, and updates for the UN Commission on Sustainable Development on progress in implementing *Agenda 21*
- *Capacity 21:* United Nations Development Programme framework to assist developing countries to implement *Agenda 21* and develop sustainability policies and plans
- Green plans and national environmental policy plans: comprehensive government action programs for environment-economy integration, with long-term objectives and commitments

NSDSs are defined by several key dimensions: a forum and context for dialogue on sustainability, including the guiding visions and values; a framework and process for identifying major issues and priorities; a mechanism for focusing policy and research to address these; an approach to building capacity and strengthening institutional arrangements for implementing agreed upon actions (IUCN 1993). A major impetus to the preparation of NSDSs was given by UNCED. Governments and international organizations are called upon to adopt *Agenda 21* and subsequently to report on follow-up to the UN Commission on Sustainable Development. National strategies, plans, and policies are identified as the main instruments for implementing commitments consistent with the capacities, circumstances, and political culture of each country. Broad guidance on the preparation of an NSDS is outlined in Chapter 8 of *Agenda 21,* which deals with the integration of environment and development decision-making:

Governments, in cooperation, where appropriate, with international organizations, should adopt a national strategy for sustainable development based on, inter alia, the implementation of decisions taken at the Conference, particularly in respect of Agenda 21. This strategy should build upon and harmonize the various sectoral economic, social and environmental policies and plans that are operating in the country. The experience gained through existing planning exercises such as national reports for the Conference, national conservation strategies and environment action plans should be fully used and incorporated into a country-driven sustainable development strategy. Its goals should be to ensure socially responsible economic development while protecting the resource base and the environment for the benefit of future generations. It should be developed through the widest possible participation. It should be a thorough assessment of the current situation and initiatives.

The general approach proposed in *Agenda 21* differs from conventional planning in several notable respects:
- It has an all-encompassing scope. National strategies should build upon and harmonize economic, social, and environmental policies and plans.
- It advocates a participatory process. Strategies should be developed through the 'widest possible' public involvement.
- It is based on assessment. Strategies require a thorough examination of the current situation.
- It is driven by issues. Strategies should be responsive to domestic priorities but can also be assessed by reference to the themes and issues contained in *Agenda 21.*
- It is built from experience. Strategies should utilize the lessons of previous planning experience.

The fundamental challenge is one of policy and institutional integration, recognizing that previous experience provides only partial and incomplete guidance to that end. *Agenda 21* itself is a massive and not especially well-organized document that deals with: economic and social trends, such as health, settlement, trade, and debt; implementing international agreements for protecting the global commons; reconsidering the role of science, technology, and education in achieving sustainability; and strengthening the information base and policy tools for environment and development decision-making and resource management. The implication is that all of these issues are to be encompassed within a single, comprehensive NSDS. Such an approach could soon become unwieldy and founder. Alternatively, an NSDS might be designed as a 'policy chapeau,' linked to and executed through a series of other plans and instruments.

At a minimum, the thrust of an NSDS should establish a concrete response to the political commitments made at Rio. To be sure, many critical matters were left unsaid at UNCED, notably about population and consumption (Figure 2.4). Much of *Agenda 21*, too, is unexceptional; as a negotiated document it represents the lowest common denominator rather than the leading edge of thinking about sustainable development (Holmberg and Timberlake 1993). Whatever criticisms one might have of the document, however, starting to implement it would end what the reconvened World Commission on Environment and Development calls the 'era of procrastination and half measures' and begin 'inescapable actions' (WCED 1992). These are the policy paths down which countries and international organizations must start in order to halt environmental deterioration and initiate the transition to sustainability.

More radically, NSDSs could be prepared as greenprints for the long-term societal transformation that many policy analysts argue is necessary to secure a common future (e.g., Milbraith 1989). This challenge involves, among other things, identifying the fundamental character of a sustainable society, specifying the guiding values and principles, and developing the ecological and socio-political design criteria for making proposed changes (see Robinson et al. 1990; Lerner 1991; Slocombe and Van Bers 1992). Within such an idealized framework, the Brundtland levers of policy, investment, and technology could be deployed to common purpose. A sustainable society, according to Meadows, Meadows, and Randers (1992), is technically possible. Except for war and disaster, however, there are few precedents for embarking on the level of coordination and intervention necessary.

Of course, sustainability strategies are not meant to return to the type of centralized, prescriptive planning that is now discredited (INGP 1994a). This would stand little chance of success. Rather, a flexible

Figure 2.4

Tallying the Rio ledger

Criticisms
- The Earth Summit did not live up to the objectives and expectations set by the UNCED secretariat.
- Key issues were not discussed, notably population and consumption, nor were linkages identified, such as those between aid, trade, and debt reduction.
- The poorest countries gained least.
- *Agenda 21* was pedestrian, bureaucratic, and contained no new ideas on sustainable development.
- No agreement was reached on new funding necessary to place developing countries on a sustainable footing.

Positive aspects
- Sustainable development was placed at the heart of the international political agenda.
- The conventions and principles represent an important, new superstructure of agreements and basic principles.
- *Agenda 21* is both an affirmation of commitment and a program of *action*.
- The process itself was transforming, affecting everyone who participated.
- For the first time, NGOs played an important role in international negotiations.
- Taken together, these developments constitute a lever on the future, through which NGOs and others can monitor government commitment and accountability.

---

approach is needed, based on a broad vision and policy options that recognize sustainability as an evolving target with many value dimensions and backed by monitoring, feedback, and adaptation (Robinson et al. 1990). At the same time, sustainability strategies must also focus on priorities, 'no regrets' actions (which deliver both environmental and economic benefits), and immediate, practical steps that begin the change of course necessary. These include, for example, wringing eco-efficiencies from the existing industrial processes to smooth the path toward new, low-impact technologies (Schmidheiny 1992; Hawken 1993).

International Experience with Sustainability Strategies

Several reviews of international experience with sustainability strategies have been undertaken. These include a guide to the preparation of NSDSs and a subsequent update on issues and dilemmas (Carew-Reid et al. 1994; Dalal-Clayton et al. 1994). Other basic sources of information are the workshop papers and discussions at the Organisation for Economic Cooperation and Development review (OECD 1993) of national plans for sustainable development and background materials prepared for the inaugural meeting of the International Network of Green Planners (INGP 1994a,b,c,d,e).

A number of key issues run through this initial round of analysis, centring on the evolving relationship of NSDSs to policy-making and instruments for implementation. In question is whether NSDSs are really breaking new ground and what their impact is or will be on decisions and actions. Such questions form criteria for examining the effectiveness of NSDSs. It must nonetheless be emphasized that NSDSs are at a relatively early stage of development. Much of the emphasis in evaluations of experience to date is on the process rather than the substance of green planning.

With few exceptions, the thrust of NSDSs is toward the implementation of *Agenda 21* rather than preparation of greenprints for societal transformation. In practice, strategy-making takes a number of directions. As might be expected, there are major differences between the NSDSs undertaken in developing countries and those in industrial countries. The transitional economies of central and eastern Europe represent a special case.

Developing Countries

In developing countries, NSDS preparation tends to be driven by the requirements of donors or initiated by international agencies. Most of the processes underway in Africa, Asia, and Latin America are based on either national conservation strategies or national environmental action plans. This reflects reality, and, in principle, has a number of potential benefits (Winpenny and Tanden 1993). Where appropriately designed, NSDSs can and should have an important capacity-building component, helping to strengthen institutions and competencies for dealing with environmental, social, and economic problems. As such, they can also provide the framework under which the supporting donor agencies can and should target projects and coordinate their activities. For the poorer countries, in particular, there may be no practical alternative to using multilateral or bilateral mechanisms to launch their NSDS processes. In some cases, there has been considerable effort to encourage a participatory, capacity-building exercise, as in Malawi and Pakistan.

Preliminary experience, however, also indicates a number of problems in this regard (see OECD 1993; IUCN 1993; Dalal-Clayton et al. 1994). At present, for example, thirty-three African countries have either completed or are drafting national environmental action plans. Many have also prepared national conservation strategies, and now the United Nations Development Programme is exploring the possibility of national agendas under the framework of *Capacity 21*. The multiplicity of approaches evidently results in duplication and inefficiencies on a continent where resources are slim at best. There is the danger of sustainability strategies becoming a pro forma rather than a problem-solving exercise, undertaken to satisfy the reporting requirements of international and donor organizations. This risk appears to be increased where outside consultants are employed to prepare NSDSs. Often, donor requirements result in a rushed approach with little opportunity for local participation and capacity building.

Tanzania provides an example. A national conservation strategy (NCS) process was initiated in 1988, renamed after UNCED as the *National Conservation Strategy for Sustainable Development* (NCSSD) and approved by the Tanzanian National Environment and Management Council (NEMC) in 1994. The process was conducted at a central level, with little public consultation, to produce a framework for integrating development and conservation. In parallel, the Ministry of Tourism, Natural Resources and Environment (MTNRE) was developing a national environmental policy, with sector-specific documents on land, tourism, population, forests, wildlife, agriculture, and water. Work also began in 1993, with support from the United Nations Development Programme (UNDP), on a national plan for *Agenda 21*. This was drawn up by MTNRE based on the proceedings of a national workshop. No process to take the plan forward is in place.

From 1992 onwards, the World Bank had argued the need for the NCSSD to include an environmental action plan as a prerequisite for receiving concessionary (i.e., interest-free) funds from the International Development Association (called the IDA-10 replenishment). Concerned over the slow progress of the NCSSD, the Bank pressed for the various policy and strategy documents to be consolidated into a national environmental action plan (NEAP). This was completed in June 1994 to meet a deadline imposed by the Bank. As a result there is now an approved NEAP document that has little or no institutional ownership and no apparent continuity beyond the World Bank's deadline date. Other overlapping processes are still ongoing with a profusion of policy drafts and unclear overall roles and relationships (Dalal-Clayton et al. 1994).

Transitional Economies

The transitional economies of central and eastern Europe also face urgent and complex environmental challenges. Widespread ecological deterioration has resulted from poorly controlled industrialization. Estimated costs of clean-up are staggering, well beyond the financial capability of the ex-socialist countries. In 1993, an environmental action program for the region was drawn up within the broad framework of *Agenda 21*. The plan is based on three main points:

(1) integration of environmental concerns into the process of economic restructuring
(2) building institutional capacities through training and education
(3) immediate assistance to regions in which there is a direct threat to human health, to resource productivity, or of irreversible ecosystem damage (Environment for Europe 1993).

On paper, the environmental action program looks promising (Figure 2.5). It constitutes a regional approach to sustainable redevelopment based on resource and ecological rehabilitation. It provides a means of targeting assistance and coordinating the activities of the European Commission, its member states, the World Bank, and other international organizations and financial institutions. This framework identifies common region-wide environmental challenges that must be addressed by all countries in the context of resource scarcity and the difficulties of adjusting to market systems. Convergence on these priorities is intended to reinforce subregional environmental programs (e.g., for the Baltic Sea and the Danube River) and to catalyze the development of national plans (Gillespie 1993).

This regional approach deserves close monitoring. It will be useful, in light of the problems of strategy conditionalities noted above, to see whether the various investment and donor agencies can focus and coordinate their activities. Also of interest is the economic thrust of the plan. It emphasizes both domestic and international investments, environmental restoration, and clean-up, linking immediate 'win-win' measures to improve industrial housekeeping to longer term market reforms that require policy reform and capacity building (Environment for Europe 1993).

Figure 2.5

___

Environmental action program for Central and Eastern Europe

The action program illustrates a range of actions that could be taken to implement a 'three-legged' approach of policy reform, institutional strengthening, and investment. The program provides a framework and guide for identifying the highest priority problems and for developing cost-effective solutions.

Criteria for setting priorities
- damage to human health
- productivity losses caused by damage and destruction of physical capital and natural resources
- deterioration of, or threat of irreversible damage to, biodiversity in general and in particular to wetlands, grasslands, coastal and marine ecosystems, forests, and mountain habitats
- low-cost/high-gain measures to address issues of growing importance in the medium to long term

Major, region-wide environmental challenges
- removing subsidies to energy and other production inputs
- reducing dependence on highly polluting industries
- establishing realistic incentives to encourage less harmful environmental behaviour
- promoting decentralized and participatory approaches to environmental management

___

Sources: Environment for Europe (1993); Gillespie (1993)

Industrial Countries
As noted, industrial countries have had a significant involvement in the development of NSDSs in developing and transitional countries. Because these processes have been linked to international institutional arrangements, they share certain features. Less attention has been paid to date to the experiences of the various OECD member states. The approaches adopted by industrial countries are, by definition, 'self-initiated.' As a result, they are more autonomous and specific to their policy and institutional context. The spectrum of response is exemplified in three levels of NSDS development:
(1) amendments to existing policy for institutional frameworks
(2) a linked series of new initiatives

(3) a comprehensive strategy or plan in draft or final form, often implemented through various elements of (1) and (2).

(1) According to *The Green Planners' Draft Guide,* the United States has to date primarily relied on a mix of amendments to existing policy mechanisms (INGP 1994e). The US Environmental Protection Agency (EPA) is currently undertaking a futures project, however, based on: critical trends assessment; examination of key issues such as urbanization, energy and climate, and biodiversity; comparison of business as usual with desired future scenarios; and identification of key challenges for the agency and the operational responses necessary. In addition the Office of Environmental Policy, the Global Environmental Affairs Office, and the President's Council on Sustainable Development have been established. The Council has the goal, inter alia, of 'formulating specific policy recommendations for a national strategy for sustainable development that can be implemented by the public and private sectors' (White House, Office of the Press Secretary 1993).

(2) Several countries have linked processes that approximate NSDSs or establish an integrated approach to meet Rio commitments. Japan, for example, is drafting a national action plan for implementing *Agenda 21*. In addition, the Japanese government has passed the Basic Environment Law and also intends to establish an environmental plan consistent with the conditions of the Earth Summit (Environment Agency of Japan 1993). A similar approach is being followed in Norway, which has national action plans on biodiversity and climate change, a strategy for environmental education, and the *Green Book,* a unique report on the environmental effects of budget expenditures (INGP 1994e).

(3) Other countries have comprehensive NSDSs and green plans in place. These include Australia, Canada, Denmark, the Netherlands, New Zealand, and the United Kingdom. All of the approaches, to date, focus primarily on the environment; links to the economy are variously developed, and social, or distributional, issues are poorly represented or absent. None of the above examples thus conforms fully to the broad guidelines laid down in *Agenda 21*. They also vary in terms of the range of issues covered, specificity of targets set, and links to other policy instruments and means of implementation.

Case Examples of Industrial Country Strategies

Several countries have prepared NSDSs with clear policy objectives, specific targets, and timeframes for achieving them. These are of interest because they represent the leading edge of strategy-making. In addition, they afford international benchmarks against which Canadian experience, discussed in the next section, may be compared. *Canada's Green Plan,* for example, is often promoted and cited as a 'model' for other countries (Canada 1992). A sober assessment of this claim requires some consideration of other case examples.

By many standards, the Dutch *National Environmental Policy Plan* (NEPP) represents the most far-reaching strategy to date (VROM 1989). Aptly subtitled *To Choose or To Lose,* the strategy was a policy response to a report that documented the cumulative risks to human health and the constraints on development associated with critical pollution and contaminant loadings (RIVM 1988). Unlike so many government statements, the NEPP contains an uncompromising assessment of the severity of environmental problems. It also explicitly recognizes that environmental quality will certainly deteriorate if current policies are followed and that radical measures are unavoidable. The key premises and principles of the plan are shown in Figure 2.6.

The initial NEPP was a medium-term strategy to attain sustainable development within the duration of one generation. It covered the policy priorities and actions necessary from 1988 to 1994 to initiate change and longer term objectives for environmental quality to 2010. It puts forward an integrated strategy for environmental management rather than the traditional sector or media approach dealing with air, water, and so on. The focus is on the interconnection of sources of human activity and their environmental effects at global, continental, fluvial, regional, and local scales. Environmental quality objectives for each scale are set at levels thought necessary to restore carrying capacity and correlated with source- and effect-based approaches.

Over 200 measurable actions, including quantified targets and timeframes, are set out in the NEPP. At all levels, the targets specified involve drastic or sharp emission reductions. The global objectives are consistent with international agreements to include stabilization of CO_2 emissions at their 1989-90 average level by the year 2000 and to phase out ozone-depleting substances. Much more impressive are the proposed reductions of between 70 and 90 per cent for hydrocarbon and heavy metals emissions to attain environmental quality goals at the continental and fluvial levels and equivalent decreases in hazardous waste volumes to cut risks to acceptable levels. These targets are shown in the final column of Table 2.2.

Policy options for achieving necessary reductions are evaluated under three different scenarios:

Figure 2.6

Premises and principles of the Dutch *National Environmental Policy Plan*

- Sustainable development requires that the functions which the environment can supply now or in the future must be maintained as well as possible. The roll-off of environmental problems to other areas, levels of scale, or generations must be prevented. This means that in principle environmental problems must be solved within the frame of one generation (20 to 25 years).
- Countering the roll-off mechanism implies the introduction of controlled feedback mechanisms. In this respect, there is a distinction between feedback at the sources and feedback through risk management. Sustainable development is pursued through feedback at the sources directed at a combination of:
  - *closing substance cycles* in the chain of raw material – production process – product – waste and the associated emissions;
  - *saving of energy* together with increasing efficiency and utilizing renewable energy sources;
  - *quality improvement* (above quantity) of products, production processes, raw materials, waste, and environment in order to prolong the usage of substances in the economic cycle.
- The setting of standards for environmental quality is based on a risk policy. This requires that risk policy does not only focus on the health and well-being of *human beings* but also on *environmental functions* and *nature values*. Separate risk limits will be developed for these three categories.
- Source-oriented measures are to be preferred to effect-oriented ones because the possibility to control is greatest at the source, one source can cause more than one effect, uncertainties about the cause-effect chain can exist, irreversible effects can occur and because it generally costs less to intervene at the source.

  Source-oriented measures can be divided into:
  - emission-oriented measures: add-on technology which reduces emissions and waste steams without changing the processes of production and consumption;
  - volume-oriented measures: legal and organizational measures which reduce the volumes of raw materials and products without changing production and consumption processes as such;
  - structure-oriented measures: structural changes of a technological or other nature which change the processes of production and con-

sumption. (Structural measures will also result in changes in volumes and emissions.)

• Effect-oriented measures are only taken if:
  • environmental quality has already been damaged by past developments or calamities, but the effects can still be mitigated;
  • there are prospects for structure-oriented measures, but they cannot be taken at short notice;
  • effect-oriented measures have significantly lower social costs and do not impede structural measures for other environmental problems.
• Everyone is expected to know his responsibility for the environment and to act accordingly. The large scale at which some environmental problems occur does not reduce this responsibility.

Source: VROM (1989)

(1) continuation of current measures
(2) maximum use of emission-related measures
(3) mix of emission and structural measures (as set out in the key principles of the NEPP).

As shown in Table 2.2, only the last approach, scenario 3, will meet or approximate the objectives set, although the costs are correspondingly higher. Of course, considerable uncertainties are involved in these calculations.

Updated as the *National Environmental Policy Plan Plus,* the second phase focuses on additional and accelerated measures for implementing the strategy (VROM 1990). These include stepping up actions to stabilize CO_2 emissions (e.g., limiting the growth of car traffic and conducting afforestation for carbon sequestering), to limit acidification of woodlands (e.g., more stringent NO_x emission norms for waste incineration), and to decontaminate soil (e.g., where soil pollution constrains urban renewal). Further changes are specified to the instruments for coordinating the NEPP with water, nature, and physical planning and to the mix of regulatory, voluntary, and fiscal incentive arrangements.

Those reacting to the NEPP initially questioned whether the package of instruments employed was, in fact, adequate to internalize environmental costs and alter processes of production and consumption (van Zijst 1993). Legislation backed by penalties and enforcement still provides a backbone of environmental standards, thresholds, and ceilings. As elsewhere, however, 'command and control' approaches are not well

Table 2.2

Percentage changes in 1985 emissions resulting from various sustainability scenarios

| | Results in 2010 | | | |
	Scenario 1 (continuation of current measures)	Scenario 2 (maximum use of emission-related measures)	Scenario 3 (mix of emission and structural measures)	Necessary emission reductions
CO_2	+35	+35	-20 to -30	-20 to -30
SO_2*	-50	-75	-80 to -90	-80 to -90
NO_x*	-10	-60	-70 to -80	-80 to -90
NH_3*	-33	-70	-80	-80 to -90
Hydrocarbons	-20	-50	-70 to -80	-80
CFCs	-100	-100	-100	-100
Discharges to Rhine and North Sea	-50	-75	-75	-75 to -90
Waste dumping	0	-60	-70 to -80	-80 to -90
Noise leading to serious nuisance**	+50	0	-15	-70 to -90
Odour**	+10	-50	-60	-70 to -90

Notes:
* relative to 1980
** Changes for noise and odour refer to per cent changes in numbers of people experiencing nuisance.
Source: VROM (1989)

suited to broadly based implementation of sustainability policy and strategy. Markets and negotiating instruments provide greater flexibility and potential for influencing economic decision-making and behaviour (Sadler 1992b).

Of interest in this regard is the use of covenants for implementing NEPP objectives. Under Dutch civil law, a covenant is a legally binding agreement between one or more government bodies and an industry association or group of companies. It is developed through a cooperative, consensus-building process to conclude a specific commitment for multi-media reduction of environmental emissions, wastes, and impact. Government co-responsibilities are also set out, such that businesses have greater certainty about permits and regulation. The NEPP designates twelve sectors of the economy as 'target groups' for this purpose, including agriculture, transportation, construction, and gas and electricity supply. Some analysts consider the use of covenants as a major breakthrough in changing the culture of environmental policy-making and administration (van Zijst 1993). This instrument is still being developed, however, and some earlier covenants have not stood up in court, either because they deprived third parties of legal rights or because they were inconsistent with existing law.

Environmental organizations have little access to the covenant negotiation process and many remain critical of the scope and pace of NEPP implementation. Their concerns focus on the gap between the objectives established for emission reduction and the estimated results of present policy. By government admission, shortfalls in reaching a number of targets are projected. Environmental policy is depicted by Friends of the Earth (FOE) Netherlands as too cautious and overly focused on technical rather than structural measures and thus, by definition, unable to alter the nature of production and consumption (Buitenkamp, Venner, and Wams 1992).

FOE Netherlands has prepared an alternative action plan for a sustainable Netherlands based on the notion of 'environmental space.' Assessing environmental space involves making rough calculations of per capita global carrying capacity for energy, water, arable land, and other crucial resources and identifying the cuts in current consumption levels in the Netherlands necessary to return to or maintain sustainability by 2010. This global perspective explicitly recognizes the ecological shadow or deficit that industrial nations have built up by appropriating the carrying capacity of developing countries (see Rees 1992). Sustainability is not just about environment-economy integration but about equitable distribution. The policy implications of this goal are funda-mental, challenge traditional notions of trade and sovereignty, and de-pend on cultural and lifestyle changes that add up to what the Netherlands alternative plan calls 'post-materialism' (Buitenkamp, Venner, and Wams 1992).

A related Dutch initiative is the 'eco-cooperation' agreement. This ap-proach is of considerable interest because it links Dutch foreign and trade policy to sustainability strategies domestically and overseas. Eco-cooperation agreements have been signed with Bhutan and Costa Rica, for example, both of which are at the forefront of sustainability initia-tives by developing countries. The mountain kingdom of Bhutan has placed strict capacities and controls on tourism to manage its social and environmental impact, and Costa Rica has undertaken a range of poli-cies and plans to preserve biodiversity, conserve forest and water re-sources, and gain energy efficiencies (Sadler and Hull 1990; Solis 1992).

The Netherlands is a relatively small, intensively settled, and highly industrialized country. With very few exceptions, other countries are neither confronted by such immediate limits to the carrying capacity of their resource base nor so evidently dependent on the annexation of environmental space. In part, this explains why other sustainable strategies are 'paler green' versions of the Dutch NEPP. This is especially the case now that the latest version, NEPP 2, promotes a broad debate regarding sustainable consumption patterns and production processes, including the concept of environmental space (VROM 1994).

Other relatively small, highly industrialized European countries such as Denmark and Great Britain also have comprehensive strategies. The British and Danish documents are both founded on concern about the state of the environment, employ sectoral policy approaches, and in-corporate specific targets for significant emission reductions (Denmark, Ministry of the Environment 1992; United Kingdom, Department of the Environment 1994). As well, the UK strategy builds on white papers and consultation with interest groups and identifies various participa-tory mechanisms to carry the process forward, including a round table on sustainable development. Although the strategy represents a definite advance on previous approaches, British environmental groups are sceptical of it and the proposed round table, fearing that it will be a government-controlled 'talk-shop,' unrelated to decision-making and action (Dalal-Clayton et al. 1994).

New Zealand is an isolated island nation, approximately the size of the United Kingdom, with a relatively small population of 3.5 million and few heavy industries. By many standards, it also has one of the world's most coherent frameworks for sustainability planning. The *Environment 2010 Strategy* provides a broad statement of the vision, values, goals, principles, and priorities that will guide government policy-making (New Zealand, Ministry for the Environment 1994). It is linked to an economic and fiscal strategy and taken forward by a nine-part agenda for action, which sets out what has to be done by 2010. The document is a first step, to be translated into specific plans and actions via existing legal and institutional frameworks.

In recent years, New Zealand has undertaken a series of statutory reforms that now provide a comprehensive framework for environmental management. A cornerstone is the Resource Management Act (1991), a path-breaking law to control the environmental effects of development activities on land, air, and water. The act consolidated over fifty separate planning and regulatory laws into a single management framework with one overriding purpose: sustainable use of natural and physical resources, excluding minerals. Under the act, the regulatory system is directed at maintaining the 'environmental bottom line,' the capacities or thresholds below which natural systems suffer irreversible or significant damage; it requires that effects be avoided, remedied, or mitigated. Early experience with practice under the act appears reasonably positive (Muntz and Dixon 1993) and shows promise in relation to the longer term implementation of the environmental sustainability strategy.

Australia is more comparable to Canada in ecological history and federal geopolitics. The Australian *National Strategy for Ecologically Sustainable Development* (Australia 1992) has a number of innovative features. Its origins lie in the earlier *National Conservation Strategy for Australia* and more immediately in the reports of the Ecologically Sustainable Development (ESD) Working Groups (1991), commissioned by the prime minister in response to the Brundtland report. A broad policy framework for decision-making and action is set out in the national strategy. It sets out, under nine sectors and twenty-two cross-cutting themes, the government's strategic approach and specific commitments to 500 recommendations made by the ESD working groups. Various provisions are made for monitoring and review, including the development of appropriate performance measures for tracking actions outlined in the strategy and overall progress toward ecologically sustainable development. A recent update of progress in implementing the ESD strategy indicates that work has commenced on most of the actions identified but

progress has been slower than hoped, in part because of financial constraints (Australia, Ecologically Sustainable Development Steering
Committee 1993). The Australian strategy is also linked to a range of
other policy initiatives and instruments, but it is not clear how these activities relate to and reinforce each other.

As well as the *National Strategy for Ecologically Sustainable Development*,
Australia has a range of issue- and sector-related strategies. These include the *National Greenhouse Response Strategy*, the *National Strategy for
the Conservation of Australia's Biological Diversity*, and the *National Forest
Policy Statement*. Of particular interest for Canada and other federal
states is the *Intergovernmental Agreement on the Environment*, which sets
out, in a series of schedules, the rules and arrangements by which the
federal, state or territory, and local levels will cooperate on a wide range
of issues related to environmental protection, nature conservation, and
the conventions on climate change and biodiversity. Numerous sectoral strategies are also being developed. With respect to tourism alone,
the initiatives include the *National Ecotourism Strategy*, the *Rural Tourism
Strategy*, and the *National Aboriginal and Torres Strait Islander Tourism
Strategy*. In addition, the states and territories are developing separate
tourism strategies based on sustainability principles (Australia, Ecologically Sustainable Development Steering Committee 1993).

Canadian Experience with Sustainability Planning
Canada has taken a leading role at the international level in promoting
sustainability principles and actions. By many accounts, Canada was a
positive and influential force in the negotiation processes that culmi-
nated in the 1992 Earth Summit. The Canadian approach – sustainability planning writ large – builds on a long tradition of support for efforts
to address global environmental issues. It was exemplified in Canadian
input and response to both the *World Conservation Strategy* (IUCN,
WWF, and UNEP 1980) and the report of the World Commission on Environment and Development (WCED 1987), both milestones on the
road from the 1972 UN Conference on the Human Environment in
Stockholm to the 1992 UN Conference on Environment and Development in Rio. During this period, a major theme of Canadian participation was the development of consensus-building processes and
mechanisms.

At UNCED, the government of Canada proposed a 'quick start'
agenda to continue international progress toward sustainable development. The proposed measures included:

- expeditious signing, ratification, and implementation of the biodiversity and climate change conventions
- support for the UN Commission on Sustainable Development as a means of holding countries accountable for progress on *Agenda 21*
- preparation of natural sustainable development strategies and plans as a key means of implementing the commitments made at Rio (FAIT 1994).

A review of trends and issues in sustainability strategy-making in Canada is given in this section. Overall, the number and range of initiatives under way in this country are quite remarkable. Many of them predate Rio and are subsequently being adapted to incorporate the provisions of *Agenda 21*. The preparation of sustainability strategies is closely related to the work of national, provincial, and local round tables, but this is neither an exclusive relationship nor a precondition for strategy development. The operating premises and principles rather than the form of round tables are important. A cornerstone is the idea that the transition to sustainability is a society-wide responsibility; its achievement is dependent on the active engagement of government, business, voluntary organizations, and individuals.

The National Level
Canadian follow-up to UNCED is moving forward on a number of tracks. These reflect the geopolitical realities of cooperative federalism, in which responsibility for environmental management and sustainability planning is divided among the federal and provincial or territorial governments, with other, subsidiary powers devolved to indigenous, regional, and local authorities. Other intergovernmental and multisectoral institutions also have an important role in this sphere, including the Canadian Council of Ministers of the Environment (CCME), the National Round Table on the Environment and the Economy (NRTEE), and the Projet de société, a broad coalition for planning for a sustainable future. With the support of the National Round Table, the Projet de société is drafting a national sustainable development strategy. Meanwhile, the current status of *Canada's Green Plan* is uncertain, and some of its components are being taken forward by other strategic processes.

Launched in 1990, the plan outlined the federal government's policy framework and approach to sustainable development (Canada 1990). Seven goals were identified, with supporting principles, a series of targets, and actions and commitments to meet them (Figure 2.7). Following a review of initial experience, the *Green Plan* was updated and broadened to include UNCED commitments (Canada 1992). Subsequently, under the Chrétien administration, the plan has become almost invisible domestically although it is still referred to internationally, most notably in Canada's report to the UN Commission on Sustainable Development (FAIT 1994).

Figure 2.7

Canada's Green Plan

Goals
- clean air, water, and land
- sustainable use of renewable resources
- protection of special spaces and species
- preserving the integrity of the North
- global environmental security
- environmentally responsive decision-making
- minimizing the impact of environmental emergencies

Principles for environmental action
- respect for nature
- environment-economy integration
- efficient use of resources
- shared responsibility for problem-solving
- leadership by government as an environmental trustee
- informed decision-making
- ecosystemic approach to planning and action

Specific targets
- 50 per cent Canada-wide reduction in waste generation by 2000
- setting aside of 12 per cent of the country as protected space, although with no timeline
- completion of the National Park System by 2000
- stabilization of CO_2 and other greenhouse gas issues at 1990 levels by 2000
- phasing out of CFCs by 1997 and of other major ozone-depleting substances by 2000
- 50 per cent reduction of SO_2 emissions in eastern Canada by 1994

Source: Canada (1992)

A critical look at the plan indicates several shortcomings. The process began on the wrong foot with well-intentioned but misplaced public consultation. Because the draft document appeared to environmental non-government organizations (ENGOs) to be at an advanced stage, the *Green Plan* never gained their full endorsement. Nor did other federal departments, in particular economic and finance agencies, appear to accept the plan fully. The plan is not, as advertised, a comprehensive, government-wide approach to environment-economy integration, let alone a national policy for sustainable development. It remains overly centred on Environment Canada, with too much of the funding and too many of the initiatives recycled from established programs and projects and too little connection with the socio-economic policies that drive federal expenditure, decision-making, and the direction of development.

Despite these flaws, the plan has a number of positive aspects on which to build. When first introduced, it was an important advance from the ad hoc culture of federal policy-making. It exemplifies a *strategic* focus and approach to environmental planning and problem-solving, based on setting goals and priorities, packaging a range of actions to deliver them, and tracking progress and responsibilities. As well, the plan initiated several innovative projects – such as the model forest program (Figure 2.8) – that otherwise might not have taken place and may catalyze changes in environmental and resource management. The main benefits from the *Green Plan* may be long term and intangible, accruing from a more integrated approach to decision-making in which the environment is taken into account in the process of weighing and selecting trade-offs.

Other components of the plan are being taken forward under new arrangements. These include the specific actions necessary to fulfil Canada's commitments under the UN conventions on biological diversity and climate change. At the time of writing, a draft biodiversity strategy was being finalized by an intergovernmental task force, with advice from a broadly based consultative group (Environment Canada 1994). The strategy outlines the actions required of all jurisdictions and parties to implement the articles of the biodiversity convention. The proposed approach appears considerably broader in scope than the protected areas and species component of the *Green Plan*. It forms a policy umbrella that encompasses parks designation, wildlife management, and sustainable use of renewable resources by the agriculture, fishery, and forestry sectors. As such, the strategy could serve as an ecological cornerstone for sustainable development, a policy assurance that the integrity of natural systems will be maintained. This will only occur,

Figure 2.8

Model forest program

Purpose
- designed to support the efforts of provincial governments and landowners to develop new approaches to resource management
- seeks to balance the various economic, environmental, and social needs of the forest's users and inhabitants

Key objectives
- to accelerate the implementation of sustainable development
- to develop and apply new and innovative techniques of integrated resource management
- to test and demonstrate the best sustainable forestry practices available

Example
Nine of the ten model working forests are in full operation. They are spread over five major forest eco-regions of Canada and reflect a variety of cultural and ecological values, such as the value of wildlife, biodiversity, watersheds, recreation, and fisheries, as well as the traditional economic value of wood supply. The Fundy Model Forest in New Brunswick, for example, covers 400,000 hectares already within an integrated management plan. A diverse group of actors – including the provincial environmental authorities, a large forestry corporation, a cooperative unit of smaller logging companies, scientists, and the public – are thrashing out what constitutes sustainable forestry management

Source: Adapted from Projet de société (1994a)

however, if the range of measures proposed are consistent with application of the precautionary principle, applied within an ecosystemic approach and comprehensively implemented by participating governments and interests. No other Canadian initiative has such potential importance as an insurance policy for environmental sustainability.

Of comparable potential significance is the Projet de société, a network of a hundred government, indigenous, business, and voluntary organizations. The Projet de société was formed in 1992 as a multistakeholder partnership for maintaining the UNCED momentum and process. Under this mandate, it has undertaken an assessment of Canadian progress toward implementing *Agenda 21* and drafted a macroframework and participatory process for a national sustainability strategy. The strategy is based on principles adopted by the Canadian delegation to Rio, and the process is designed to be transparent, accountable, and inclusive.

The key elements are as follows:

- Each partner and each sector is encouraged to identify and take responsibility for its own contribution to sustainability.
- Dialogue and cooperation among sectors and communities are key elements of problem-solving.
- A shared vision and agreement on key policy, institutional, and individual changes are necessary for the transition to sustainability.
- Strategy and action must be linked and must build on previous and ongoing initiatives.
- Canada's practice of sustainable development and its contribution to global sustainability should be exemplary (Projet de société 1994a).

The Projet has prepared a series of documents entitled *Towards a National Sustainable Development Strategy for Canada*. Volume 5, *Canadian Choices for Transitions to Sustainability*, outlines a set of policy values, guidelines, principles, options, and instruments for this purpose (Projet de société 1994b). An innovative aspect of the Projet's latest version of a draft sustainability strategy is the use of 'choice work' tables for policy engagement. The tables are designed to clarify the consequences and trade-offs of various strategies and to provide examples of policy measures that will help Canada to realize nine sustainability goals (Figure 2.9).

In its current form, the document is intended to serve as a guide to future options, one that builds on and adds value to existing sustainability plans and activities and facilitates their linkage. The most recent version was endorsed at the 4th National Stakeholders Assembly, the general forum for member organizations, and will serve as a basis for wider consultation. Strictly interpreted, the Projet's function is near completion, but no alternative process for taking a national strategy forward has been developed yet (See Postscript).

As a bottom-up, consensus-building process, the Projet's evolving approach to strategy development has pros and cons. Its strength lies in its emphasis on process and in the clarification of choice. Much of what the Projet de société is attempting exemplifies what Meadows, Meadows, and Randers (1992) call 'committed experimentation,' net*working* with others to establish a vision, confront problems, and identify actions that can lead toward a sustainable society. This process is primarily one of exploring, learning, and adapting our thinking and behaviour

Figure 2.9

Sustainability goals for Canada proposed by the Projet de société

Goal 1: Air
Ensure that all Canadians have safe air to breath at all times while maintaining socio-economic activities that do not threaten global climate security.

Goal 2: Fresh and salt water
Provide access to safe drinking water and economical supplies of water for other purposes without reducing the capacity and quality of water resources, including salt-water resources.

Goal 3: Food
Ensure a sustainable system of food production, distribution, processing, consumption, and recycling that promotes healthy diets and strong economies, both at home and around the world.

Goal 4: Habitat, human and natural
Provide adequate shelter and a sense of community for all Canadians without threatening the natural habitat, upon which people and all other species depend.

Goal 5: Human relationships
Develop a society in which people respect one another for their differences and their common human values, and in which people are able to develop to reach their full potential, without compromising similar opportunities for future generations.

Goal 6: Health
Create a healthy environment and an affordable healthcare system that will improve the physical and mental well-being of all Canadians.

Goal 7: Security
Develop a community, a country, and a world in which there is much less danger, fear, and worry.

Goal 8: Mobility
Ensure levels of mobility and communication that support basic human needs without denying future generations similar opportunities.

Goal 9: Sources and sinks
Use resources at a rate that ensures that the regenerative (source) and assimilative (sink) functions of ecological systems are maintained.

Source: Projet de société (1994a)

accordingly. By definition, it is *not* about authoritatively prescribing *the* course of action to be followed.

The downside of this approach is that consensus-building takes time, and initial results may seem disappointing. At the national level, in particular, policy options and actions tend to approximate the lowest common denominator on which groups with diverse values and interests can agree. In the case of the Projet de société, the stakeholders may have come to that point in the choice work tables. Still to be addressed in the latest document – or in the *Green Plan* – are the hard questions of sustainable development: whether, when, and how to move away from political and economic reliance on throughput growth and population increase as the basis for improvement of social welfare.

The Projet de société also remains unconnected to federal policy-making processes and institutions. In particular, there appears to be little if any coordination between the work of the Projet and the efforts reportedly under way either to overhaul the *Green Plan* or to replace it with another federal government sustainability strategy. Under these circumstances, the conclusion of one commentator that Canada is working on not one but two national strategies for sustainable development is not surprising (Prescott-Allen 1993). The reasons are not entirely clear but no doubt involve a certain degree of infighting over turf. Whatever the background, at a minimum there is a need to ensure that information is shared and activities cross-referenced. The National Round Table, which has recently assumed greater administrative responsibility for the strategy development component of the Projet's mandate, is in a position to address this issue with Environment Canada. It should also be able to facilitate wider contact with regions, groups, and communities outside Ottawa and central Canada, still the predominant geographical focus of Projet activities.

The Provincial, Regional, and Local Levels
Within the compass of the present chapter, it is not possible to provide a complete review of the sustainability strategies in preparation at the provincial, regional, and local levels. Nevertheless, some reference to these is essential for three reasons. First, in a federal state like Canada, the national perspective provides only a very partial and incomplete picture of trends and developments. Second, the relationship of national, regional, and local strategies should be complementary and reinforcing. Third, the transition to sustainability takes place through myriad decisions and actions on development and environment (see

Roseland 1992). In large measure, these occur in Canada at the provincial and local level. Some examples of sustainability strategies in these jurisdictions follow.

The Arctic Region
The *Arctic Environmental Strategy* (AES) is a corollary of the *Green Plan*. It focuses on, among other things, cleaning up more than 800 hazardous solid waste dumps and industrial sites strung across the region. It also emphasizes the provision of job and skill opportunities for northerners and promotes community-based resource management. The last of these is extended in the *Inuit Regional Conservation Society,* which defines 'eco-development' as the touchstone of cultural sustainability and the expression of the Inuit relationship to land, water, and wildlife. Community-based resource management is also given an international dimension in the *Arctic Environmental Protection Strategy* (AEPS), which commits the eight circumpolar states to sustainable use of natural resources, including their use by local populations and indigenous peoples. Inuit remain concerned about the pollution from outside sources, however, they consider that the region continues to be developed in a manner unacceptable to them, and they argue that the AEPS and AES fall short of their vision of the North (Inuit Circumpolar Conference 1993).

This vision is expressed in a regional conservation strategy outlined in the report of the Inuit Circumpolar Conference. The core elements are:
- a register of Inuit experts to build and maintain a database
- a manual of Inuit management to document traditional and modern experience and knowledge
- development of a database to gather and generate the detailed information needed in all areas in order to make informed choices
- a protected areas network to protect, for example, habitats and breeding areas, with the aim of achieving both conservation and sustainable development goals
- sustainable development demonstration projects to promote the concept and demonstrate successes
- education and communication to inform people within and outside the Arctic about Arctic issues (Inuit Circumpolar Conference 1993)

Comprehensive land claim agreements are providing new institutions and methods to manage land, water, and wildlife. These are broadly supported by the innovative Yukon 2000 exercise and the NWT Sustainable Development Policy, but each component is insufficient in and of itself, and we still need a comprehensive picture to guide us in assembling them. This is why we need a national sustainable development strategy with an explicit northern dimension that incorporates indigenous values (Sadler and Fenge 1993). For urban Canadians, these values are ecological and cultural bellwethers.

The Status of Provincial Strategies
At the provincial level, the preparation of sustainability strategies has been undertaken primarily by round tables on environment and economy. Most provincial strategies are in final or draft form. These are individually and comparatively reviewed in outline in two recent reports (Weichel 1993; Clement 1993). Although each provincial strategy takes a distinct approach, they have some common elements:
- There was considerable public consultation in strategy development by all jurisdictions.
- Three organizing formats may be recognized, based on sector, cross-cutting, or strategic approaches to identifying goals and recommending actions.
- The three dimensions of sustainability are dealt with variously, with social or equity aspects referred to the least.
- A mix of policy instruments and mechanisms for initiating change are identified with education, round table processes, and state of the environment reporting widely cited.
- The responsibility for strategy implementation varies considerably. In some cases, provincial governments have formally adopted the reports (e.g., Manitoba and Nova Scotia); in other cases, they remain advisory.

The British Columbia experience exemplifies both the progress and the problems in translating frameworks into action. In 1992, the provincial round table released an assessment of the state of sustainability in British Columbia, concluding 'that, in many cases, present patterns of human activity and trends in expectations are not sustainable' (BCRTEE 1992, 15). It also provided a comprehensive statement of the principles, criteria, tools, and identified decision-making reforms necessary to turn this situation around. The statement was seen as a first step toward developing a strategy – a plan of action – that set out clearly how sustainability could be achieved. Less than one year later, however, the BC round table was closed down, with unfinished business on the books.

On the positive side, aspects of the sustainability agenda were incorporated into the mandate of the Commission on Resources and the Environment (CORE). The commission is developing a province-wide strategy for land use planning and resource and environmental management. As part of its approach, CORE (1992) has developed a land use charter that defines principles of sustainability and consensus decision-making. It is also applying these to strategic regional planning for major regions of the province, using public consultation and multi-party negotiation to try to resolve long-standing and contentious issues of resource use allocation, notably timber versus conservation (Owen 1993). Finally, CORE (1994) has just released its proposed provincial land use strategy, with a sustainability act as its cornerstone. The government response to recommended legislation will be a test case of its commitment to sustainability, recognizing that land use is only one dimension of sustainability.

Local and Community Networks

There is what Doering (1994) calls a 'wonderful explosion' of sustainability planning and action at the local level in Canada. Only the broad contours can be traced here. From a macro-perspective, local sustainable strategies are being prepared by several routes, including municipal government plans, local round tables, and the Canadian Healthy Communities Network or equivalent programs.

At the local government level, the goal or principle of sustainable development is incorporated into many of the most recently completed municipal plans. There are also other indications of the greening of municipal planning: statements of environmental protection, conservation, and rehabilitation goals; endorsement of an ecosystemic approach, consideration of cumulative effects, and development of urban growth management principles; and, in some cases, recognition of the wider ecological footprint of built areas, exemplified by attempts to reduce or offset greenhouse gas emissions (MacLaren 1994).

Local round tables are in place across Canada and operate under various auspices, goals, and rules. These processes appear to be most solidly established in British Columbia, Manitoba, and Ontario. In Manitoba alone, there are fifty-two local round tables, approximately 40 per cent of which have completed sustainability vision statements or strategies. Equally important are the grass roots activities to conserve energy, reduce waste streams, or support zero tillage agricultural production (see Sopuck 1994). Often sustainability at the local level is characterized by 'doing something, not only talking,' and may involve, in the words of the chair of one local round table, 'an unlikely mix of business people ... and environmentalists' (Edwards 1994, 15).

The Canadian Healthy Communities Network is another catalyst for local sustainability planning and action. Based on principles of participation and partnership, the aim of the program is to create the kind of local environment that contributes to 'a state of physical, mental and social well being,' the UN definition of health. Launched as a government-sponsored project in 1989, the process continues in over 200 communities. It is most strongly represented in British Columbia and Québec, where the healthy communities concept is strongly linked to activism and problem-solving. The process has been used to initiate a domestic hazardous waste collection program in Sherbrooke, for example, and to prepare an action plan for tackling the complex and contentious issue of lead contamination in the mining town of Rouyn-Noranda (Lacombe 1994).

Equivalent networks and processes are in place in other parts of the country. Local sustainability is an urgent, immediate issue for resource-based communities in Atlantic Canada, struggling to overcome economic hardship and the collapse of the east coast fisheries. The Sustainable Communities Network of Nova Scotia, for example, was established in 1993 to facilitate strategies for community resilience and a measure of self-reliance (Laine 1994). Similar approaches and activities have been undertaken by other networks in Nova Scotia. The sustainable community pilot project, coordinated by Mount Allison University, aims to develop and implement sustainability action plans, and the Envirotowns Program, run by the Clean Nova Scotia Foundation, focuses on self-assessment, practical environmental improvements such as recycling, and changing attitudes and behaviour. In the final analysis, achieving a sustainable community depends on more than simply participation; it involves empowering people to make changes, making use of local knowledge, and tapping latent skills (Harvey 1994).

Lessons and Recommendations

National sustainable development strategies and their equivalents at other levels are rapidly evolving policy instruments. This process is at the forefront of the post-Rio struggle toward making sustainability an operational reality. A rich seam of experience with strategy preparation is being built up in Canada and internationally. Nonetheless, it is also at a relatively early stage of evolution, and so the track record of progress is mixed and subject to qualification. Even so, the real issue is whether NSDSs are or will have any lasting effect on public policy, economic development, and social attitudes and behaviour, or whether they will sit on bureaucratic bookshelves gathering dust like earlier generations of master plans (Rowley 1993).

A brief summing up of the pros and cons of NSDSs in these terms is undertaken below. First, some guiding principles for strategy design and implementation are identified, building on earlier work (Carew-Reid et al. 1994; Dalal-Clayton et al. 1994; INGP 1994c,d). These are refocused as keys to success, and by extension they serve as criteria for evaluating the effectiveness of current approaches. Under each principle, some concluding observations are made about Canadian and international progress with strategy development. On this basis, several recommendations are made for moving ahead with Canada's national sustainable development strategy.

Seven Principles of Strategy-Making

(1) Take an integrative approach. National sustainable development strategies are integrative, forward-looking, cross-sectoral processes for linking together and balancing environmental, social, and economic policy objectives. They encompass ends and the means to achieve them, often applying elements of traditional approaches to policy-planning, such as gathering information, setting objectives, and so on. Not surprisingly, however, making sustainability operational in this way has proved elusive. In practice, the predominant approach is still to treat sustainable development as primarily an environmental matter. So far, very few national strategies appear to have satisfactorily integrated the ecological, economic, and equity dimensions of sustainability. A number have integrated environmental and economic concerns, the Dutch *National Environmental Policy Plan* perhaps being the furthest advanced. The *Green Plan* and the draft national strategy of the Projet de société have both made credible efforts in this direction, but ironically the Canadian example that probably comes closest to an integrated approach is the now abandoned BC draft sustainability strategy.

(2) Focus on the issues. National sustainable development strategies should directly address the major structural issues and constraints on achieving an economically viable, socially desirable, and ecologically maintainable future. This involves addressing current problems within a longer term policy horizon, applying the type of criteria set out in the environmental action program for central and eastern Europe, for example. Canadian examples of current problems are resource stock depletions such as the collapse of the east coast fishery and environmental health risks such as the build up of contaminants in arctic marine sys-

tems. An assessment of carrying capacity is at the centre of the Dutch NEPP and is a strong dimension of Australia's national strategy too. It is less explicitly stated in the *Green Plan* and the Projet de société's draft strategy but is represented in their goals and principles. State of the environment reporting provides a basis for examining the risks associated with further net loss of natural capital in managed resource systems and the extent to which this may be traded off against economic gains.

(3) Base strategies on goals. National sustainable development strategies should be based on clearly defined objectives and priorities with measurable targets and timeframes for meeting them. A long-term vision of a sustainable society is a useful starting point, because it can be framed in terms of broad, shared values and hopes for the future, as outlined in the Projet de société strategy document. Establishing specific goals and targets to achieve sustainable development is a more difficult, qualified, and contentious process, involving painful trade-offs among ecological, social, and economic objectives. Often countries need to be faced with immediate, real health risks or constraints on development before making these choices. The Dutch NEPP, again, represents the leading edge of setting quantitative targets for emission reductions. Both the *Green Plan* and the Projet de société's strategy contains a mix of both soft and hard, or measurable, goals, although in the case of the Projet these do not represent government commitments.

(4) Make sure that strategies are workable within policy processes. National sustainable development strategies must be adjusted to the policy cycle and institutional culture and must initiate change in the direction and process of decision-making. Far too many strategies are pro forma exercises that exert little or no influence on government policy-making. This appears to be the case in certain developing countries, even though preparation of NSDSs has become an integral aspect of international assistance requirements. Many industrial countries are not much further ahead, often seeming strong on green conditionalities for developing countries and short on their application to domestic macroeconomic and fiscal policy. A notable exception is Norway, where each government department must estimate the environmental effects of its proposed expenditures. Internationally, the *Green Plan* rates moderately well in terms of its general application to government agencies. The Projet de société currently lies outside the policy mainstream.

(5) Seek consensus. National sustainable development strategies are developed with and through wide public involvement and consultation. Public involvement is a vital aspect of the process for several rea-

sons. It is indispensable to founding strategies on societal values and ethics, to ensuring that they incorporate the visions and aspirations of citizens, and to facilitating lifestyle and behavioural changes. Depending on the socio-political context, public involvement may involve consultation with interest groups, community-wide participation, or building consensus among major sectors and interests. The national and provincial strategy processes undertaken in Canada have been at the forefront of these approaches. Still in question, however, is the extent to which consensus-based negotiations can develop a sustainability strategy that breaks new ground and tackles deep-rooted structural and institutional problems.

(6) Keep strategies action oriented. National sustainable development strategies should lead to immediate, practical steps that lay the ground for a longer term, systemic transition in patterns of production and consumption. Win-win and 'no regrets' measures, such as site remediation and resource rehabilitation, are obvious priorities, and form the basis of the environmental action program for central and eastern Europe. There are many other examples in renewable resource management, as documented in the Australian national strategy and the *Green Plan,* which is particularly strong on demonstration projects. Achieving more far-reaching changes in economic behaviour will require wider use of green taxes and other market instruments. These are referred to in the *Green Plan* and incorporated into the matrix of policy options in the Projet de société's choice work tables.

(7) Design strategies to enhance capacity. National sustainable development strategies are capacity-building processes that strengthen institutions, sharpen concepts and tools of sustainability, improve skills and competencies, and promote public awareness. Such benefits are difficult to measure. They are perhaps most evident in developing countries, where external agencies provide long-term support to base national strategies on cultural traditions and reinforce existing commitments. Pakistan's NSDS was developed with the advice of the World Conservation Union (formerly the International Union for the Conservation of Nature [IUCN]) and the support of the Canadian International Development Agency and is widely regarded as a model of capacity-building as well as a practical success. In Canada, the self-education, as well as instrumental, benefits of using multi-party processes for national and provincial strategy-making constitute the articles of faith of the Projet de société and the round table movement.

Strengthening Canada's Process

At present, our best chance of achieving a viable NSDS probably rests with the Projet de société. Several recommendations are made below for strengthening the Projet's NSDS approach and its relationship to other processes. These cover three broad categories: policy linkages (recommendations 1 and 2), strategy development (recommendations 3 and 4), and process outreach (recommendation 5). As such, they incorporate elements of approach that could be applied by other institutions that replace or supplant the Projet.

(1) Coordinate the relationship of the Projet de société's draft NSDS, the federal government's *Green Plan,* and the *Canadian Biodiversity Strategy.* In principle, their roles are complementary and reinforcing; in practice, policy and process coordination is hindered by scepticism on the part of government officials about the political viability of multistakeholder activities. Given these constraints, the way forward lies in a linking arrangement, in which the next draft of the NSDS (see recommendation 3, below) would outline the long-term, across-the-board process of change necessary to establish a sustainable society and economy, the *Canadian Biodiversity Strategy* could serve as a cornerstone for maintaining ecological integrity and resource productivity, and a strengthened *Green Plan* would provide the federal government's action plan. Other sustainability strategies and sectoral plans can round out the approach once these baseline processes are in place.

(2) Clarify the function of an NSDS in federal policy-making. The relation of the Projet de société to the National Round Table should be used as a conduit to link NSDS preparation firmly to the policy-making institutions of the federal government. First, the work of the Projet de société and the NRTEE should be integrated in a number of areas, notably in the conduct of further research and policy dialogues (see recommendation 4, below). Second, through its advice to the prime minister the NRTEE could recommend that the federal government review and adopt all or part of the NSDS after public consultation. On its own, an NSDS will only work if public policy signals and sectoral institutions are aligned in the areas of economics, finance, environment, research, and technology development, and if institutional arrangements are enabling and support necessary initiatives by government, the private sector, and individual Canadians. At the federal level, this will be a primary responsibility of the incoming auditor general for environment and sustainable development.

(3) Refocus the strategy on the substantive issues of sustainable development in Canada. Under the Projet de société, major issues, roadblocks, and some policy options for achieving sustainable development in Canada are listed but still remain to be analyzed and addressed in depth. In the next draft of an NSDS it should be possible to

- expand on the initial vision and of a sustainable society and Canadian goals for a sustainable future
- analyze the policy, economic, and technological implications
- schedule policy dialogues on major cross-cutting issues of sustainable development
- repackage and critically analyze existing targets and timeframes for implementing international and national commitments to achieve sustainability
- link these objectives to initiatives under way at the federal, provincial, and local levels
- demonstrate the use of policy and planning instruments, such as environmental impact assessment, for implementation of the draft national strategy.

Figure 2.10 outlines proposed core elements of a revised strategy.

(4) Under the auspices of the National Round Table, conduct a series of policy dialogues on key issues, eventually resolving the hard questions of sustainable development. By definition, the hard issues and choices are subject to sharply differing opinions. Initially, policy dialogues might focus on win-win initiatives such as research development and investment in the environmental industry, or energy conservation and efficiency. Eventually, however, the more intractable issues must be dealt with, including those that presently elude national political debate in Canada: population, consumption, and immigration levels in the context of national and regional carrying capacities. This will probably not result in consensus or anything approximating it, but a well-structured policy dialogue could identify areas of agreement and disagreement, with alternative views and reasons for them. By clarifying the trade-offs, the federal government would be in a position to make clear policy choices.

(5) Broaden the membership base of the Projet de société. At present, the Projet largely draws its membership from central Canada, and the Ottawa, Toronto, Montreal area in particular. More diverse participation is necessary if a truly national strategy is to be drafted, one that builds on and adds value to activities under way at the provincial and local levels. In addition, sectoral representation in the Projet de société

Figure 2.10

Core elements of a national sustainable development strategy

Introduction
- the rationale and benefits of an NSDS

State of the nation
- assessment of global trends, national issues, regional prospects
- Canada in a global context

Vision for tomorrow
- values and ethics of a sustainable society
- images and aspirations for the future

Goals, objectives, and targets
- overall goal
  e.g., to improve quality of life consistent with obligations to future generations
- objectives
  e.g., to improve social welfare and individual well-being
  e.g., to provide an equitable distribution of opportunities
  e.g., to maintain natural capital at or above current levels
- targets for meeting economic, social, and environmental objectives
  e.g., to adopt minimum standards to guarantee environmental sustainability
  e.g., to pay down the environmental deficit through rehabilitation measures

Guiding principles
- integrated decision-making
- market harnessing
- shared responsibility
- consensus-building
- public awareness
- accountability of decisionmakers
- transparency of decision-making
- empowerment of people

Cross-cutting elements
- institutional reform
  e.g., harmonizing environmental regulations

(continued on next page)

Figure 2.10 (continued)

- greening the economy
  e.g., 'clean industry' strategies
- resource and environmental stewardship
  e.g., biodiversity strategy
- healthy communities
  e.g., urban renewal, promotion of rural and traditional livelihoods
- individual action and initiative
  e.g., environmental citizenship
- population and immigration
  e.g., replacement and growth options
- scientific and technical innovation
  e.g., raw materials substitution
- global commitments
  e.g., response to convention on climate change

Sectoral plans and initiatives
- directions and dimensions for achieving sustainability in major policy and economic sectors
- detailed plans to be drawn up by each industry sector
  e.g., energy, transportation, agricultural, forestry, fisheries, tourism, chemicals, etc.

Regional dimensions
- links to provincial and local sustainability strategies
- responses to regional issues and concerns
- the North and the national interest

Indigenous peoples
- use of traditional knowledge and lifestyles
- land and resource use
- community and economic development

Means of implementation
- communication and outreach
- policy dialogue on cross-cutting sectoral issues
- monitoring progress on implementing the strategy
- supporting measures
  e.g., research agenda, information tools and technologies
- policy tools and instruments

Source: Adapted from Sadler and Fenge (1993)

needs strengthening, especially from the private and research sectors. The initial thrust of the draft NSDS is toward environment-economy integration; business, commerce, and industry concerns are central to any evolving policy dialogue. Finally, the work of the Projet needs to become more analytical by drawing on the considerable scientific and policy research on sustainable development being done in various universities, institutions, and centres.

A Postscript on Canadian NSDS Processes

Some time has elapsed between the writing and the publication of this chapter. In the interim, events have changed the Canadian picture with regard to the preparation of a national sustainability strategy. The *Green Plan* has been terminated, replaced, in part, by *A Guide to Green Government*. A final draft of *Canadian Choices for Transitions to Sustainability* (Projet de société 1995), has been completed but the survival of the Projet itself is now in question. Following a change of membership, the National Round Table on the Environment and the Economy has closed the file on the Projet, passing the decision whether to continue it to an informal working group. What this means, in effect, is that there is no viable, national sustainable development strategy, although numerous other related initiatives carry on, such as the *Canadian Biodiversity Strategy* and the National Action Programme on Climate Change. As far as an NSDS along the lines recommended in *Agenda 21* is concerned, the nearest reasonable substitute may be the coordinating functions performed by the incoming commissioner for environment and sustainable development. It will be interesting to see how he or she responds to the absence of an NSDS and to follow the line of green argument put forward in the next national report to the UN Commission on Sustainable Development. But perhaps that commitment is also negotiable?

References

Australia, Commonwealth of. 1992. *National Strategy for Ecologically Sustainable Development*. Canberra: Australian Government Publishing Service

Australia, Ecologically Sustainable Development Steering Committee. 1993. *Summary Report on the Implementation of the National Strategy for Ecologically Sustainable Development*. Canberra: Department of the Prime Minister and Cabinet

Australia, Ecologically Sustainable Development Working Groups. 1991. *Final Report – Executive Summaries*. Canberra: Australian Government Publishing Service

British Columbia Round Table on the Environment and the Economy (BCR-TEE). 1992. *Towards a Strategy for Sustainability*. Victoria: Queen's Printer

Brown, L.R., W.U. Chandler, C. Flavin, J. Jacobson, C. Pollock, S. Poster, L. Starke, E.C. Wolf. 1987. *State of the World 1987*. New York: Norton and Worldwatch

Brown, L., A. Durning, C. Flavin, H. French, N. Lenssen, M. Lowe, A. Misch, S. Postel, M. Renner, L. Starke, P. Weber, J. Young. 1994. *State of the World 1994*. New York: Norton and Worldwatch

Buitenkamp, M., H. Venner, and T. Wams, eds. 1992. *Action Plan Sustainable Netherlands*. N.p.: Friends of the Earth Netherlands

Canada. 1990. *Canada's Green Plan*. Ottawa: Government of Canada

–. 1992. *Canada's Green Plan and the Earth Summit*. Ottawa: Government of Canada

–. 1995. *A Guide to Green Government*. Ottawa: Supply and Services Canada

Carew-Reid, J. 1993. Learning to Care for the People. *People and the Planet* 2 (4):6-9

Carew-Reid, J., R. Prescott-Allen, S. Bass, and D.B. Dalal-Clayton. 1994. *Strategies for National Sustainable Development: A Handbook for Their Planning and Implementation*. London: Earthscan

Clement, P. 1993. National Overview of Strategic Planning of Sustainable Development in Canada's Provinces and Territories. National Round Table on the Environment and the Economy, Working paper no. 18. National Round Table, Ottawa

Colby, B.E. 1990. *Environmental Management in Development*. Discussion paper no. 80. Washington, DC: World Bank

Commission on Resources and the Environment (CORE). 1992. *Land Use Charter*. Victoria: Queen's Printer

–. 1994. *A Sustainability Act for British Columbia*. Vol. 1 of *The Provincial Land Use Strategy*. Victoria: Queen's Printer

Costanza, R. 1989. What is Ecological Economics? *Ecological Economics* 1:1-7

Dalal-Clayton, D.B., S. Bass, B. Sadler, K. Thompson, R. Sandbrook, N. Robins, and R. Hughes. 1994. *National Sustainable Development Strategies: Experience and Dilemmas*. London: International Institute for Environment and Development

Daly, H.E., and J. Cobb. 1989. *For the Common Good*. Boston: Beacon Press

Denmark, Ministry of the Environment. 1992. *Environmental Initiatives in the 1990s*. Copenhagen: Government of Denmark

Doering, R. 1994. Sustainable Communities: Progress, Problems and Potential. *National Round Table Review* (Spring):1

Edwards, G. 1994. Actions Speak Louder Than Words. *National Round Table Review* (Spring):15

Ehrlich, P., and A. Ehrlich. 1990. *The Population Explosion*. London: Hutchinson

Elkington, J. 1992. Going Green. In *The Greening of Business*, edited by B. Sadler, 101-6. Vancouver: GLOBE 92

Environment Agency of Japan. 1993. Overview of Japan's Experience Regarding National Plans for Sustainable Development. Discussion paper for OECD Workshop on National Plans for Sustainable Development. (See OECD 1993.)

Environment Canada. 1994. *Draft Biodiversity Strategy.* Ottawa: Environment Canada

Environment for Europe. 1993. *Executive Summary: Environmental Action Program for Central and Eastern Europe.* Booklet. N.p.

Foreign Affairs and International Trade (FAIT). 1994. *Report of Canada to the United Nations Commission on Sustainable Development.* Ottawa: Supply and Services Canada

Fukuyama, F. 1992. *The End of History and the Last Man.* New York: Free Press

Gillespie, B. 1993. Environmental Action Program for Central and Eastern Europe. Paper prepared for OECD Workshop on National Plans for Sustainable Development. (See OECD 1993)

Harvey, J. 1994. Sustainability in Atlantic Canada: A Grass Roots Movement. *National Round Table Review* (Spring):18-19

Hawken, R. 1993. *The Ecology of Commerce: A Declaration of Sustainability.* New York: Harper-Collins

Holmberg, J.K., and L. Timberlake. 1993. *Facing the Future.* London: Earthscan and International Institute for Environment and Development

International Network of Green Planners (INGP). 1994a. Approaches to Strategic Environmental Management. Paper 1. First Meeting of INGP, Maastricht, Netherlands

–. 1994b. Developing Plans and Strategies. Paper 2. First Meeting of INGP, Maastricht, Netherlands

–. 1994c. Implementing Plans and Strategies. Paper 3. First Meeting of INGP, Maastricht, Netherlands

–. 1994d. Moving from Environmental to Sustainable Development Strategies. Paper 4. First Meeting of INGP, Maastricht, Netherlands

–. 1994e. Green Planners Guide. Part 2, Country Information Sheets. Background paper. First Meeting of INGP, Maastricht, Netherlands

Inuit Circumpolar Conference. 1993. Circumpolar Sustainable Development and the Projet de société. Report prepared for National Stakeholders Assembly, Ottawa

International Union for the Conservation of Nature (IUCN, now World Conservation Union). 1993. *The IUCN Joint Program on Strategies for Sustainability: Activities and Lessons Learned.* Gland: IUCN

International Union for the Conservation of Nature (now World Conservation Union), World Wildlife Fund, and United Nations Environment Programme (IUCN, WWF, and UNEP). 1980. *World Conservation Strategy: Living Resource Conservation for Sustainable Development.* Gland: IUCN, WWF, UNEP

International Union for the Conservation of Nature (now World Conservation Union), United Nations Environment Programme, World Wide Fund for Nature (IUCN, UNEP, and WWF). 1991. *Caring for the Earth: A Strategy for Sustainable Living.* Gland: IUCN, UNEP, WWF

Lacombe, R. 1994. Villes et Villages en Santé: The Rouyn-Noranda Community of Notre-Dame. *National Round Table Review* (Spring):24-5

Laine, K. 1994. Building Sustainable Communities in Nova Scotia. *National Round Table Review* (Spring):26-7

Lerner, S. 1991. Socio-Political Design Criteria for a Sustainable Canadian Society. Sustainable Society Project Working paper no. 3, University of Waterloo, Ontario

MacLaren, V.W. 1994. Sustainable Urban Development: Signs of Progress. *National Round Table Review* (Spring):2, 10

MacNeill, J., P. Winsemius, and T. Yakushiji. 1991. *Beyond Interdependence.* New York: Oxford University Press

Meadows, D.H., D.L. Meadows, and J. Randers. 1992. *Beyond the Limits.* Toronto: McClelland and Stewart

Milbraith, L.W. 1989. *Envisioning a Sustainable Society: Learning Our Way Out.* Albany, NY: State University of New York Press

Muntz, B., and J. Dixon. 1993. From Law to Practice: EIA in New Zealand. *Environmental Impact Assessment Review* 13 (1):89-108

New Zealand, Ministry for the Environment. 1994. *Environment 2010 Strategy.* Wellington: Ministry for the Environment

Ogilvie, S.C. 1979. *The Park Buffalo.* Calgary: National and Provincial Parks Association of Canada

Organisation for Economic Cooperation and Development (OECD). 1993. Workshop on National Plans for Sustainable Development. Annotated Agenda and Issues Paper, plus various background papers for general distribution or limited circulation at the workshop, 13-15 October, Ottawa. OECD/GD (93) 154

Owen, S. 1993. Participation and Sustainability: The Imperatives of Resource and Environmental Management. In *Law and Process in Environmental Management,* edited by S. Kennett, 335-6. Calgary: Canadian Institute of Resources Law

Pfirman, S., K. Crane, and R. deFur. 1993. Arctic Contaminant Distribution. *Northern Perspectives* 21 (4):8-15

Prescott-Allen, R. 1993. Where Loggers and Tree Huggers Play. *People and the Planet* 2 (4):25-8

Projet de société. 1994a. *Overview of the Projet de société.* Ottawa: National Round Table on the Environment and the Economy

–. 1994b. *Canadian Choices for Transitions to Sustainability.* Vol. 5 of *Towards a National Sustainable Development Strategy for Canada.* Ottawa: National Round Table on the Environment and the Economy

–. 1995 *Canadian Choices for Transitions to Sustainability.* Final draft. Ottawa: National Round Table on the Environment and the Economy

Rees, W. 1992. Ecological Footprints and Appropriated Carrying Capacity: What Urban Economics Leaves Out. *Environment and Urbanization* 4 (2):121-30

Richardson, N. 1989. *Land Use and Sustainable Development in Canada.* Ottawa: Canadian Environmental Advisory Council

RIVM (Netherlands National Institute of Public Health and Environmental Protection). 1988. *Concern for Tomorrow.* Alphen aan den Rija: Samson H.D. Tjeenk Villik

Robinson, J.B. 1994. In Defense of Sustainable Development. *Sustainable Development Research Institute Newsletter* (December):1-2

Robinson, J.B., G. Frances, R. Legge, and S. Lerner. 1990. Defining a Sustainable Society: Values, Principles and Definitions. *Alternatives: Perspectives on Society, Technology and Environment* 17 (2):36-46

Roseland, M. 1992. *Toward Sustainable Communities: A Resource Book for Municipal and Local Governments*. Ottawa: National Round Table on the Environment and the Economy

Rowley, J. 1993. Confounding the Cynics. *People and the Planet* 2 (4):3

Sadler, B. 1990. Sustainable Development and Water Resource Management. *Alternatives: Perspectives on Society, Technology and Environment* 17 (3):14-24

–. 1992a. The Enterprise of Sustainable Development. In *The Greening of Business*, edited by B. Sadler, 3-9. Vancouver: GLOBE 92

–. 1992b. Instruments for Change for Sustainability: An Agenda for Business and the Environment. In *Environmental Strategy Europe 1992*, 66-80. London: Campden Publishing

–. 1994. Environmental Assessment and Development Policy Making. In *Environmental Assessment and Development*, edited by R. Goodland and V. Edmundson, 3-30. Washington, DC: World Bank

–. 1995. Ecology, Economics and the Assessment of Sustainability. In *Balancing the Scale: Integrating Environmental and Economic Assessment*, edited by B. Sadler, E.W. Manning, and J.O. Dendy, 1-35. Toronto: Foundation for International Training

–, ed. 1985. *Environmental Protection and Resource Development: Convergence for Today*. Calgary: University of Calgary Press

Sadler, B., and B. Hull. 1990. *In Business for Tomorrow: The Transition to Sustainable Development*. Ottawa: Conference Board of Canada

Sadler, B., and T. Fenge. 1993. A National Sustainable Development Strategy and the Territorial North. *Northern Perspectives* 21 (4), Supplement

Schmidheiny, S. 1992. *Changing Course*. Cambridge, MA: MIT Press

Schneider, S.H. 1989. The Changing Climate. *Scientific American* 261 (3):70-80

Slocombe, D.S., and C. Van Bers. 1992. Ecological Design Criteria for a Sustainable Canadian Society. *The Environmentalists* 12 (4):243-54

Solis, V. 1992. Conservation Based Development in Costa Rica. In *The Greening of Business*, edited by B. Sadler, 142-4. Vancouver: GLOBE 92

Sopuck, R. 1994. Local Round Tables: Celebrating Success in Manitoba. *National Round Table Review* (Spring):13-14

United Kingdom, Department of the Environment. 1990. *This Common Inheritance, Britain's Environmental Strategy*. London: HMSO

–. 1994. *Sustainable Development: The UK Strategy*. London: HMSO

United Nations Department of Public Information (UNDPI). 1993. *Agenda 21: Programme of Action for Sustainable Development, Rio Declaration on Environment and Development; Statement of Forest Principles*. Final text of agreements negotiated by governments at the United Nations Conference on Environment and Development (UNCED), 3-14 June 1992. New York: UN Department of Public Information

van Zijst, H. 1993. A Change in the Culture. *The Environmental Forum* (May-June):12-17

VROM (Netherlands Ministry of Housing, Physical Planning and Environment). 1989. *National Environmental Policy Plan: To Choose or To Lose*. The Hague: SDU Publishers

–. 1990. *National Environmental Policy Plan Plus*. The Hague: VROM Department for Information and International Relations

–. 1994. *National Environmental Policy Plan.* Update. The Hague: VROM Department for Information and International Relations

Weichel, B. 1993. Common Destination: An Analysis of Canadian Strategies for Sustainable Development. Report for Canadian Council of Ministers of the Environment, Winnipeg

White House. Office of the Press Secretary. 1993. On Earth Summit Anniversary President Creates Council on Sustainable Development. Press release, 14 June

Winpenny J., and N. Tanden. 1993. Overview Paper on Non-OECD Member Countries' Experiences. Paris. OECD/GD (93) 156

World Commission on Environment and Development (WCED). 1987. *Our Common Future – Report of the World Commission on Environment and Development.* Oxford: Oxford University Press

– (reconvened). 1992. *Statement* (of London meeting 22-4 April). Geneva: Centre for Our Common Future

Connections

3
Growing Wisely:
Reconciling Competitiveness and
Sustainability in a Shrinking World
Ted Schrecker

Growth, Competitiveness, and the Canadian Situation

This chapter is being revised immediately after the October 1995 Québec referendum. That political event was preceded by considerable economic uncertainty and would have been followed by far more had the secessionist side won. Those of us who are in our early fifties or younger, and who were born and raised in one of the industrial countries, know the economic world as one in which stability is unquestioned and expansion the rule. This is true despite the vicissitudes of our personal situations and despite increasingly severe cyclical recessions. The referendum and the anticipated consequences of a secessionist victory provided an overdue reminder that such stability cannot be taken for granted; in an increasingly open and interdependent international economy, a variety of events can trigger a rapid descent into severe recession, or worse.

Why are these observations relevant to reconciling sustainability and competitiveness? While taking economic stability for granted, most Canadians with personal or professional commitments to sustainable development are sceptical about organizing public policy around the idea of competitiveness, for at least three reasons. First, enhanced competitiveness seems to imply accepting a variety of environmental costs in the interests of increased profitability and market share at the company level and rapid economic growth at the national level. The resulting trade-offs are anathema to environmentalists who insist, on ethical grounds, that people should not be required by circumstances outside their control to make hard choices between their livelihoods on the one hand and their health and quality of life on the other (Schrecker 1987). Second, cost minimization in the pursuit of competitive advantage appears to require limited consideration of the consequences of environmental damage and the degradation of key resource bases, if such matters are formally considered at all. Competitiveness may constrain the actions of companies and governments alike with reference to the priorities of their more desperate competitors, as when an Ontario government spokesperson explained the province's choice of permissible effluent levels for the chemical industry by saying, 'We could say zero discharge but they would all close their plants and move to Mexico' (quoted in Westell 1994). Third, competitiveness is often dismissed as a mantra chanted in support of any effort to drive down wages and working conditions toward an internationally determined common denominator. This perception is strengthened when corporate executives argue that 'until we get real wage levels down much closer to those of the Brazils and Koreas we cannot pass along productivity gains to wages and still be competitive' (a Goodyear Tire and Rubber executive speaking in 1987, quoted in Palmer 1994, 101), or when the Thatcher government's efforts to break unions and drive down labour costs through high unemployment are praised for having attracted an influx of foreign investment in northeast England (Stevenson 1995).

Unfortunately, such misgivings about the competitiveness agenda are well founded. At the same time, if Canada wants to avoid economic decline it can ill afford to ignore the imperative of enhancing competitiveness, at least if we define that imperative rather broadly in terms of improving the marketability of Canada's products and the attractiveness of Canada as a venue for investment. Stated in these terms, better competitiveness is demanded by a variety of changes in the international economic environment. One such change is the gradual reduction of both tariffs and non-tariff barriers to trade as a result both of successive GATT rounds and of the Canada-US Free Trade Agreement and the North American Free Trade Agreement (CUFTA and NAFTA). Trade liberalization is obviously significant in the continental context. It is even more significant in the global context, given the rapid growth in the percentage of the world's economic activity – and the world's labour force – that has been integrated into the global economy. Harvard economist Jeffrey Sachs points out that 'just 25 years ago only a third of the world's population ... lived in economies of countries that engaged in open, market-based international trade.' Now, 'perhaps 90% of the world's population is linked via trade and financial flows' (Sachs 1995, 49; see also World Bank 1995, 54-60).

Trade liberalization was explicitly, if contentiously, endorsed in *Agenda 21* (Chapter 2.A) because of the expected economic benefits to the developing world. It has also facilitated transnational reorganization of production of many kinds of goods and of provision of some services. The speed with which one pattern of production, or 'commodity chain' (Gereffi and Korzeniewicz 1993), replaces another depends on several industry- and product-specific factors, but the general implications for global distribution of income and employment are inescapable. The pattern of economic activity in which mass North American consumer markets for automobiles were fuelled by the wages of the workers who assembled the product, which admittedly was always partly mythical, is being replaced by the pattern of affluent North American and European consumers snapping up designer running shoes stitched together by Indonesian workers earning 15 cents an hour, who can never hope to buy them (Donaghu and Barff 1990; Ballinger 1992).

Although trade liberalization has been the most high-profile dimension of transnational economic integration, global economic competition among political jurisdictions has at least as much to do with attracting investment as it does with trade (Julius 1990; WorldLink Survey 1993). Furthermore, deregulation of national financial markets and the emergence of genuinely global stock, bond, and currency markets has meant that national economies must now routinely compete on a world stage for a substantial portion of the savings of their own residents.

Canada's future economic prospects are thus inextricably linked to competitiveness, whether we concentrate on the resource-based industries that have historically financed our imports of manufactured goods or on the knowledge-based industries characteristic of what some observers have called the new economy, the 'new techno-economic paradigm' (Freeman and Perez 1988). One approach is to reject growth as a primary goal of economic policy in favour of a more egalitarian vision of a society whose economic product as measured by conventional indicators might actually be shrinking. Of several objections to this view, the most compelling is based on equity. Canada's current distribution of income and wealth is by almost all accounts ethically unacceptable. This is why eliminating child poverty in Canada by the year 2000 attracted unanimous rhetorical support from all parties in the House of Commons in 1989 and strong multipartisan endorsement by a parliamentary committee in 1991 (Canada, House of Commons 1991). At the same time, policies of progressive redistribution within societies and economies are politically fragile at the best of times but especially unworkable when future growth cannot be relied upon to reduce the negative impact on powerful losers from redistribution.

Daniel Bell (1977, 20) has called economic growth a 'political solvent' for at least the most serious distributional conflicts. This is the rationale, unfortunately not explained effectively enough, behind the Brundtland Commission's observation that 'in most situations, redistributive policies can only operate on increases in income' at the national level (WCED 1987, 50-1). The commission made this observation in order to link the imperative of economic growth in poor countries with the prospects for reducing absolute poverty, but it is just as relevant to the politics of redistribution within rich countries and, of course, to the prospects for transfers from rich to poor countries that are not motivated solely by commercial considerations or the search for geopolitical advantage. The argument being made here is that growth is a necessary, rather than a sufficient, condition for progressive redistribution. It is incumbent on proponents of a kinder, gentler (but no-growth) Canada to show that such barriers to progressive redistribution could be overcome, and they have not done so (Schrecker 1993). The question confronting economic policy is therefore not whether growth should continue but rather how best to achieve it. If we assume for the sake of argument the limited viability at the national scale of a variety of inward-looking development strategies emphasizing regional self-sufficiency, then growth means competitiveness, and the policy challenge is that of enhancing competitiveness within the constraints imposed by both sustainability and equity.

Sustainability and What It Means

There are both weak and strong concepts and definitions of sustainability (Pearce, Markandya, and Barbier 1989); they are most easily distinguished from one another with reference to often unstated assumptions about how effectively technology and human ingenuity (human or technological capital) can be assumed to substitute for natural resources and ecological services (natural capital). Strong definitions of sustainability assume that the possibility for such substitution is limited enough, or at least uncertain enough, to make continued industrial growth ecologically precarious. Weak definitions tend to assume that efficiency in use of resources, reflecting the substitution of ingenuity for resource inputs, will continue to increase as it has done in the past (Cairncross 1991, 47; Daly and Cobb 1989, 72-3).

Historical patterns of technological change tend to support the second point of view (Ayres 1989a), one that Krier and Gillette have referred to as 'techno-optimism' (1985). The tension between strong and weak definitions of sustainability is simply not susceptible to empirical resolution, however, except after the fact. For policy purposes, that determination depends on one's relative aversion to various kinds of economic, political, and ecological risks (Goodland, Daly, and El Serafy 1987; Krier and Gillette 1985; Netherlands Scientific Council for Government Policy 1995, ch. 2). Direct trade-offs may be involved in the sense that aversion to one set of risks implies increased willingness to contemplate another set, on behalf of present and future generations and various groups and sub-populations within them. Thus Paul Ehrlich's familiar analogy between present environmental management practices and the uninformed removal of rivets from the wing of an airplane (Ehrlich 1981, 19) is undeniably powerful yet ignores the possible range of undesirable consequences of refusing to get on the plane for a flight whose risks are admittedly uncertain. If the metaphorical flight is one's best or last chance of escape from poverty or worse, the risks suddenly look more bearable. Ehrlich's position is that of the business or even recreational traveller, rather than of the refugee, and it must not be forgotten in the global context that the economic situation of much of the world's population is better described by the latter analogy than by the former. This is why, for instance, *Agenda 21* points out that 'environmental standards valid for developed countries may have unwarranted social and economic costs in developing countries' (ch. 2.B).

A weak and explicitly economic definition of sustainability would be organized around an industry's or a region's ability to continue providing income either directly through employment or indirectly through the multiplier effects of local spending of that income. Canadian resource management practices often conspicuously fail to meet even this weak criterion. The most familiar example is the collapse of the east coast offshore fishery. The federally appointed task force that surveyed the resulting economic wreckage pointed out that evidence of overcapacity in the fishing and fish-processing industries was ignored or dealt with ineffectively over more than a decade (Task Force 1993; see also Gomes, Haedrich, and Villagarcia 1995; Ommer, in press). Long overdue reductions in allowable catches were resisted by the federal Department of Fisheries and Oceans until the resource base collapsed. At that point, in the words of a fish-processing industry executive, 'the moratorium [had] already been imposed by the fish' (quoted in Feschuk 1992). Forty thousand fishery workers were left without a source of livelihood, and the federal treasury has been left with a bill of $1.6 billion, so far, for income support and retraining costs.

Newfoundland-style economic crises may be brewing for other resource industries and by extension for the economies of the regions of Canada that depend on them. Economist Peter Pearse, who headed a royal commission on the future of British Columbia's forest industry in the 1970s, recently warned that organizing public policy around the maintenance of employment levels in the industry has meant a four-fold growth in the annual timber harvest since the end of the Second World War: 'Companies have been systematically – and deliberately – harvesting forests more rapidly than they have been growing.' Pearse says that the inevitable eventual decline in harvest volumes, profits, and employment 'has been continually postponed because the industry has expanded into poorer and more remote areas and learned to extract more from the areas it cuts' (Pearse 1993, A23). This pattern is characteristic of the management of other Canadian resource bases as well. Zoologist Henry Regier and forester Gordon Baskerville have pointed out that the subregional economies supported by the New Brunswick forest products industry and the Great Lakes commercial fishery have survived only through the exploitation of progressively lower quality renewable resources: 'Industry, broadly defined, was sustained, but the productive structure of the *resource* was not' (Regier and Baskerville 1986, 82, emphasis in original).

Economic crisis in the regions studied by Regier and Baskerville has so far been avoided, but many environmentalists would not therefore regard those practices as sustainable. In one variant of a weak criterion for sustainability, the liquidation of British Columbia's forests and Newfoundland's offshore fish stocks might not be considered unsustainable *as long as* the proceeds were invested in the development of other productive activities that could provide a comparable income stream in the future (cf. Cairncross 1991, 47). For a thoughtful critique of this position see Goodland and Ledec (1987, 36-8). There is nevertheless no evidence that this is happening in such cases, arguably continuing an historically persistent pattern of the dissipation of rents from natural resource harvesting and extraction in Canada. The distribution of rents is not the reason most Toronto and Vancouver environmental activists object to present Canadian resource management practices, but even in this definition those practices fail the sustainability test. This means quite simply that we are not getting even the analytically easy challenges right!

Fishery- and forestry-based examples suggest that sustainable development is a concept relevant primarily to Canada's resource industries and to the communities and regions that depend on them for income and employment. An important line of argument identifies unsustainable practices at least as strongly with patterns of predominantly urban consumption as with patterns of resource extraction or harvesting. William Rees has argued that urban economies 'appropriate carrying capacity' (1992; Rees and Wackernagel 1994) in the sense that they cannot function without the resources provided by a land area many times the size of the one within their borders. If one accepts this view, then achieving sustainable development depends heavily on changing the behaviour of rich-country consumers, manufacturers, and service providers. *Agenda 21*, in fact, devotes an entire chapter (Chapter 4) to the need for such changes, ranging from reductions in packaging volumes to basic redesign of industrial processes.

Often, there will be few reasons to consider such changes incompatible with enhanced national competitiveness. Land use planning policies that limit road construction, control urban sprawl, and promote more compact, higher density cities along the lines envisioned by Calthorpe (1993) are bitterly resisted by local growth coalitions organized around land speculators and municipal governments. At the same time, such changes would probably have minimal impact on the cost of doing business internationally and might well make our cities more attractive in terms of the quality of life they offer the managers of footloose firms. In addition, some management scholars argue that demanding environmental standards can be a source of competitive advantage for a nation's manufacturers over the long run by providing valuable incentives for innovation (Porter and van der Linde 1995). A counterargument, suggested by the case of Ontario's chemical industry standards, is that pressures for cost reduction will create strong incentives for 'downward harmonization' of environmental standards among nations competing for industrial investment and in highly cost-sensitive product markets (see, for example, Shrybman 1990; Daly and Goodland 1994). This is undoubtedly a real hazard, but as I argue in the concluding section of the chapter it will probably be far more serious for the poor countries than the rich ones.

It is probably fair to say that the stronger one's definition of sustainability, the less likely one is to consider the imperatives of sustainability and competitiveness to be compatible or reconcilable. This is at least partly because strong definitions of sustainability tend to assume limits on 'carrying capacity' that in turn imply constraints on continued increases in economic output in the rich countries, even given dramatic increases in the efficiency with which technology transforms resource and energy inputs into marketable outputs (Goodland 1992) – a process described with increasing frequency as 'industrial metabolism' (Ayres 1989b). Once again, such controversies are not susceptible to empirical resolution except after the fact. My concern in the next section of this chapter is both more immediate and more modest: I identify some changes in the principles around which Canadian economic policies are organized that have the potential to advance the goals of sustainability and competitiveness simultaneously.

Managing Economic Transitions: From Place Prosperity to People Prosperity

Queen's University economist Thomas Courchene (1992a,b) has described Canadian economic policy as focusing on 'place prosperity,' or the preservation of jobs, incomes, and firms in particular provinces or regions, rather than 'people prosperity.' There are several distinct elements to this pattern. Direct federal spending on regional development has a long history and by an extremely conservative estimate amounted to more than $1.1 billion in 1993-4, including more than $300 million in support for the economically and ecologically questionable Hibernia offshore oil project (Canada, Department of Finance 1994). Historically, an even more significant policy instrument used to further place prosperity was trade protection for uncompetitive but regionally significant industries, such as textile and clothing manufacture, dairy farming, and dairy product processing (Trebilcock, Chandler, and Howse 1990).

Canada's commitment to liberalized regimes of international trade has somewhat limited the effectiveness of these policy options in the future, although they have by no means been eliminated. It is less clear what effect, if any, this commitment will have on the corporate bailouts involving direct grants or subsidized loans. These are another element of the pattern and have been a distinguishing feature of recent Canadian economic policy with respect to both resource industries and a variety of ailing manufacturing firms or plants (Trebilcock et al. 1985; Lush 1994; Séguin 1994; Saunders 1995). With the advantage of hindsight, a few such bailouts appear successful but many others emerge as disastrous failures even on strictly economic grounds, suggested by the fact that for each job protected, both trade protection and direct corporate bailouts often cost consumers or taxpayers several times as much per year as the affected workers earn (Allen 1991; Trebilcock, Chandler, and Howse 1990, 56-76). This observation suggests strong elements of both economic irrationality and policy inconsistency.

Various Canadian industries have also enjoyed place-related subsidies in the form of routine renegotiation or non-enforcement of pollution control and waste management requirements. The value of this subsidy is hard to calculate but is certainly substantial; as with other kinds of firm- or industry-specific bailouts, it is not infrequent for specific instances of renegotiation or non-enforcement to be defended explicitly in terms of protecting local employment and the economic base that such employment provides. The effects are likely to be economically perverse since often the least efficient firms in a given industry will have greatest difficulty in meeting environmental requirements and thus will benefit most from the subsidy implicit in regulatory relief (Sinclair 1991, 101; see also Trebilcock 1986, 338-9).

Economic irrationality emerges even more clearly in the final element of the place prosperity pattern: permitting exploitative development of a variety of resource bases long after the direct economic hazards of doing so become clear. The east coast fishery collapse is an obvious case in point; it is directly attributable to 'the use of the fishery as the employer of last resort' by governments (Task Force 1993, 14), and emphasizes, as if emphasis were needed, that a policy of trying to preserve place prosperity by hoping for the magical recovery of mismanaged natural resources simply will not work.

This observation must be placed in a broader context. Historically Canada – and certainly most of Canada outside the Québec-Windsor corridor – has relied on abundant and cheaply available natural resources to sustain incomes and employment, to provide government revenues, and to finance imports of manufactured goods. The uncertainty associated with jobs in resource-based industries and regions is now compounded by the emergence as formidable international competitors of a number of similarly resource-rich countries whose costs are far lower. Chile, for instance, has embarked on an aggressive program of encouraging industrial forestry (Clapp 1995; Marchak 1995, 79-81, 303-23). Its rich ore deposits also made the country a preferred destination for investment by the Canadian mining industry well before Chile's intent to join NAFTA was announced (Vincent 1993). The imperative of cost reduction in resource industries selling into international markets will therefore lead to substantial employment reductions in Canada's primarily export-oriented resource industries, with associated effects on the regional economies that depend on them, even if market share is maintained and the relevant resource base managed in a way that will avoid exhaustion. The level of automation and computer control in Canada's most modern and lowest cost pulp mills, such as those recently built in Alberta to serve the Japanese export market, means that employment levels are extremely low (Marchak 1995, 41, 63; Pratt and Urquhart 1994, 138). Technological and organizational changes are having a similar impact on employment in Canadian mining (Dansereau 1992).

These findings suggest yet another dimension to the argument that trying to maintain place prosperity through reliance on resource industries is doomed to failure. Even if we ignore ecological considerations and are willing to accept temporary maintenance of Canadian firms' competitive position by destroying the viability of the resource base, all we are doing is postponing Newfoundland-style reckonings, whether imposed by the fish, or the trees, or the international marketplace.

Is the postponement worth its costs, broadly defined? There may be a socially desirable and even ethically compelling outcome: the temporary preservation of individual incomes and regional social stability. Individual incomes at least, however, could be preserved in other ways. One of the most valuable pieces of research for the Macdonald Commission on Canada's economic future was carried out by economist Michael Trebilcock, whose comparison of approaches to economic adjustment in seven countries concluded that 'those countries which possess an industrial policy framework which is conducive to factor mobility' – the movement of both labour and capital investment out of declining sectors and into more productive ones – 'will be better able to ensure that national wealth is maximized by directing resources to their most valuable uses' (Trebilcock 1986, 293). Trebilcock further argued that policies of facilitating rather than resisting change are economically preferable to policies that aim to preserve existing industries and regional patterns of economic activity, not least because of the high economy-wide cost of protecting jobs by way of place-oriented strategies. In the long run, what he called worker-oriented, as distinct from firm-oriented, adjustment policies can make almost all of us better off. The study went on to outline a range of alternative policy directions, starting with financial assistance for worker retraining and relocation to areas where job prospects are brighter and going on to more specific measures to address the problems associated with declining industries:

'generous severance packages for older workers, compensation for loss of resale value on houses and loss of social amenities, and compensation to the residual elements of the community to offset higher per capita public services (through assistance to municipalities)' (Trebilcock 1986, 338-43).

Such measures would be costly, sometimes, although by no means always, more costly than the firm-oriented policies they replaced, but in the long run the economy-wide gains realized by reducing understandable resistance to change on the part of workers and communities whose livelihoods are at risk might well outweigh the added short-term costs. Have policymakers taken Trebilcock's advice to heart? The federal task force on the Atlantic fishery appears to have grasped the importance of worker education in the economic equation, stressing the general need for special support for education and retraining and arguing as well that 'special emphasis must be given to community-based adult education,' ranging from basic literacy and numeracy training to college and university access. 'Post-secondary education and the opportunity to get that education are fundamental requirements in building a long-term strategy of social and economic adjustment,' and indeed the task force argues that universities and colleges should be given special assistance in return for which they would 'have a special responsibility to develop and implement an affirmative action plan for the educationally and economically less advantaged' (Task Force 1993, 92-4).

Encouragingly, the same emphasis on education is found in a recent discussion paper from the British Columbia Round Table on the Environment and the Economy (BCRTEE), which identifies high dropout rates from school and barriers to postsecondary education and retraining as among the province's key economic weaknesses (BCRTEE 1993, 63). Less encouragingly, although the report assumes 'the near-certainty of continued decline in some of British Columbia's traditional industries' (BCRTEE 1993, 85), its economic strategy recommendations do not seem to appreciate fully either the social impact of that decline or the indirect political links among sustainable resource management, environmental protection, and economic policy. In particular, the report does not explicitly reject policy approaches organized around maintaining place prosperity based on resource extraction or harvesting. Neither, for that matter, does the report of the fishery task force. It does not fully acknowledge the hard choice to be made between two policy options: establishing an attractive environment for private investment to create relatively high-wage employment in activities unrelated to the fishery, or enhancing individuals' marketable skills so that large numbers of them can leave the region to seek work elsewhere.

Both sustainability and competitiveness dictate that these are the only two options with respect to the future of most resource-reliant regions. With respect to Canada as a whole, a shift in policy emphasis from resource endowments to knowledge as a basis for economic growth appears promising economically as well as ecologically. The example of foreign investment in northeast England suggests that a major alternative source of comparative advantage is low labour costs, but it is not the only one (Barrows 1992). Consider, for instance, the situation of Virginia and the Carolinas. These are admittedly relatively low-wage jurisdictions in the North American context, but their success in attracting investment appears less directly related to that than to the availability of infrastructure and such public investments as those in 'customized training' (Kanter 1995a, 57; see also Kanter 1995b). Advertisements run by the Economic Development Authority of Fairfax County, Virginia, boast of 'the largest pool of Ph.D.s in the country, more than 20,000 strong. And 96% of all adults in the County have high school degrees, while 55% have graduated from college.' Few Canadian jurisdictions could make a similar case to prospective investors without risking accusations of false advertising. The advertisements go on to boast of 'one of the nation's best public school systems.'

These anecdotal examples reflect the declining importance of resource endowments as a source of competitive advantage (Streeten 1993), while knowledge endowments and the associated infrastructure are becoming crucially important. Industries of all kinds, ranging from medical devices to retailing and long-distance trucking (see, for example, Lappin 1995) are now knowledge based in the sense that both ingenuity and accurate and timely (often almost instantaneous) access to and control over information are essential to lower costs and better quality. These elements depend, in turn, on the education and training of the workforce. In the twenty-first century this may be the crucial determinant of economic success or stagnation. 'Workers ... are immobile in important senses in which other factors of production are not. And because a *nation* wishes to retain or gain comparative advantage, it must focus on the quality of its domestic workforce, the only ingredient of comparative advantage that, in the long-term, will resist globalization' (Trebilcock, Chandler, and Howse 1990, 190).

What is true of nations is just as true of regions within nations, perhaps even more so given the diminished economic significance of national boundaries (Florida 1995; Kanter 1995a,b; Storper and Allen 1995). The most recent survey of the best Canadian cities in which to do business, conducted by *Report on Business Magazine,* looked for so-called 'smart cities,' characterized by such attributes as a research university actively engaged in university-industry partnerships, a highly educated workforce, a highly developed communications infrastructure, and 'plenty of PCs in high schools,' as well as 'the more traditional business considerations, such as cost, transportation and the degree to which a city was business-friendly' (Walmsley 1995, 45). This shift in emphasis reflects the emergence of what economic geographer Richard Florida (1995, 528) has called 'learning regions' that 'function as collectors and repositories of knowledge and ideas, and provide an underlying environment or infrastructure which facilitates the flow of knowledge, ideas and learning.'

In ecological terms, many of the technologies underpinning today's knowledge-based economy seem consistent with the dematerialization of economic growth. This is partly because the information-based consumer products now in high demand embody limited energy and raw material content: portable compact disc players, compact discs themselves, computer software, direct-broadcast satellite television receivers, and the program content that makes them marketable. Perhaps more significantly, as industries of all kinds become more knowledge intensive they will probably increase the efficiency with which they use energy and resource inputs. Further research is urgently needed on the global ecological and equity implications of a shift toward knowledge-based economic activity. The concept of ecological footprints requires that we ask whether we are genuinely reducing the resource intensiveness of economic activity and the extent to which industrialization relies on 'the discipline of labour by the state' (Amsden 1990, 18), and whether that discipline is imposed by way of direct restrictions of political freedoms or by way of macro-economic policies. Alternatively are we simply shifting low-wage and environmentally destructive activities offshore as part of a global division of the costs and benefits of industrialization that is also beginning to incorporate Third World style wages and work arrangements into the North American social fabric (Mead 1992)? This possibility is suggested by the Nike example outlined above and by the severity of industrial pollution and exploitative working conditions associated with the *maquiladora* plants of northern Mexico (dePalma 1993; Kelly 1992; United States General Accounting Office 1992).

Conclusion: Sustainability and Competitiveness in the National and Global Context

This disturbing possibility is just one question among many requiring further inquiry. Another, more immediate issue is whether Canada's political system is currently equipped to manage large-scale inter- and intraregional shifts in employment, income, and population on any basis other than the invocation of external causes for collapses that could have been anticipated well ahead of time. Those external causes may involve the resource base itself, the markets for it, or, in the case of manufactured goods, the changing basis of comparative advantage in an international context.

Unfortunately the answer is unclear, especially because the structure of Canadian political institutions is strongly conducive to the effective articulation of regional and local interests (Cairns 1991). A proactive approach to structural economic adjustment 'acknowledge[s] that an industry has no long-term future,' or at least has a future that involves reduced employment levels, 'and that politicians have elected to acquiesce in its fate' (Trebilcock 1986, 34). As a result, particularly when easing the process of adjustment out of declining industries will involve substantial expenditures, 'politicians will feel constrained to ask whether expenditures on such a scale anywhere else across the political landscape will yield more positive political returns.' The answer will almost always be yes, because of the geographically concentrated and therefore politically sensitive nature of the short-term economic losses that will result from refusal to bail out the troubled firm, plant, or industry (Trebilcock 1986; see also Trebilcock et al. 1985, 348-50).

Was the *Atlantic Groundfish Strategy* the best use of scarce resources? There was no candid national debate to consider whether those funds could have been better spent elsewhere in restructuring the national economy. Perhaps there should not have been one, given the desperate situation of the individuals and communities involved. On the other hand, what is the principled basis for distinguishing between Newfoundland workers whose livelihoods were lost with the collapse of the fishery and the far larger number of industrial workers in Ontario whose jobs and economic futures have disappeared as a result of the decline and restructuring of North American manufacturing? The geographic isolation of Newfoundlanders may or may not provide an adequate answer, but given the fiscal constraints now facing Canadian governments it is not absurd to ask the question and its more fundamental corollary: What is the extent of government obligation to individuals whose economic futures are jeopardized by structural economic change? There is, as Trebilcock notes, a strong ethical case, quite apart from the economic arguments, for organizing assistance around support for workers and communities rather than around the insulation or compensation of major shareholders and creditors, who are usually those best informed about the potential risks of the business in question, those best placed to reduce them, and those who can best afford to bear the costs.

The question of government obligation becomes politically strategic and contentious for at least two reasons. First, adopting economic policies that would minimize economic losses to workers and communities would almost certainly require substantial additional expenditures: 'new money' above and beyond that allocated to existing programs. This is particularly true of ambitious initiatives like the Workers' Superfund proposed in the United States. Patterned after a federally administered program for cleaning up industrial waste disposal sites, the proposal would 'provide those displaced from environmentally destructive or military industries with four years of support for further education and/or training at an institution of their own choosing,' including both tuition costs and lost earnings 'at the average union wage in the geographical region and industrial sector in which they were employed' (Wykle, Morehouse, and Dembo 1992, 54). Even more modest proposals, such as the Atlantic fishery task force's recommendation for special assistance to postsecondary institutions, come at a time when federal transfer payments are shrinking and provincial governments are engaging in deep and ongoing cuts to education funding. The present political climate is unremittingly hostile to such expenditures, although Trebilcock's analysis suggests that the longer term economic consequences of programs requiring substantial added expenditure in the short term might well be positive.

Second, an even more formidable challenge is presented by the likely impression that policies supporting the emergence of knowledge-based industries not only countenance the economic decline of regions whose economies are heavily reliant on resource extraction or harvesting and traditional manufacturing but also favour other, primarily urban, regions. Such policies are therefore likely, at least in some contexts, to reinforce already strong intraregional cleavages like those associated with forest policy in British Columbia.

To return to the theme with which the chapter began, those of us born and raised in the industrial countries since the end of the Second

World War are the quintessential postmaterialists, to use the phrase coined by Ronald Inglehart (1981, 1990; Inglehart and Rabier 1986). Our experience, however, is not shared by the majority of the world's population. Juan Martinez-Alier (1995, 83) has asked about the possibility of a 'contrast ... between a post-materialist environmentalism of affluence and a materialist environmentalism of the poor? This is too simple,' he concludes, noting the existence of materialist and postmaterialist, or at least non-materialist, environmentalisms in both rich and poor countries. It remains the case that the environmental problems confronting poor countries and their people are, with some exceptions, dramatically different from those we experience. They are also far more serious, often life threatening. Addressing them will require not only economic growth in the poor countries, but also the policy initiatives detailed throughout *Agenda 21*.

It is here that the most serious tension may emerge between sustainability and competitiveness. Rich countries such as Canada have already solved many of the environmental and resource management problems – like access to safe drinking water and some categories of urban air pollution – that routinely threaten life and health throughout much of the world. We also have the resources, if we choose to allocate them in this way, that would enable us to address many other such problems and to ease the social and economic consequences of adjustment to a changing international economy. Poor countries that are trying to cope simultaneously with population growth, the interactive downward spiral of poverty and environmental degradation, rapid urbanization, *and* the pressures associated with international competition for investment and product markets have no such luxury. They are therefore likely to become the loci of deadly and increasingly common resource-related political conflicts (Homer-Dixon 1994) from which we can probably remain insulated by virtue of national wealth. Often overlooked in discussions of the changing international economy is that such countries are competing not only with the industrialized world but also, and primarily, with each other for markets as well as for highly mobile capital (O'Reilly 1992; World Bank 1995, 50-64). In early 1993, Mexican officials expressed concern that wage increases in the wake of NAFTA might make the country's labour costs uncompetitive with those of Thailand, Malaysia, the Philippines, Indonesia, and China (Robinson 1993, 139). A further complication is the absence of the democratic domestic political institutions that offer at least minimal protection against the most exploitative economic and environmental circumstances (cf. Boyce 1995).

On a global scale, the question of whether competitive advantage can be pursued and achieved on some basis other than a race to the bottom in terms of such parameters as wages, working conditions, and environmental quality remains open. We must keep in mind that the stakes are high: competitiveness and sustainability are the two necessary conditions for national economic survival in a world that is shrinking both economically and ecologically.

Acknowledgments

Part of the research for the chapter was indirectly supported by Social Sciences and Humanities Research Council Canada grant 806-93-0002, which funds the operation of a strategic research network on sustainable development, growth, and distributive justice. The research assistance of Racquel Lindsay, Edith Richardson, and Derek Swartz is gratefully acknowledged, as are the comments of Jean Dalgleish and the editors of this volume on much earlier drafts of this chapter.

References

Allen, G. 1991. Ontario Hydro saves 600 Elliot Lake jobs. *Globe and Mail,* 18 June, sec. A

Amsden, A. 1990. Third World Industrialization: 'Global Fordism' or a New Model. *New Left Review* 182 (July-August):5-31

Ayres, R.U. 1989a. *Technological Transformations and Long Waves.* RR-89-1. Laxenburg, Austria: International Institute for Applied Systems Analysis

–. 1989b. Industrial Metabolism. In *Technology and Environment,* edited by J. Ausubel and H. Sladovich, 23-49. Washington, DC: National Academy Press

Ballinger, J. 1992. The New Free-Trade Heel: Nike's Profits Jump on the Backs of Asian Workers. *Harper's Magazine,* August, 46-7

Barrows, D. 1992. International Trade and Investments. In *Meeting the Global Challenge,* edited by J. Dermer, 31-56. North York, ON: Captus Press

Bell, D. 1977. Are There 'Social Limits' to Growth? In *Prospects for Growth,* edited by K.D. Wilson, 13-26. New York: Praeger Press

Boyce, J.K. 1995. Equity and the Environment. *Alternatives: Perspectives on Society, Technology and Environment* 21 (1):12-17

British Columbia Round Table on the Environment and the Economy (BCRTEE). 1993. An Economic Framework for Sustainability. Draft discussion paper, Round Table on the Environment and the Economy, Vancouver

Cairncross, F. 1991. *Costing the Earth.* London: Economist Books

Cairns, A. 1991. Constitutional Change and the Three Equalities. In *Options for a New Canada,* edited by R. Watts and D. Brown, 77-100. Toronto: University of Toronto Press

Calthorpe, P. 1993. *The Next American Metropolis: Ecology, Community, and the American Dream.* Princeton: Princeton Architectural Press

Canada, Department of Finance. 1994. *Federal Spending: Background.* Ottawa: Department of Finance

Canada, House of Commons. 1991. *Canada's Children: Investing in Our Future.* Second Report of the House of Commons Standing Committee on Health and Welfare, Social Affairs, Seniors and the Status of Women, Sub-Committee on Poverty. December. Ottawa: House of Commons

Clapp, R.A. 1995. Creating Competitive Advantage: Forest Policy as Industrial Policy in Chile. *Economic Geography* 71:273-96

Courchene, T. 1992a. The Meaning of No: A Political Era Dies. *Globe and Mail,* 27 October, sec. A

–. 1992b. Global Competitiveness and the Canadian Federation. In *Rearrangements: The Courchene Papers,* edited by T. Courchene, 108-44. Oakville, ON: Mosaic Press

Daly, H., and J. Cobb. 1989. *For the Common Good: Redirecting the Economy toward Community, the Environment, and a Sustainable Future.* Boston: Beacon Press

Daly, H., and R. Goodland. 1994. An Ecological-Economic Assessment of Deregulation of International Commerce under GATT, Part II. *Population and Environment* 15:477-503

Dansereau, S. 1992. Technological Change in the Canadian Mining Industry. *Raw Materials Report* 8 (3):10-21

dePalma, A. 1993. Law Protects Mexico's Workers, But Its Enforcement Is Often Lax. *New York Times,* 15 August, sec. A

Donaghu, M., and R. Barff. 1990. Nike Just Did It: International Subcontracting and Flexibility in Athletic Footwear Production. *Regional Studies* 24:537-52

Ehrlich, P. 1981. Environmental Disruption: Implications for the Social Sciences. *Social Sciences Quarterly* 62:7

Feschuk, S. 1992. Only One Big Processor Ready for Cod Clobbering. *Globe and Mail,* 3 July, sec. B

Florida, R. 1995. Toward the Learning Region. *Futures* 27:527-36

Freeman, C., and C. Perez. 1988. Structural Crises of Adjustment, Business Cycles and Investment Behaviour. In *Technical Change and Economic Theory,* edited by G. Dosi, C. Freman, R. Nelson, G. Silverberg, and L. Soete, 38-66. London: Frances Pinter

Gereffi, G., and M. Korzeniewicz, eds. 1993. *Commodity Chains and Global Capitalism.* New York: Praeger Press

Gomes, M.C., R.L. Haedrich, and M. Guadalupe Villagarcia. 1995. Spatial and Temporal Changes in the Groundfish Assemblages on the North-east Newfoundland/Labrador Shelf, North-west Atlantic, 1978-1991. *Fisheries Oceanography* 4 (2):85-101

Goodland, R. 1992. The Case That the World Has Reached Limits: More Precisely That Current Throughput Growth in the Global Economy Cannot be Sustained. *Population and Environment* 13:167-82

Goodland, R., and G. Ledec. 1987. Neoclassical Economics and Principles of Sustainable Development. *Ecological Modelling* 38:19-46

Goodland, R., H. Daly, and S. El Serafy. 1987. Introduction. In *Environmentally Sustainable Economic Development: Building on Brundtland,* edited by R. Goodland, H. Daly, and S. El Serafy. Environment working paper no. 46, July. Washington, DC: World Bank

Homer-Dixon, T. 1994. Environmental Scarcities and Violent Conflict: Evidence from Cases. *International Security* 19:5-40

Inglehart, R. 1981. Post-Materialism in an Environment of Insecurity. *American Political Science Review* 75:880-900

–. 1990. *Culture Shift in Advanced Industrial Society.* Princeton: Princeton University Press

Inglehart, R., and J.-R. Rabier. 1986. Political Realignment in Advanced Industrial Societies: From Class-Based Politics to Quality-of-Life Politics. *Government and Opposition* 21:456-79

Julius, D. 1990. *Global Companies and Public Policy: The Growing Challenge of Foreign Direct Investment.* London: Royal Institute of International Affairs

Kanter, R.M. 1995a. The New World Class: How Local Goes Global. *WorldLink* (September-October):52-8

–. 1995b. Thriving Locally in the Global Economy. *Harvard Business Review* 73 (5):151-60

Kelly, M.E. 1992. Free Trade: The Politics of Toxic Waste. *Report on the Americas* 26 (2):4-7

Krier, J., and C. Gillette. 1985. The Un-Easy Case for Technological Optimism. *Michigan Law Review* 84:405-29

Lappin, T. 1995. Truckin': It Isn't about Weed, Whites, and Wine Anymore. *Wired* 3 (1):118-23, 166

Lush, P. 1994. Cominco, B.C. Cut Deal on Smelter, Power. *Globe and Mail,* 5 March, sec. B

Marchak, P. 1995. *Logging the Globe.* Montreal: McGill-Queen's University Press

Martinez-Alier, J. 1995. Political Ecology, Distributional Conflicts, and Economic Incommensurability. *New Left Review* 211 (May-June):70-88

Mead, W.R. 1992. Bushism, Found: A Second-term Agenda Hidden in Trade Agreements. *Harper's Magazine,* September, 37-45

Netherlands Scientific Council for Government Policy. 1995. *Sustained Risks: A Lasting Phenomenon.* Reports to the Government no. 44. The Hague: Scientific Council for Government Policy

Ommer, Rosemary. In press. Deep Water Fisheries, Policy and Management Issues, and the Sustainability of Fishing Communities. In *Deep Water Fisheries of the North Atlantic Slope,* edited by A.G. Hopper. Proceedings of the NATO Advanced Research Workshop. Dordrecht: Kluwer

O'Reilly, B. 1992. Your New Global Work Force. *Fortune,* 14 December, 52-66

Palmer, B. 1994. *Capitalism Comes to the Backcountry: The Goodyear Invasion of Napanee.* Toronto: Between the Lines

Pearce, D., A. Markandya, and E.B. Barbier. 1989. *Blueprint for a Green Economy.* London: Earthscan

Pearse, P.H. 1993. Growth Fells the Foresters. *Globe and Mail,* 21 October, sec. A

Porter, M., and C. van der Linde. 1995. Green and Competitive: Ending the Stalemate. *Harvard Business Review* 73 (5):120-34

Pratt, L., and I. Urquhart. 1994. *The Last Great Forest: Japanese Multinationals and Alberta's Northern Forest* Edmonton: NeWest Press

Rees, W. 1992. Ecological Footprints and Appropriated Carrying Capacity: What Urban Economics Leaves Out. *Environment and Urbanization* 4:121-30

Rees, W., and M. Wackernagel. 1994. Ecological Footprints and Appropriated Carrying Capacity: Measuring the Natural Capital Requirements of the Human Economy. In *Investing in Natural Capital: The Ecological Economics Approach to Sustainability,* edited by A. Jansson, M. Hammer, C. Folke, and R. Costanza, 362-90. Washington, DC: Island Press

Regier, Henry, and Gordon Baskerville. 1986. Sustainable Redevelopment of Regional Ecosystems Degraded by Exploitive Development. In *Sustainable Development of the Biosphere,* edited by W.C. Clark and R.E. Munn, 75-101. Cambridge: Cambridge University Press

Robinson, Alan. 1993. Pressures Mount on Maquiladoras. *WorldLink* (January-February):138-9

Sachs, J. 1995. Keep Baby in the Bath Water. *WorldLink* (September-October):49-50

Saunders, J. 1995. Helping the Helpless: Case Studies of NDP Government Aid to Industry in Ontario. *Globe and Mail,* 27 May, sec. B

Schrecker, T. 1987. Risks versus Rights: Economic Power and Economic Analysis in Environmental Politics. In *Business Ethics in Canada,* edited by D. Poff and W. Waluchow, 265-84. Scarborough: Prentice-Hall Canada

–. 1993. Missing the Point about Growth. In *Crosscurrents 2: International Relations in the Post-Cold War Era,* edited by M. Charlton and E. Riddell-Dixon, 535-41. Toronto: Nelson

Séguin, R. 1994. Hyundai Returns to Haunt Liberals. *Globe and Mail,* 23 March, sec. B

Shrybman, S. 1990. International Trade and the Environment. *The Ecologist* 20 (1):30-4

Sinclair, W. 1991. Controlling Effluent Discharges from Canadian Pulp and Paper Manufacturers. *Canadian Public Policy* 17:86-105

Stevenson, R.W. 1995. Smitten by Britain, Business Rushes In: Thatcherism's Industrial Evolution. *New York Times* 15 October, sec. 3

Storper, M.S., and J. Allen. 1995. The Wealth of Regions: Market Forces and Policy Imperatives in Local and Global Context. *Futures* 27:505-26

Streeten, P. 1993. Markets and States: Against Minimalism. *World Development* 21:1281-98

Task Force on Incomes and Adjustment in the Atlantic Fishery. 1993. *Charting a New Course: Towards the Fishery of the Future.* Ottawa: Communications Directorate, Department of Fisheries and Oceans

Trebilcock, M. 1986. *The Political Economy of Economic Adjustment.* Toronto: University of Toronto Press

Trebilcock, M., M. Chandler, M. Gunderson, P. Halpern, and J. Quinn. 1985. *The Political Economy of Business Bailouts.* 2 vols. Toronto: Ontario Economic Council

Trebilcock, M., M. Chandler, and R. Howse. 1990. *Trade and Transitions: A Comparative Analysis of Adjustment Policies.* London: Routledge

United States General Accounting Office. 1992. *U.S.-Mexico Trade: Assessment of Mexico's Environmental Controls for New Companies.* GAO/GGD-92-113. Washington, DC: US Government Printing Office

Vincent, I. 1993. Chile's Prospects Entice Canadians. *Globe and Mail,* 27 April, sec. B

Walmsley, A. 1995. Smart Cities: *Report on Business Magazine*'s Fourth Annual Survey of the Best Cities for Business in Canada. *Report on Business Magazine* 12 (2):44-73

Westell, D. 1994. New Rules to Cut Toxic Wastes 47%. *Globe and Mail,* 14 September, sec. B

World Bank. 1995. *World Development Report 1995: Workers in an Integrating World.* New York: Oxford University Press

World Commission on Environment and Development (WCED). 1987. *Our Common Future – Report of the World Commission on Environment and Development.* Oxford: Oxford University Press

WorldLink Survey. 1993. Regional Competitiveness: The World's Best Regions. *WorldLink* (November-December):31-4

Wykle, L., W. Morehouse, and D. Dembo. 1992. *Worker Empowerment in a Changing Economy: Jobs, Military Production, and the Environment.* New York: Apex Press

Action

4
Biodiversity Conservation: A Decision-Making Context
Ann Dale and Stuart B. Hill

The worst thing that can happen is not energy depletion, economic collapse, limited nuclear war, or conquest by a totalitarian government. As terrible as these catastrophes would be for us, they can be repaired within a few generations. The one process ongoing that will take millions of years to correct is the loss of genetic and species diversity by the destruction of natural habitats. This is the folly our descendants are least likely to forgive us (Wilson 1992).

From the beginning of the 1960s, environmental concerns were included more and more often on national and international agendas. Previously, governments had focused on single, smaller scale effects such as pollution control, acid rain, single species preservation such as fur seals and whales, migratory wildlife, toxic contamination, and the domestic management of natural resources. The scale of these issues began to shift dramatically, however, in the late 1960s, from apparently local, relatively contained effects to larger, global phenomena. Single, local species loss enlarged into biodiversity loss globally; pollution control expanded to encompass ozone depletion and climate change; local fisheries and marine mammal issues progressed to the broader concern of stewardship of ocean resources and attendant issues of dying coral reefs and deep-seabed mining. There is now emerging scientific consensus that the maintenance of the earth as a suitable habitat for humans, and for most other species, is at stake.

It has been estimated that humans already appropriate over 40 per cent of net primary production (Vitousek et al. 1986). Fortunately, ecological constraints on human activities are beginning to be recognized at various levels. Although some of these constraints may have temporary technical solutions, it is becoming clear to many that because of the increasingly consumptive and disruptive habits of our growing population, we are fast approaching and may even have exceeded the carrying capacity of the planet. The concept of ecological limits is, however, open to debate. Whereas some argue that these limits are fixed and inelastic, others believe that ecological carrying capacity is plastic, normative, and not reducible to a simple measure. Such debates reflect what societies value and define as their needs (Regier 1995).

In general, however, it appears that human carrying capacity can be increased only at the expense of other species (Dale, Robinson, and Massey 1995). For some time, we have been living in an anthropogenic era because of our ability to transcend time, place, and scale through technology.

The five most urgent challenges currently facing humanity, which will continue to persist well into the twenty-first century in the overall context of sustainable development, are global warming, ozone depletion, biodiversity loss, overpopulation, and equity. Equity may prove to be the overarching social imperative, particularly if current population rates continue to rise, environmental degradation accelerates with attendant further decline in the quantity and quality of natural resources, and access to basic needs for life continues to diminish for certain groups and regions. These five issues are interactive, overlapping, and complex, and each embodies some aspect of the others (Caldwell 1990).

An analysis of various reports over the last twenty years shows that the same recommendations for action keep appearing. What is missing is the political and personal will to effect change (Dale 1990). The solutions to these problems do not lie primarily in science and technology but in political, corporate, and personal decision-making. The very nature of the challenges, and the fact that they continue to worsen demands immediate changes in the process of decision-making at all political levels. The increasing globalization of biophysical phenomena, trade, and large-scale human migration collapses traditional notions of sovereignty and scale dependency. We are therefore witnessing an intensification of the problems across both space and time (Holling 1993). Effects extend from local to global, as in harvesting practices in tropical rain forests that affect climate everywhere.

Ecosystem responses to these effects are non-linear, interactive, and often spatially and temporally unexpected (Holling 1993). Societal solutions lie in our understanding the dynamics of both complex ecosystems and social systems with their perception of multiple realities and associated need for multiple approaches. Thus our knowledge in general, and the contributions from science in particular, will always be incomplete and inadequate. Efforts for improvement must take into account a plurality of interests. Both multipartite and interdisciplinary forms of decision-making are therefore needed, and explicit references to values are at the heart of the process.

We are living in a period between myths. The positivist modernism myth claims that we can understand nature with science, control it with technology, and create well-being with material abundance through the marketplace. We are now beginning to realize the naïveté of this and witnessing the numerous unexpected negative side effects (Norgaard 1994).

The postmodern myth recognizes that systems are complex, interactive, co-evolving, and to some extent self-organizing, and that they exhibit unique properties within different contexts. It builds on the insights of quantum mechanics, irreversible thermodynamics, information theory, organic evolution, constructivism, and pluralism rather than on the limited mechanistic insights of René Descartes and Isaac Newton. For our species this implies that we must conduct our affairs in such a way that we can conserve our cultural and natural capital and facilitate their positive co-evolution by means of suitable institutional structures and processes.

The current capacity of our institutions of governance to effect significant change in these areas, however, remains weak because of the dominant organizational structures and modes of decision-making. Government decision-making is still opaque, often inaccessible, and based on a positivist, expert-driven rational model. Its emphasis on control-oriented management has led to more and more brittle and rigid organizational structures and associated growing pathologies (Walters and Holling 1990). Moreover, the fragmentation and isolation of processes resulting from present departmental separation of institutional structures leads to a plethora of economically perverse and ecologically damaging incentive structures and barriers. Overall efforts to promote growth at almost any cost are thus frequently in conflict with the stated aims of departments concerned with health, the environment, and social justice.

Because it has widespread acceptance both domestically and internationally the definition of sustainable development from the Brundtland Commission – as development that meets the needs of the present without sacrificing the needs of future generations – provides us with a framework for bridging these issues (WCED 1987). Sustainable development is receiving attention partly because we now have such high levels of economic interdependence and it raises fundamental questions about the distribution of wealth, power, and resources between the North and South (Hurrell and Kingsbury 1992). The ability of the term to forge new links and at the same time remain paradoxical should perhaps be viewed as its greatest strength, rather than criticized as a weakness.

In Canada, in spite of ongoing debate about and criticisms of an acceptable definition, there is increasing consensus that sustainable development implies the integration of environmental and economic decisions, although there remains less openness to the inclusion of social issues. As a consequence one can easily assemble over a hundred definitions for the term, and it is not our intention to enter this debate. We do, however, take the position that the term implies reconciliation of ecological, social, and economic imperatives. Although these may vary according to the biophysical and socio-economic features of particular regions, we nonetheless hope that common elements will emerge through such reconciliation. Within this overall context, and accepting the Brundtland definition, we will use the specific issue of biodiversity conservation to highlight the complexities of decision-making for sustainable development. It is therefore useful to take a brief look at the meaning of biodiversity first.

The following taxonomy is modified from the *Global Biodiversity Strategy* (WRI, IUCN, and UNEP 1992). Biodiversity is the totality of genes, species, and ecosystems within a region. The wealth of life on earth today is the product of hundreds of millions of years of evolutionary history. Over the course of time, human cultures have emerged and adapted to local environments, discovering, using, and altering their biotic resources. Many areas that now seem 'natural' bear the marks of millennia of human habitation, crop cultivation, resource harvesting, and waste production. The domestication and breeding of local varieties of crops and livestock have further shaped biodiversity.

For convenience, biodiversity can be divided into three hierarchical categories: genes, species, and ecosystems. These describe quite different aspects of living systems and scientists measure them in different ways.

Genetic diversity refers to the variation of genes within species. There occur distinct populations of the same species, such as thousands of traditional rice varieties in India, and genetic variation within a single population, which is very high among Indian rhinos, for example, and very low among cheetahs. Until recently, measurements of genetic diversity were applied mainly to domesticated species and populations held in zoos and botanical gardens, but increasingly these techniques are also being applied to wild species.

Species diversity refers to the variety of species within a region. Such diversity can be measured in many ways, and scientists have not settled on the best method. The number of species in a region – its species 'richness' – is one often used measure, but a more precise measurement, 'taxonomic diversity,' also considers the relationship of species to one another. An island with two species of birds and one species of lizard, for example, has greater taxonomic diversity than an island with three species of birds and no lizards.

Ecosystem diversity is harder to measure than species or genetic diversity because the 'boundaries' of communities – associations of species – and of ecosystems are elusive. Nevertheless, as long as a consistent set of criteria is used to define communities and ecosystems, their number and distribution can be measured. Until now, such schemes have been applied mainly at national and subnational levels, although some coarse global classifications have been proposed.

Many other expressions of biodiversity can be important. These include the relative abundance of species, the age structure of populations, the pattern of communities within a region, changes in community composition and structure over time, and ecological processes such as predation, parasitism, and mutualism. To meet specific management and policy goals, it is crucial to examine not only compositional diversity – genes, species, and ecosystems – but also diversity in ecosystem structure and function.

Human cultural diversity could be considered part of biodiversity. Like genetic and species diversity, some attributes of human cultures, such as nomadism and shifting cultivation, represent 'solutions' to the problems of survival within particular environments. Like other aspects of biodiversity, cultural diversity helps people adapt to changing conditions. It is evident within language, religious beliefs, land management practices, art, music, social structure, crop selection, diet, human relationships, and numerous other attributes of human society.

We have selected the issue of biodiversity rather than one of the other four identified above – global warming, ozone depletion, overpopulation, and equity – because we believe that its irreversibility makes it one of the most important issues now facing our society. Expert assessments of the scale and temporality of the decline vary greatly, although as early as 1980 it was predicted that 500,000 to 2 million species would become extinct worldwide by the year 2000 (Lovejoy 1980) and that the rate of decline would increase from one per day in 1970 to one per hour by the end of the century (Myers 1979). We may be exceeding even these early estimates with respect to tropical forests, which are now disappearing at a rate of some 17 million hectares a year, and they are estimated to contain over three-quarters of the species on the planet (WRI, IUCN, and UNEP 1992). Estimates of potential species extinction in the tropics in general vary from 20 to 50 per cent over the next thirty years. Thus, these species are predicted to either die out or be reduced to such small populations that extinction is inevitable (Lovejoy 1980; Myers 1983; Oldfield 1984; Ehrlich 1982; Simberloff 1983; Wilson 1988).

Losses at this rate of magnitude are clearly undesirable (Ehrlich 1982; Kim 1993; Myers 1993; Reid and Miller 1989; Wilson 1988). Ehrlich, Ehrlich, and Holdren (1977) estimated that in the closing decades of the twentieth century the rate of species extinction will be some forty to 400 times the rate that has prevailed through most of geological time. Much of this accelerating loss is occurring before we have had a chance even to name these taxa, much less to appreciate the unique services they provide within ecosystems. Because so few habitats have been adequately investigated, estimates of the total number of species on the planet vary by orders of magnitude from 3 million to over 30 million. In any event, only 1.4 million of these have been named and just a fraction of these have been studied in any detail (Wilson 1988). Our knowledge of most invertebrates, primitive plants, and microorganisms remains particularly fragmentary.

The loss and degradation of terrestrial and aquatic habitats are continuing at an alarming rate and the existing mechanisms to ameliorate this are inadequate. The main cause of biodiversity loss is habitat destruction from increasing population growth and technological expansion (Ehrenfeld 1988; Ehrlich and Wilson 1991; McNeely et al. 1990; Reid and Miller 1989; WRI, IUCN, and UNEP 1992). In 1993, 87 million extra people were added to the planet, bringing the world population to nearly 5.6 billion. The United Nations now projects that world population will not peak until after 2200, when it will have reached over 11 billion (Brown, Kane, and Roodman 1994).

As our numbers increase, we inevitably displace other species. In the process of designing and managing human habitats, we also tend to create conditions in which pest and disease species and species with requirements similar to our own such as rats, cockroaches, and houseflies are favoured, and efforts to control them inevitably result in further negative effects. Even in those countries where burgeoning human numbers do not appear to be a problem, we are continuing to displace other species from the highest quality space through deforestation, agricultural expansion and intensification, and urbanization.

Every other sustainable development issue, therefore, without exception, affects and is affected by biodiversity. Biodiversity may be viewed as a library of historical and emergent information, and as such provides not only a multiplicity of evolutionary and adaptive pathways for future development of life on earth but also the essential regenerative capacity for all living systems (Ehrenfeld 1988; Regier 1995). Put simply, we need high biodiversity to ensure our own survival. Wilson (1988) estimates, for example, that the full information contained in the DNA of the common house mouse is equivalent to the text in the fifteen editions of the *Encyclopedia Britannica* published since 1768, if the former were translated into ordinary printed letters. Schneider and Kay (1994) have developed this idea further. They describe the gene as

> a record of successful self-organization. Given that living systems go through a constant cycle of birth, growth, death and renewal, at many temporal and spatial scales, a way of preserving information about what works and what doesn't so as to constrain the self-organization process is crucial for the continuance of life. This is the role of the gene. At the larger scale, it is the role of biodiversity (p. 36).

Because certain species are known to play a keystone role within ecosystems, they especially ought to be conserved because they have a disproportionate effect on the persistence of all other species (Bond 1993). Such species include large predators that 'manage' competitor populations, mutualists such as pollinators and dispersers that facilitate reproduction, and nitrogen fixers and mycorrhizae that affect rates of nutrient transfer (Boucher 1985). As well as affecting the survival of other species, keystone species play a major role in maintaining community integrity and environmental quality (Paine 1966). Thus the loss of a keystone species will eventually lead to a multitude of linked extinctions by means of a ripple effect through the ecosystem (Myers 1990).

In addition to being scientifically complex, biodiversity conservation is normative and involves profound social, ethical, and aesthetic questions. What value does the polar bear have to Canadians? Or the common loon? Will our society be affected by their disappearance or decline? Do we consider that we would be worse off or are we indifferent to their extinction? Do we save only the attractive birds and mammals, or do we consider the trade-offs between species that are essential for the maintenance of ecosystems? As more and more keystone species disappear we may well find ourselves – as a result of our changing role and growing numbers – with the unenviable responsibility not only for rates of extinction but also for maintenance of the many ecological processes on which we depend for our survival.

Biodiversity conservation forces us to adopt a broad systems perspective because it involves complex interactions both at the individual, community, and species levels and between ecosystem functioning and the ecological services that keystone species provide for all life. These indispensable, irreplaceable 'eco-services' include maintenance of the gaseous composition of the atmosphere, regulation of the earth's hydrological cycle, soil formation and maintenance, disposal of wastes and cycling of plant nutrients, biogeochemical cycles, and pest control and pollination (Ehrlich 1982). Conservation of biodiversity therefore necessarily involves protection and regeneration of habitat through appropriate ecosystem management.

Ecosystems are unique, holarctic, and often highly dynamic open systems characterized by complex, non-linear relationships between the parts and the whole. They exhibit self-organizing maintenance and regulatory and co-evolutionary processes, some of which may be fairly resilient and others highly susceptible to disruption by imposed stresses. The task in working with ecosystems is to support these processes – thereby building negentropy – while knowing that our understanding of them is fragmentary and often inadequate to provide a solid foundation for wise decision-making. Uncertainty and surprise are the norm (Walters and Holling 1990). In taking ecosystemic approaches to ecosystem management, it is important to remember that all species are the product of co-evolutionary processes, a few species being highly adaptable but most being highly specialized, with narrow environmental requirements and tolerances that must be weighed when designing management plans. It is particularly important to consider this when endeavouring to conserve endangered keystone species because of their broad influence on overall biodiversity. Appropriate decisions must be based on an understanding of this complexity; we must assign priorities with the implications of irreversible (biodiversity) versus reversible (economic) crises in mind. As well, it is necessary to be proactive and to appraise the needs of future generations and the interrelationship of biodiversity initiatives and other environmental and cultural issues.

The complex and interlocking nature of biodiversity therefore demands changes in the way we make decisions. Our present institutional arrangements – academic, professional, and governmental – are incapable of adequate collaboration because they are physically isolated from one another and their procedures conflict. Their current organization is also incompatible with the realities of complex and self-organizing open systems. Dryzek (1987), for example, has argued that instrumental rationality lies at the root of society's failure to deal with ecosystemic complexities, primarily because the dominant science implicitly assumes that complex systems are best handled by disaggregating them into their many parts. Needless to say, this reductionism then allows the parts to be dealt with in isolation, and therefore inappropriately, by different disciplinary experts. Dryzek proposes new forms of communicative competency to facilitate discourse that reveals and deals with complexities in some kind of direct, participatory manner (Dryzek 1992). Linear, hierarchical, and deterministic ways of thinking and organizing tend to be antithetical to understanding and working with the complex, open, self-organizing, and nested systems found in nature. If we are to conserve the complexity and richness of biodiversity effectively, we need to develop organic organizational structures that can support the development of appropriate policies.

Biodiversity conservation initiatives can be achieved neither in isolation from other program and policy goals nor without recognizing the plurality of interests involved. For specific programs to be effective, they must be part of a broader, integrative program that facilitates an evolution in values and world views emphasizing recognition of and respect for natural limits, the rights of other species and our responsibilities toward them, equity, more appropriate non-monetary measures of value, participation in political processes, and many more factors.

There are five key aspects of biodiversity conservation, and these must be understood before appropriate decisions can be made. First, we will never attain scientific consensus over the systems under examination, partly because knowledge will always be incomplete (Walters 1986; Collie and Walters 1993). Second, change in managed ecosystems and in the societies with which they are co-evolving is inherently unpredictable (Holling 1993). Third, a dynamic, situation-specific, adaptive management system is preferable to a generalized passive one or to maintenance of the status quo because our ability to forecast and plan for change will always be limited (Walters 1986). Fourth, decision-making must focus on ecosystem processes for effective habitat conservation. Fifth, since complex bio-ecological, aesthetic, moral, and social dimensions are involved, biodiversity conservation incorporates the notion of multiple stakeholders, broadening the constituency in time and space to include other voices not normally considered in traditional decision-making forums.

The constituency can be broadened only by establishing pluralistic forums in which the multiplicity of legitimate perspectives can be expressed and questions of biodiversity policy and valuation can be addressed. The valuation of those characteristics of life that are irreversible and for which there are no substitutes is particularly problematic for decisionmakers. Conventional market mechanisms are inappropriate for such valuations, which must consider both methodology and ethics. Biodiversity conservation therefore has to be addressed within forums that represent the bio-ecological, technological, economic, socio-political, aesthetic, and ethical dimensions and consider them interactively. Multi-stakeholder dialogue is crucial to accommodate the broad range of interests involved.

Adoption of an adequately broad perspective is a central challenge for the current expert-driven, rational decision-making model. As Brewer argues,

> prevailing attitudes and styles of knowledge creation and uses have too often done precisely the opposite – by denying the legitimacy of different perspectives and preferences, by adhering narrowly to intellectual paradigms ill-suited to the challenges (and then dissolving into brittle squabbles when the limitations of each are exposed), and by favoring tools and methods used to solve problems only remotely like those facing us (and continuing to use them despite lack of success) (n.d., p. 467).

Interdisciplinarity and integrated modes of inquiry are needed for understanding sustainable development because competence in this area, which can never be based on complete knowledge, must rely on the best available information and expertise, intuition, responsible experimentation, and common sense. Interdisciplinarity must necessarily integrate the various disciplines within the natural and social sciences, given the complex interactions of environmental and social systems and the current difficulty of reconciling social and ecological imperatives. It should be noted that whereas many ecological imperatives relate to absolutes such as each species' needs for food and space, social imperatives are relative and much more flexible, although it may not seem so. In the long term, ecology determines the bottom line of culture, not vice versa.

Both interdisciplinarity and multi-stakeholder processes are dependent upon the development of a shared 'pre-analytic vision' (Daly 1995), or what Holling (1993) refers to as the entry point of problems. Developing the pre-analytic vision makes explicit the dominant paradigms and world views with their associated assumptions and values. This is essential to transcending the status quo and creating new solutions based on knowledge emerging from an interdisciplinary perspective and participatory processes. That 'prevalent analytic paradigms and particular intellectual perspectives are extremely limited as a means to comprehend and inform realistic choices' (Brewer n.d., p. 467) must not be underestimated.

One interesting technique for exposing dominant thought patterns and methodologies is strategic questioning. Strategic questions, as defined by Peavey (1994) are questions that make a difference. They help extricate our thinking from fixed positions, open up options and liberate creativity, expose the roots of prevailing paradigms, avoid asking 'why' or provoking defensiveness, avoid yes-no questions, empower rather than manipulate, question assumptions, support expressions of our higher values, and facilitate our positive co-evolution. Examples of strategic questions that can be used to broaden thinking prior to planning for the conservation of biodiversity are given in the appendix to this chapter.

Because habitat preservation is a prerequisite for biodiversity conservation – particularly for the preservation of mega-species, which have extensive space requirements – policies designed to promote it are of immediate concern. They require a fundamental understanding of the structure and dynamics of ecosystems and of non-linear dynamics and complex, evolving systems. Because the properties of ecosystems are uncertain and unpredictable (Ludwig, Hilborn, and Walters 1993), appropriate policies and actions must accommodate an evolving understanding of them while meeting our also evolving social goals (Holling 1989-90). Just as ecosystems are constantly evolving, policies and planning must evolve in parallel organic ways. Users of resources need to be encouraged and supported to become conservers of them, with the attendant responsibility for monitoring and evaluation thereby facilitating a positive co-evolution of nature and culture.

Building models of both hard and soft systems can help to identify gaps in our knowledge about complex systems and serve as effective planning tools for policy analysts, decisionmakers, and stakeholders (Checkland and Scholes 1990). They have six functions. First, they are capable of linking research information and analysis directly to those making resource management decisions without a filter of bureaucratic interpretation. Second, they make explicit the uncertainties and difficult choices related to risks and planning time frames. Third, they can expose innovative policies by making use of spatial replication, allowing decision-makers to see the effects of their trade-offs. Fourth, they can facilitate more flexible responses to natural and human surprises. Fifth, they can expose gaps in information and knowledge, leading to the development of more precise research agendas. Sixth, by creating a visual image, they can evoke an emotional response, leading to more direct action (F. Westley, personal communication).

Questions of space, time, energy, and information (Schneider and Kay 1994) are paramount for the conservation of biodiversity and for sustainable development decision-making. The knowledge systems required therefore integrate not only disciplines but also whole metafields, with their diverse ontologies, epistemologies, and methodologies. Modelling that is informed by holartic theory, spatial dynamics, event models, satellite imagery, geographical information systems, and gender balance and other forms of socio-cultural awareness will start to address some of the inherent complexities.

Analysis should be cognizant of the interactions between slow and fast phenomena and should monitor long-term, slow changes in structural variables (Holling 1993). The political window that emphasizes quick fixes simply leads to increasingly unforgiving conditions for future decisions, more fragile natural systems, and more dependent and distrustful citizens (Holling 1993). It must be recognized that the environment and society interact in co-evolutionary ways at regional, national, international, and planetary levels (Holling 1993). Forums for biodiversity decision-making, therefore, should attempt to develop practices that can take into account natural time spans for key ecological processes within the realities of the electoral processes.

When values are both ecologically and socially high, the stakes must be recognized as correspondingly higher for present and future generations. Pluralistic forums cannot have all voices reflected at the table; most obviously they cannot include those of other species and future generations. Yet their 'interests' are where the stakes are likely to be the highest. Only the widest possible diversity of representation can balance this inadequacy. By paying attention to gender balance, for example, much broader and deeper considerations of the difficult trade-offs to be made may be achieved.

Useful knowledge, good policy, and effective communication – and incidentally artistic endeavour – are produced through simplicity and focus. Models to enhance decision-making in the context of both knowledge systems and politics must therefore be simple and easily understood by a wide variety of stakeholders. It must be appreciated, however, that such models will miss most of the complexities of the systems under study, and it may therefore be prudent first to identify the crucial keystone species and model their functions and the effects of their elimination. The accuracy and relevance of information selected is key to the success of these pluralistic forums and to meaningful decision-making.

The integrity of this information is limited by the ability of our sociopolitical institutions to generate both active, adaptive management systems (Holling 1978) that promote learning and innovation and policies that recognize the interrelation of process and product. Figure 4.1 depicts how these pluralistic decision-making forums could be structured to enhance decision-making for biodiversity conservation in particular and sustainable development generally. The model represents only a first step in broadening the concept of experts and stakeholders, who will necessarily vary depending on the specific issue in sustainable development being addressed and on its particular dimensions of time and place. The separation between disciplinary and stakeholder inputs reflects the current isolation of the research community from the wider community of which it is a part.

It is only through the interface of the three overlapping circles shown in the figure that the most innovative and effective solutions for sustainable development will emerge from the synergism of new insights from several fields and multiple interests represented at the table (Kay 1994). This dynamic and 'untidy' interface represents the paradox of decision-making for uncertainty and surprise. The ability to live within this paradox requires individuals with the ability to transcend disciplinary perspectives and resolve paradoxes of stability and change, of order and chaos, of order and disorder, of sustainability and development (Holling 1989-90), and of simplicity and complexity. They must transcend gaps in knowledge to make decisions with irreversible

Figure 4.1

Pluralistic decision-making

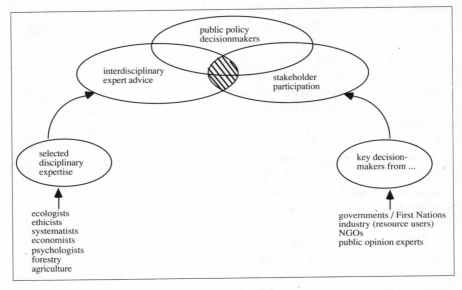

consequences for future generations. They must simultaneously deal with the parts and the whole, and balance the needs of our species with the needs of the many 'others' with which we share this planet. Such changes in decision-making will require a massive shift in our appreciation of our role in the universe, our relationships with other species, and our understanding of the value of diversity and beauty in our world, perhaps leading to an appreciation that there is really no 'other.' We close with the strategic question we ask ourselves each day: If not us, then who will take responsibility?

Appendix: An Illustrative List of Strategic Questions for Biodiversity Conservation

Having a 'shopping list' of strategic questions – questions that facilitate movement away from dominant paradigms – is essential to the process of implementing positive change. Questions can be used to obtain essential information, to clarify assumptions and values, to develop new visions, to identify and involve relevant stakeholders, to recognize barriers and ways to remove them, to act on opportunities for making progress, to highlight priorities, and to encourage creativity and collaboration.

Information and Knowledge

(1) What gaps in our knowledge are preventing us from developing effective local, provincial, national, and international strategies for the conservation of biodiversity? How can they best be addressed?

(2) What are the ecological, economic, and social consequences of loss of biodiversity in each area? How are these likely to influence one another over the long term?

(3) What are the primary threats to biodiversity within each region and what can we do about them?

(4) What level of species diversity is required to maintain the various ecosystem services within each region?

(5) What keystone species can we least afford to lose?

(6) If we had detailed knowledge of the bio-ecology and ecosystem functions of all of the species within Canada, would this guarantee that all or most would be conserved? If not, why not? What else is limiting effective action and what needs to be done to address this situation?

(7) If access to quantitative information is not a significant limit to effective action, is the lack of other kinds of knowledge limiting? Do we need to know more about what determines human behaviour, for example, or about the process of change, or about holistic and systemic approaches to habitat restoration and maintenance? How should we assign priority to these factors and how could we redesign biodiversity conservation programs accordingly?

(8) What will it take for me, my local community and businesses, and the various levels of government to initiate responsible action for biodiversity conservation?

(9) How can we define and value biodiversity in ways relevant for those who decide policy?

(10) What existing information systems need to be amalgamated and further developed to produce a clear biodiversity map for Canada?

Paradigms and Processes in Academic Institutions

(1) Can success be achieved within the boundaries of the present dominant paradigms of learning, research, development, and extension of programs to the wider community? If not, what needs to change?

(2) How could participatory action research approaches be used effectively for biodiversity conservation?

(3) Have our approaches overemphasized the values given on the left, overleaf, and underemphasized those on the right?

- hierarchical, patriarchal
- single discipline

- short-term
- national, state, polit-zone
- econocentric, anthropocentric, ethnocentric
- single, linear, direct, deterministic, rigid

- focus on problems and cures

- product, single focus, isolated goals
- institutional territoriality, competition
- secret, owned, inaccessible, authored
- big science, capital and resource intensive, centralized

- life-stage limited, synthetic, systemic, learning based

- unidirectional, doctrinaire learning

- systemic, participatory
- inclusive, holistic, organismic systems, transdisciplinary

- short- to long-term
- global, regional, local
- ecosystem, ecocentric, equicentric
- multifaceted, cyclical, complex, indirect, chaotic, flexible

- healthy systems promotion, problem prevention

- maintenance, multiple, focus on integrated goals
- transinstitutional collaboration
- open, accessible, anonymous
- scale- and resource-appropriate science, decentralized, subtle, catalytic

- life-long, experiential, imposed learning on own agenda

- intentional, multidirectional, evolving learning

(4) Do models exist in other countries that have more success in promoting academic, industry, and government linkages, which might provide a structural basis for effective biodiversity conservation programs? How could they be applied in Canada?

(5) What role does academia have to play in disseminating research findings? How can this be done?

Individual Responsibility

(1) Do I have a well-developed vision of how I can live in an environment in which biodiversity is appreciated and maintained? Describe it. If not, what is my partial vision and what is limiting its further development?

(2) What brings an issue into the moral arena, what makes it a matter of moral concern, and how can we deal with our conflicting values relating to biodiversity conservation?

(3) What would it take to extend our moral concern to other organisms? How might this affect our sense of personal fulfilment?

(4) Is the argument of species superiority based on intellectual and spiritual difference a defensible criterion for moral concern that applies varying standards?

(5) What relationship, if any, is there among hierarchical systems, gender, the concept of dominion over nature, and regard for other life forms?

(6) What am I willing to give up to help achieve my biodiversity conservation goals? How would I describe my projected gains?

Resources

(1) What would it take to redirect resources from other, less critical areas to biodiversity conservation?

(2) What skills and training are necessary for biodiversity conservationists? What do these people need to do, and where, to be successful?

(3) Do women and indigenous peoples bring different and inherent values to our appreciation of other species? How can we draw on these human resources?

Governance

(1) What cultural, social, and ethical principles could provide a context for the conservation of biodiversity? Which of these are currently widely accepted, which are not, and how can the latter be promoted?

(2) What aspects of the current political system constitute barriers to effective biodiversity conservation? How can they be removed or transformed?

(3) What kinds of forums should be established to generate more appropriate applied policy research in designing effective conservation programs over the long and short term?

(4) What mix of decisionmakers must be at the table to develop regional and national biodiversity strategies? What process will be most effective in facilitating appropriate action?

(5) Is the preservation of all species desirable and achievable? If not, is it possible and feasible to adopt selective strategies? On what basis should we choose species for conservation?

(6) What constitutes an appropriate mix of social and market mechanisms for biodiversity? How can they be mobilized to maximize biodiversity in the short term and develop an appropriate ethos among the general public over the longer term?

(7) Can we measure the value of biodiversity? If we cannot devise appropriate forms of measurement, how can we enable politicians to make informed decisions about the trade-offs with other public spending priorities?

(8) If human survival and quality of life depend on biodiversity conservation, what institutional structures and procedures are required to ensure that the public, government, and business are aware of this?

(9) Have we overemphasized the characteristics shown on the left, below, and underemphasized those on the right?

Dominant worldview	*Alternative worldview*
• national, state	• global bioregional, local
• anthropocentric, present generation, existing elite	• ecocentric, future generations, social justice, equity
• ethnocentric	• equifinality (diverse paths to just goals)
• dependent, closed systems	• self-organizing and maintaining open systems
• mechanistic, formulaic, patterned	• organismic, instinctual, spontaneous
• rigid, defensive, highly resistant to change	• flexible, adaptive, co-creative, co-evolutionary
• linear determinism, irrespective of time and space	• flexible, able to adapt to temporal and spatial uniqueness
• disciplinary, sectoral, vertical, hierarchical, patriarchal	• transdisciplinary, transsectoral, horizontal, interactive, participatory
• decisions re politically defined geographical boundaries	• ecologically and culturally defined
• interagency and institutional non-cooperation and competition (gridlock)	• collaboration, cooperation
• adversarial, winners and losers	• mediated processes, conflict resolution

- exclusivity of information, ad hoc coordinative processes with limited information exchange
- specialized and sectoral decision-making with little consultation other than with groups with vested interests

- integrated, accessible information technologies, transparency, openness
- integrated local, regional, and global decision-making, participatory politics in action

Industry

(1) What sectors within industry and business are most supportive of biodiversity conservation? How can their approaches be disseminated to other sectors? How can these initiatives be strengthened and developed more rapidly?

(2) What sectors and practices constitute barriers to biodiversity conservation and how can they be transformed?

(3) How could the industries based on renewable resources – agriculture, fisheries, forestry – be redesigned to promote biodiversity conservation?

(4) How can the ongoing shift to an information society be made more supportive of biodiversity conservation?

(5) How can business and professional codes of conduct be modified to take the conservation of biodiversity into account?

(6) How can ecotourism be managed so that it fully supports biodiversity conservation?

(7) What market incentives could be most effectively deployed to conserve biodiversity?

Acknowledgments
The authors are indebted to the staff of both Environment Canada Library and the resource centre of Ecological Agriculture Projects, in particular Marie Jetton and Debbie Viskilis, for their reference support, unfailing courtesy, and promptness. Their professionalism has greatly contributed to the integrity of the research for this chapter. Une mille fois merci. We would also like to thank Dr. Terry Wheeler for providing valuable feedback on an earlier draft of the chapter. And finally, in honour of Odessa, Aba, and Civa, who have left an outstanding legacy of strength, determination, loyalty, gentleness, and love.

References
Bond, W.J. 1993. Keystone Species. In *Biodiversity and Ecosystem Function 99*, edited by E.D. Schulze and H.A. Money, 237-92. Berlin: Springer-Verlag

Boucher, H., ed. 1985. *Biology of Mutualism? Ecology and Evolution.* New York: Oxford University Press

Brewer, G.D. N.d. *Methods for Synthesis: Policy Exercises.* Banff, AB: Banff School of Management Course Materials

Brown, L.R., H. Kane, and D.M. Roodman. 1994. *Vital Signs 1994.* New York: W.W. Norton

Caldwell, L. 1990. *International Environmental Policy.* London: Duke University Press

Checkland, P., and J. Scholes. 1990. *Soft Systems Methodology in Action.* Chichester: John Wiley

Collie, J.S., and C.J. Walters. 1993. Models That 'Learn' to Distinguish among Alternative Hypotheses. *Fisheries Research* 18:259-75

Dale, A. 1990. *An Inventory of Environmental Recommendations.* Ottawa, ON: National Round Table on the Environment and the Economy

Dale, A., J. Robinson, and C. Massey, eds. 1995. *Reconciling Human Welfare and Ecological Carrying Capacity.* Vancouver: Sustainable Development Research Institute, University of British Columbia

Daly, H. 1995. Preliminary Workshop. In *Reconciling Human Welfare and Ecological Carrying Capacity,* edited by A. Dale, J. Robinson, and C. Massey. Vancouver: Sustainable Development Research Institute, University of British Columbia

Dryzek, J. 1987. *Rational Ecology: Environment and Political Economy.* Oxford: Blackwood

–. 1992. Ecology and Discursive Democracy: Beyond Liberal Capitalism and the Administrative State. *Capitalism, Nature, Socialism* 3 (2):18-42

Ehrenfeld, D. 1988. Why Put a Value on Biodiversity? In *Biodiversity,* edited by E.O. Wilson, 212-17. Washington, DC: National Academy Press

Ehrlich, P.R. 1982. Human Carrying Capacity, Extinctions and Nature Reserves. *BioScience* 32 (5):331-3

Ehrlich, P.R., A.H. Ehrlich, and J.P. Holdren. 1977. *Ecoscience: Population, Resources, Environment.* San Francisco: W.H. Freeman

Ehrlich, P.R., and E.O. Wilson. 1991. Biodiversity Studies: Science and Policy. *Science* 253:758-62

Holling, C.S. 1993. An Ecologist's View of the Malthusian Conflict. Paper presented at the Population-Environment-Development Lecture Series, Royal Swedish Academy of Sciences, Stockholm

–. 1989-90. Integrating Science for Sustainable Development. *Journal of Business Administration* 19 (1-2):73-83

–, ed. 1978. *Adaptive Environmental Assessment and Management.* Wiley International Institute for Applied Systems Analysis, International Series on Applied Systems Analysis. London: Pitman Press

Hurrell, A., and B. Kingsbury. 1992. *The International Politics of the Environment.* Oxford: Clarendon Press

Kay, J.J. 1994. Some Notes on the Ecosystem Approach: Ecosystems as Complex

Systems. University of Waterloo, Department of Environment and Resource Studies. Typescript

Kim, C.K. 1993. Biodiversity, Conservation and Inventory: Why Insects Matter. *Biodiversity and Conservation* 2:191-214

Lovejoy, T.E. 1980. A Projection of Species Extinctions. In *The Global 2000 Report to the President. Entering the Twenty-First Century.* Washington, DC: Council on Environmental Quality, US Government Printing Office

Ludwig, D., R. Hilborn, and C. Walters. 1993. Uncertainty, Resource Exploitation, and Conservation: Lessons from History. In *Ecological Applications* 3(4):547-9

McNeely, J.A., K.R. Miller, W.V. Reid, R.A. Mittermeier, and T.B. Werner. 1990. *Conserving the World's Biological Diversity.* Gland: IUCN, WRI, Conservational International, WWF-US, and World Bank

Myers, N. 1979. *The Sinking Ark.* Oxford: Pergamon Press

–. 1983. Conservation of Rain Forests for Scientific Research, for Wildlife Conservation, and for Recreation and Tourism. In *Tropical Rain Forest Ecosystems, Structure and Function,* edited by F.B. Golley. Amsterdam: Elseview

–. 1990. Mass Extinctions? What Can the Past Tell Us about the Present and the Future? *Global Planet Change* 82:175-85

–. 1993. Biodiversity and the Precautionary Principle. *Ambio* 22 (2-3):74-9

Norgaard, R.B. 1994. *Development Betrayed: The End of Progress and a Coevolutionary Revisioning of the Future.* New York: Routledge

Oldfield, M.I. 1984. *The Value of Conserving Genetic Resources.* Washington, DC: US Department of the Interior, National Park Service

Paine, R.T. 1966. Food Web Complexity and Species Diversity. *The American Naturalist* 100:65-75

Peavey, F. 1994. *By Life's Grace: Musings on the Essence of Social Change.* Gabriola Island, BC: New Society Press

Regier, H. 1995. Workshop Report #1. In *Reconciling Human Welfare and Ecological Carrying Capacity,* edited by A. Dale, J. Robinson, and C. Massey. Vancouver: Sustainable Development Research Institute, University of British Columbia

Reid, W.V., and K. Miller. 1989. *Keeping Options Alive: The Scientific Basis for Conserving Biodiversity.* Washington, DC: World Resources Institute

Schneider, E.D., and J.J. Kay. 1994. Complexity and Thermodynamics: Towards a New Ecology. *Future* 24 (6):626-47

Simberloff, D. 1983. Are We on the Verge of Mass Extinction in Tropical Rain Forests? Typescript

Vitousek, P., P. Ehrlich, A. Ehrlich, and P. Matson. 1986. Human Appropriation of the Products of Photosynthesis. *BioScience* 36:368-73

Walters, C.J. 1986. *Adaptive Management of Renewable Resources.* New York: Macmillan

Walters, C.J., and C.S. Holling. 1990. Large-scale Management Experiments and Learning by Doing. *Ecology* 71 (6):2060-8

Wilson, E.O. 1988. *Biodiversity.* Washington, DC: National Academy Press

–. 1992. *The Diversity of Life.* Cambridge: Belknap Press

World Commission on Environment and Development (WCED). 1987. *Our*

Common Future – Report of the World Commission on Environment and Development. Oxford: Oxford University Press

World Resources Institute, International Union for the Conservation of Nature, and United Nations Environment Programme (WRI, IUCN, and UNEP). 1992. *Global Biodiversity Strategy. A Policy-Makers Guide.* New York: World Resources Institute

5
Industrial Ecology: Efficient and Excellent Production
Raymond Côté and Thomas Plunkett

In Kalundborg, Denmark, ten industries and activities are engaged in a system of mutually beneficial symbiosis. From the oil refinery and the power plant to the fish farm and the pharmaceutical company, one firm's waste is another's feedstock and one firm's by-product is another's raw material. The Kalundborg case (Figure 5.1) is a model of industrial ecology because as a system it mimics, albeit in a limited manner, the cycling of materials and energy that occurs in a natural ecosystem (Knight 1992).

Figure 5.1

Symbiotic relationships among companies in Kalundborg, Denmark

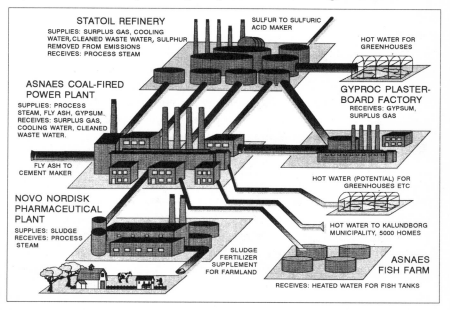

This chapter is an introduction to the emerging concept and field of study called industrial ecology. The concept is still evolving, and this chapter describes it and many of the supporting ideas as they are currently understood. It also explores strategies and tools that are being developed and refined to enable government and industry to apply the concept to the design and operation of industrial systems. Government has a significant role to play in encouraging this approach to industrial development. The chapter goes on to discuss elements of a strategic framework for Canada and an example of the way in which the concept can be applied at a manageable spatial level. Finally, a few conclusions are drawn.

Not until the Industrial Revolution did humans systematically disrupt natural cycles and begin to strain the natural environment's assimilative capacities through resource exploitation, through the creation of synthetic substances, and through a low regard for the impact of waste products. The natural environment is being increasingly stressed and may have difficulty recovering from the assault of these substances and wastes in the short term. According to such bodies as the World Commission on Environment and Development, the results could be life threatening in the long term. We believe that the trend of ecosystem disruption begun through the industrial economy can be slowed by adopting new development strategies that mimic ecological functions and take note of carrying capacities.

The Concept
Ecology is the study of the interrelationships of biota with their physical-chemical environment. An ecosystem is a bounded system of dynamic, interdependent relationships between living organisms and their physical, chemical, and biological environment. The system has mechanisms by which nutrients are retained and recycled and by which water and respirable gases are disseminated and replenished. Through the co-evolution of species, ecosystems acquire self-stabilizing mechanisms and a dynamic, internal balance (McMichael 1993). The goal of industrial ecology is to integrate production systems and product cycles with natural ecosystems and material cycles. The processes of the natural ecosystem have evolved over long periods into more or less stable communities because they are efficient, meaning that materials are not wasted but conserved and reused in various forms (Odum 1993). This is in sharp contrast to the increasing burden of waste that the industrial

economy has imposed on the natural environment in the air, soil, and water through its linear, once-through pattern of material use.

A natural ecosystem involves cyclical processing of biomass and transfer of energy through progressive trophic levels, from producers through multiple stages of consumers to scavengers and finally to decomposers. Materials and nutrients are continuously recycled. Industrial ecosystems must mimic many of the features and processes of natural ecosystems. As in natural ecosystems, the cycling of materials must become the underpinning of industrial ecosystems. These cycles should be targeted at 'making maximum use of recycled material in new production, optimizing use of materials and energy, minimizing waste generation and reevaluating wastes as raw materials for other processes' (Tibbs 1992, 8). Material webs must be established linking producers, consumers, and scavengers (recyclers) and multimaterial, multidimensional recycling must begin to emulate the complex webs in nature. Wherever possible, symbiotic relationships should be encouraged, especially those that are mutualistic, although commensal relationships should also be fostered. Incentives and disincentives must be found to improve the efficiency of metabolic processes within individual firms or production processes.

In another application of biology to industrial production, Farrell (1993) refers to hybrids, mutants, recombinants, and metamorphs. This brings to mind recycling in which the parts that are recovered are combined in various ways to create new products. Some products might be hybrids, combining parts from dissimilar original products; other products, dramatically different from the original ones, might be formed from waste materials through a metamorphosis. Another important feature of an ecosystem is diversity, which allows an ecosystem to recover after a stress is imposed. Industries that rely on a single source of supply or option for waste disposal are at greater risk of collapse than those that have diverse sources of materials or waste disposal options.

Industrial ecology is the study of industrial development policies and practices and the interrelationship of industrial and natural systems. It emphasizes material cycling and webs of producers, consumers, scavengers, and decomposers, encouraging resource conservation and waste prevention. In business terms, industrial ecology is aimed at reducing energy and material throughput per unit of product or service, thereby allowing industry to become more efficient and competitive (Lowe 1992). Some measures of the processes and products by which one can determine whether an ecological approach has been taken are: reusability, recyclability, reducibility, durability, reliability, adaptability, serviceability, and remanufacturability. In addition, industrial ecology can be studied at different spatial or geographic levels: within companies, between companies, within industrial zones such as parks or estates, within communities, and at the provincial or national level (Figure 5.2).

Figure 5.2

Spatial levels of increasing magnitude and complexity at which industrial ecosystems can be studied

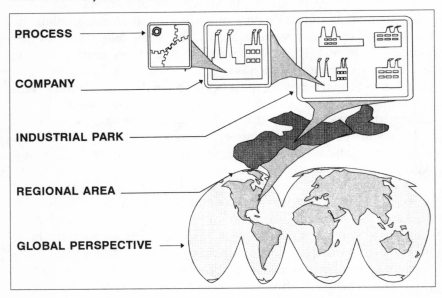

Frosch and Gallopoulos (1989) have written what is viewed by many as the seminal article for industrial ecology and have thus acted as catalysts for many of the ideas in this chapter. They saw that 'the traditional model of industrial activity in which individual manufacturing processes take in raw materials and generate products to be sold plus waste to be disposed of should be transformed into a more integrated model: an industrial ecosystem' (p. 98). They noted that products of industrialization must be kept within cycles or within recoverable, controllable loops, minimizing the dissipative elements of the production process. Their article emphasized a global perspective that envisioned the cycling of iron, plastic, and platinum in ways that mimic natural hydrological cycles, nitrogen cycles, or those of other nutrients.

Tibbs (1992, 6) has called for a broader, more long-term perspective from government and industry for 'industrialization that is not only more efficient but that is intrinsically adjusted to the tolerances of natural systems.' Tibbs notes that 'industrial ecology takes the pattern of the natural environment as a model for solving environmental problems, creating a new paradigm for the industrial system in the process' (p. 5).

Industrial ecology is a rational and increasingly practicable route to sustainable development. It supports sustainable development by recognizing the reality of human development and the interconnectedness of humans and the rest of the natural environment. In industrial ecology, technological progress is viewed as a precondition for success, since progress will develop solutions to the problems we have created for ourselves. Yet progress must be managed deliberately and carefully so that its negative consequences are substantially reduced. Thus, industrial ecology fits easily into the guiding definition of sustainable development as 'development that meets the needs of the present without compromising the ability of future generations to meet their own needs' (WCED 1987, 8).

Related Concepts

A number of principles and concepts have been described in the literature since 1987 that are aimed at making industrial processes more efficient and ecologically sustainable. These include the precautionary principle, conservation strategies, soft material paths, and the e-factor.

The industrial ecology concept represents a paradigm shift in the evolution of industrial pollution control approaches. Although the polluter-pays and precautionary principles are in theory consistent with industrial ecology, they are still not being applied fully in a preventive mode that encourages efficiency and excellence. In a recent paper, Dethlefsen, Jackson, and Taylor (1993, 57) argue in reference to the precautionary principle that 'a logical extension of the principle ... seems to call for a reduction of all inputs to the environment.' Although in practical terms it is not reasonable to expect that all inputs can be eliminated, Dethlefsen's extension brings the principle closer to industrial ecology.

The industrial ecology approach is acknowledged in the 1991 update of the *World Conservation Strategy* (WCS). The revision calls on industry and government to identify as one of their priorities the task of committing business to sustainability and environmental excellence expressed in high performance standards and advanced by economic instruments. In satisfying this goal, there will be a need to consider the occupational health and safety of workers; energy, material and water efficiency of practices, processes and products; control over the life-cycle of manufacturing; and integrated approaches to pollution prevention and control (IUCN, UNEP, and WWF 1991, 97-8).

Although the document does not refer specifically to an ecological approach, many of the strategies and tools underpinning industrial ecology are mentioned.

Young (1991, 40) has argued for another version of industrial ecology, a 'soft materials path': 'From the attempts of people around the world to find alternative solutions to waste problems, a "soft materials path" can be mapped out. Its operating principle is efficiency: Meeting people's needs with as little as possible of the most appropriate materials available.' Indeed, this is the case with mature ecosystems, which have developed over long periods of time and are arguably the most efficient systems in terms of material use and recycling.

Kumar and Murck (1992) note that the general goal of maintaining levels of resource use within the carrying capacity of geographical areas will involve regulating supply and demand and monitoring waste production and dispersal. This happens automatically in natural ecosystems and, of course, market economists will argue that the market will naturally regulate the supply and demand of materials. Unfortunately, because ecology and economy were separated after birth (both words derive from *oikos,* meaning house), the market is imperfect and does not fully account for externalities such as waste production and disposal. Kumar and Murck emphasize that governments and industries must collaborate in 'creative and aggressive investment and design decisions with a view towards reducing materials and energy use' (p. 188).

In adopting the ecological context, Ayres (1989) introduced the notion of industrial metabolism, perhaps the single most important framework for understanding industrial ecology. This concept views an industrial process as a parallel to the metabolic processes of a living organism. The process has inputs, such as materials and energy, and outputs, such as biomass and work. According to Ayres, that the inputs and outputs of living organisms are in balance with the ecosystem and the inputs and outputs of the industrial process are not, is the cause of great concern. He also introduces the materials balance concept, a means of identifying the dissipative elements within an industrial process in order to reduce that dissipation.

Makower (1993) has described something akin to industrial ecology that, in our view, goes beyond the concept. He has dubbed it the e-factor, the bottom-line approach to environmentally responsible business. The e-factor encompasses economics, enforcement, empowerment, education, efficiency, and excellence. In Makower's view, emphasis should be placed on excellence, thus linking the idea to total quality management (TQM). The common themes between the e-factor and TQM are: improvement in productivity and profits; new corporate culture and leadership; emphasis on long-range planning; more flexibility within organizations; improvement in information exchange, training, and accountability; and continuous self-auditing. In terms of industrial ecology, Makower argues that implementing the e-factor will lead to reduced underdelivery, handling losses, cleaning losses, process losses, scrap, overspecification, and overfilling. All of these difficulties relate to inefficiencies in current production systems.

Supporting Tools
Along with the elaboration of new principles and concepts, new tools have been developed to support environmentally conscious companies. These tools and variations on them will enable industries to take an ecological approach to their raw materials, production processes, products, and waste materials. The Kalundborg example is held up as a model of successful integration of industrial metabolisms (Figure 5.1). In Kalundborg, wastes from the metabolic activity of one industry are utilized as material inputs for another. Waste steam from the power plant, for example, is used by the refinery, and the sludge from the treatment system of a pharmaceutical plant is used by farmers, creating an industrial symbiosis.

The 3 Rs – reduce, reuse, and recycle – have been discussed extensively in the past decade by non-government organizations, municipalities, and businesses. Practising the 3 Rs is a precondition for industrial ecology. They represent a hierarchical approach in the practice of industrial ecology and must be adopted as an operating principle themselves for the long term as a form of continuous improvement. The 3 Rs represent a move toward nature's hallmarks of efficiency and material cycles and the most obvious means of economic benefit to industry. Firms will lower operating costs by decreasing expenses for treatment or disposal of wastes. They can also increase revenues by finding markets for their by-products or wastes. In fact, as of 1991, there were six non-profit information exchanges for waste materials and six for-profit waste material exchanges in Canada; in the United States there were eleven information exchanges and five material exchanges. For each case of recycle and reuse, the natural environment is spared the dual burden of assimilating waste and of giving up more of the required virgin raw material.

Contributing to the implementation of the 3 Rs and the creation of industrial symbioses are a number of tools and concepts. The first of these is the application of life cycle analysis (LCA), or eco-balancing. In its most basic form, this concept calls for analysis of each element or material manipulated by the industrial process: the impact of its introduction, the phases of use, reuse, and transformation within the industrial process, and its final reintroduction into the natural environment. Some synthetic materials have obviously been created without any thought at all given to their metabolic destiny. Strategists and decision-makers could assess alternatives for industrial processes and products in a manner that links their industrial and natural metabolisms.

Winsemius and Hahn (1992) introduced environmental options assessment, a concept that combines elements of life cycle analysis and environmental impact assessment. According to Winsemius and Hahn, the managers of industries should include environmental criteria in their analyses of product development and strategies. The methodology allows managers to generate, assign priority to, and plan options in four aspects of material management: raw materials used, products consumed, substances emitted, and wastes recycled. This method gives managers a more structured basis for decision-making, essentially an environmentally sensitive investment system.

The Elmwood Institute, an ecological think tank dedicated to fostering new concepts and values for a sustainable future has introduced the concept of eco-auditing, which Capra (1991) differentiated from the current practice of environmental auditing. Eco-auditing requires an holistic approach, rather than the traditional mechanistic one, to evaluating the impact of an industrial process on the environment. This is a preventive management concept similar to LCA and eco-balancing, as opposed to the reactive compliance of an environmental audit.

Total environmental quality management (TEQM) refers to the expansion of traditional approaches to TQM and ISO 9000 standards of quality assurance in order to incorporate environmental issues (Canadian Standards Association 1992). A company that has adopted an environmental ethic can do much to alter the industrial economy by considering the environmental impact of the products it manufactures. Just as quality can be built into a product and become a buying criterion, so can a vendor's environmental impact become a factor in a buyer's choices. Canadian companies selling newsprint and other paper in Germany and the United Kingdom have been faced with this kind of pressure. An environmentally conscious company will be able to improve its competitive advantage by marketing its environmentally friendly product line and image.

While practising the 3 Rs is the most expedient way to introduce industrial ecology objectives into industry in the short term, more fundamental approaches are required for true long-term improvements. Allenby and Fullerton (1992) describe how the design for environment (DFE) concept is a way to design industrial processes and products so that they are integrated into ecosystems, whether industrial or natural, from their inception. Similarly, Frosch and Gallopoulos (1989) refer to 'designed offal' and 'engineered scrap,' items that are intended to be reintegrated into other cycles.

Developing these tools further will enable economic development to proceed in a more deliberate, conscientious, and responsible manner. It is through the use of these tools that traditional 'externalities' can be identified and internalized. It is also in recognizing opportunities for manufacturing loops and designing products to facilitate reuse and recycling within loops that industrial ecologists will best apply their knowledge. In the combustion process, for example, fly ash is no longer permitted to leave the loop and be dispersed uncontrolled into the airstream; it is now kept in the loop via capture by scrubbers, and the residue can be used as a concrete stabilizer.

Government Policies and Programs

Freeman et al. (1992) have published a critical review of the interaction between the practices of industry and government regulations in the United States. The review describes economic incentive packages that encourage industry to practise the tenets of industrial ecology and reports a degree of success in preventing pollution in different situations. Some government initiatives can be positive but others are negative. Initiatives to reuse and recycle hazardous materials in the United States, for example, can actually be impeded by the 'derived from' rule. This rule forces waste generators to consider specified types of wastes as hazardous and subjects them to considerable regulation if the wastes are derived from certain sources. Once materials are listed in regulations as hazardous wastes, it becomes almost impossible to manage them in any other fashion, and particularly as secondary materials for reuse and recycling. The legislation that controls disposal of hazardous wastes and transportation of dangerous goods in Canada may also act in a similar fashion.

Industry Canada is the federal government's flagship for the development of industrial and economic development policy, the promotion of the competitiveness of Canadian businesses, and the administration of services to business, science, and consumer groups. Among the many policies, programs, and tasks described in a 1994 document *Industry Canada: A Partnership to Serve You Better,* there is no mention of the link between environment and economy. The document does mention international competitiveness, research and technology, a modern regulatory framework, standards, best business practices, and access to information. These words are also relevant to a link between environment and economy and particularly to the adoption of an industrial ecology approach to industrial development. Unfortunately, the connection between Industry Canada's and Environment Canada's policy directions has not been explicitly made. There is cooperation in programs designed primarily for development and adoption of environmental technologies and establishment of the Canadian Environmental Industries Association. Although important, these links are ancillary rather than integral to Canada's industrial and economic development policy.

Governments must determine what their long-term policies are and understand the implications of initiatives taken within their jurisdictions. In recent years, governments have sought to strike an attractive and appropriate balance between economic and environmental conditions. Within developed countries, the trends in regulation are unmistakably concerned with the environment, and apparently, in the view of some, at the expense of traditional commercial interests, as in the example of the Endangered Species Act in the United States. Recent amendments to the Clean Air and Clean Water acts in the United States have begun to recognize the connection between the economy and the environment to a degree. This was also seen in the *Green Plan* in Canada and is being reflected further in revisions to the Canadian Environmental Protection Act (Canada 1995a).

Yet global jurisdictions must find some parity among regulations so that mobile industries are discouraged from polluting more environmentally permissive locales. The permissiveness may spring from a lack of legislation and regulations or a lack of enforcement. The Montreal Protocol on CFC emissions, the North America Free Trade Agreement negotiations, the Earth Summit agreements, and many UN proposals seek to establish parity among jurisdictions. When combined with the consumptive tendencies of the more developed countries, the industrialization and mushrooming population growth of the developing world pose a potentially devastating risk to the globe's assimilative capacity. As argued by the World Commission on Environment and Development, well-managed industrial development can mean that developing countries improve their standards of living without necessarily making this threat a reality. It is hoped that as developing countries industrialize, they will import technologies from the top of the learning curve of environmentally benign processes. This requires learning from the experiences of the more industrialized countries, rather than following their example or importing their less efficient technologies.

Within some developed nations, the basic groundwork has been laid for industrial ecology to flourish. Regulations to localize waste, such as Germany's 'take back' laws for packaging and Canadian restrictions on the transport of hazardous wastes and disposal of municipal garbage, will force consumers and producers to focus more closely on the consequences of their actions. Also, the US and Canadian federal governments have caused industries to identify their dissipative processes and waste emissions through the Toxic Release Inventory and the National Pollutant Release Inventory respectively. Wastes can only be eliminated or exchanged after having been identified, accounted for, and integrated into a material loop.

Yet governments have a long way to go to establish policies consistent with environmental sustainability. As discussed earlier, some regulations actually hinder the reuse and recycling of materials. And in many cases in North America, industries have greater incentives to exploit virgin raw materials than to reuse and recycle. Incentives to promote environmentally benign processes are perceived to be government's most effective tool, since they tend to encourage progress in benign technologies. This tendency will be further supported by the efforts of the International Standards Organization and corresponding national organizations, which are devoted to promoting the worldwide application of sustainable industrial development by producing standards for environmental management systems, environmental

auditing, environmental labelling, environmental performance evaluation, industry mobilization, life cycle analysis, and products (ISO 1992).

Elements of a Strategic Framework for Industrial Ecology in Canada

Policy
It is no longer adequate to consider environmental protection and management as a modifier or regulator of industrial development. Canada and
other nations require a new type of industrial development policy in
which economic and ecological objectives are integrated from the beginning. The policy must be based on resource and energy conservation and
aimed at efficiency and excellence. As indicated in Figure 5.3, the policy
and legal framework must shift from controlling pollution after the fact
and compensating for the damages to causing society and industries to
question the need for products and services that consume resources and
generate waste. In essence, this reflects the ultimate application of the precautionary principle. The policy must encourage a supporting infrastructure and a hierarchy of industries that reflects trophic levels in an ecosystem. The chain in the figure reflects the scope of industrial ecology. A step
in the right direction has been taken by the federal government, which released its pollution prevention strategy in 1995. The strategy focuses on
the 'use of processes, practices, materials, products or energy that avoid or
minimize the creation of pollutants and waste' (Canada 1995b, n.p.).

Thus, the hierarchy of industries must not only include producers
and primary, secondary, and tertiary consumers but also scavengers
(recyclers) and decomposers (composters). The infrastructure must include incentives to create businesses that mimic scavengers and decomposers. As essential components of a material web in an ecosystem,
these types of businesses must be given a higher profile and greater
recognition in terms of their contribution to society, economic development, and environmental quality.

This industrial development policy will have to be implemented at
several geographic levels, although certain levels are more amenable to
change than others in the short to medium term. In our view, industrial
ecology is most effectively implemented at two levels: within corporations producing a diversity of products in one jurisdiction; and within
industrial parks where a diversity of businesses and therefore materials
and wastes can be found. This is not to suggest that a national government should ignore cycling materials within a broader geographic area.
The area could be the country as a whole, two adjoining countries, or a

Figure 5.3

Cause and effect linking environmental protection, environmental management, and sustainable development

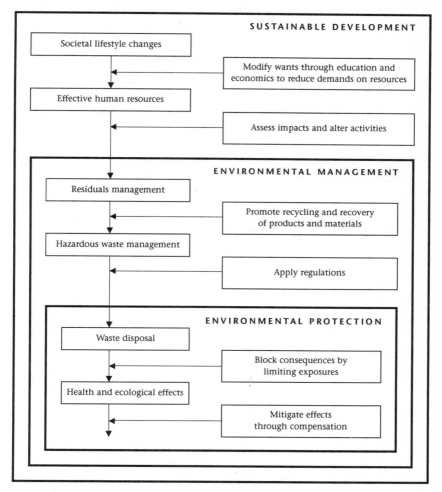

region such as North America. One of the issues to be resolved is whether wastes are in fact resources or secondary materials, which therefore could be viewed as tradeable commodities.

Government Instruments

There has been increasing recognition that a combination of economic instruments and 'command and control' regulations are needed to influence environmentally appropriate behaviour by producers and consumers. Nevertheless, regulation based on objectives and targets appears to be more effective than formal, precise rules supported by more or less literal interpretation of these rules. In some jurisdictions, implementation of these 'precise' rules is inconsistent and exacerbates the problem. Recent experience in the United States and in the Netherlands suggests that a regulatory approach beginning with a voluntary stage, such as the 33/50 program in the United States, has a better chance of obtaining industry's support and therefore of succeeding. An announcement by the Grocery Products Manufacturers of Canada – endorsed by the Canadian Soft Drink Association, the Canadian Council of Grocery Distributors, and the Retail Council of Canada – accepting the national target to cut packaging waste in half by the year 2000 promotes a combination of a target and a voluntary but industry-driven approach. The associations therefore have launched the Canadian Industry Packaging Stewardship Initiative, which will support a coordinated and comprehensive recycling system in cooperation with the provinces (Janowitz 1993).

A policy that integrates economy and environment from the beginning will have to make greater use of the market economy in reaching its objectives. This in turn means greater use of economic instruments (Cairncross 1991; Repetto et al. 1992). Governments in Canada are just beginning to investigate all of the possibilities. Some of course have been used for years now, such as deposit-refund schemes and water rates. Unfortunately, the incentives have not been set at a level that encourages greater conservation or recovery of materials. A wide range of economic instruments is available to assist the development of interlocking industrial ecosystems. These include deposit-refund schemes (containers), tax rebates (purchase of equipment, waste reduction), tax differentials (leaded and non-leaded gasoline in some countries), depreciation (on waste reduction equipment), grants (studies, audits, or equipment), product charges (pesticides, oil products), user charges (water, sewerage), emission charges and trading (SO_2, NO_x, CO_2), administrative charges (permit processing relating to quantity), and sanction charges (fines and penalties) (Neale 1993).

Another type of economic instrument is now beginning to have a major influence on the way in which business conducts its affairs. In order to determine the potential for liability in the future, banks and other lending agencies now require assessment of environmental damage and future risks when properties are bought and sold, new products are developed, and new manufacturing facilities are constructed. Assessments of the hazards of new chemicals and of the environmental impact of development projects are also dictated by government. In fact these assessments may be required by lending institutions even when government does not call for them. This is likely to have more impact on small and medium-sized businesses because federal and provincial governments pay less attention to them.

Government Procurement
The third area in which government can exert substantial influence is the procurement of goods and services. Governments at all levels in Canada purchase billions of dollars of goods and services annually, and the manufacture, use, and disposal of these have cumulative effects that have not been measured but are predicted to be significant in local as well as global terms.

Some corporations have already taken steps, as called for in the Business Charter for Sustainable Development (in Schmidheiny 1992), to pressure their suppliers into providing products that will reduce environmental impacts. Government procurement policies and practices, when combined with those of industries that have already moved in this direction, would send a very strong message to thousands of businesses. If governments adopted procurement policies for electric and electronic appliances supported by regulations of the type promulgated by Germany in January 1994, for example, this would encourage changes in product design and materials, reuse of product parts, and reparability (vanWeenen and Lafleur 1993). Products designed with the environment in mind, along with appropriately designed regulations and economic instruments, would ensure that significant progress could be made toward efficient and excellent production.

With this in mind, the government of Canada released *A Guide to Green Government* in mid-1995. In this guide, the federal government discusses the importance of leading by example by greening government operations and recommends several guidelines on procurement, waste management, water usage, energy use, transportation, land use, and human resource management (Canada 1995c).

Research
One of the reasons for the limited Canadian progress in adopting waste minimization and cleaner production technologies and techniques is that the research programs of government, universities, and private organizations have not recognized them as an opportunity in the context

of sustainable industrial development. This is in contrast to the United States and Europe, where government, universities, and private corporations have established partnerships to investigate efficient technologies, recyclability, degradability, durability, and intensity of materials and energy (Zweers 1992). In addition, research into new materials should be lead by considerations of health and environment.

Some positive steps have been taken in Canada. Under the auspices of the *Green Plan,* a package of applied research programs sponsored by Industry Canada and Environment Canada was launched, and although the plan itself has been eliminated, initiatives taken by these departments have continued and expanded. The Technology for Solutions Program will promote research into prevention technologies, and at least three environmental technology transfer centres are expected to be established. In addition, the Canada Nova Scotia Cooperation Agreement on Sustainable Economic Development, the first of its kind in the country, funded the Centre for Environmentally Sustainable Economic Development (CESED). The goal of the centre was to encourage, with some financial support, greater collaboration between universities, industry, and government in developing new technologies, information systems, economic instruments, and educational materials designed to make Nova Scotia businesses more efficient and excellent. This in turn was expected to enhance their competitiveness and sustainability. Unfortunately, federal and provincial funding was withdrawn in the summer of 1995, and the impact of the centre's demise is not yet clear.

Information
Lack of information has been identified as a major impediment to change in industry and particularly in small and medium-sized businesses. Canadian governments have devoted some financial and human resources to the establishment of easily accessible and simple information management and dissemination systems on technologies, techniques, materials, and programs to support environmental management and pollution prevention. There are a number of accessible information clearinghouses in the United States. These include the US Environmental Protection Agency's Pollution Prevention Information Clearinghouse, the University of Wisconsin Solid and Hazardous Waste Education Center, and the Waste Reduction Resource Center of North Carolina. Efforts in Canada to date have concentrated on the environmental choice program, which provides an eco-label for products that have met specified standards, and on the development of the Canadian

Standards Association standards for environmental management systems. Federal officials are considering a networking tool, possibly called ENVIRONET, for encouraging pollution prevention.

Many Canadian initiatives have focused on the protection of the Great Lakes. Information systems in support of the Great Lakes Water Quality Program, and specifically the Remedial Action Programs in various harbours around the lakes, are being developed through the Great Lakes Pollution Prevention Centre. As those information systems are constructed, they could be designed to include information from other parts of Canada with the intent of building a nationally accessible system. Pollution prevention guides are also being prepared, initially targeting industrial sectors in the Great Lakes region. The industries include automotive parts manufacturing, medical institutions, aerospace industries, pulp and paper mills, metal finishing, petrochemical industries, and painting and the graphic arts.

A research project undertaken by Dalhousie University and the Nova Scotia College of Art and Design is currently investigating the components for a database management system to support an ecosystemic approach to the design and operation of industrial parks. Figure 5.4 is an outline of the system as it is now envisaged. The researchers are proposing that such information should be available on-line and on request to business managers and owners. To facilitate access to information and assess different information transfer mechanisms, the researchers have established the Burnside Cleaner Production Centre, a technical and educational outreach facility, in the park.

Canada is perceived to be a supplier of natural resources to the world and primarily a nation of large, resource-based industries. This is not the case, at least in terms of the number of businesses. In reality, Canada is mainly a nation of small and medium-sized businesses; more than 95 per cent of businesses fall into this category. Unfortunately, much of the emphasis of government's environmental regulatory programs continues to revolve around large, visible industries such as pulp and paper mills, mines, and petrochemical plants. This should not be interpreted to suggest that little or nothing of what is learned about pollution control and prevention in those industries can be transferred to other sectors and scales of industries, but more research into cleaner production strategies, technologies, and practices should be oriented to small and medium-sized businesses.

The cumulative impact of the energy, resources, and chemicals used, the transport requirements, and the wastes generated by these businesses

Figure 5.4

Supporting framework for operating industrial parks as ecosystems

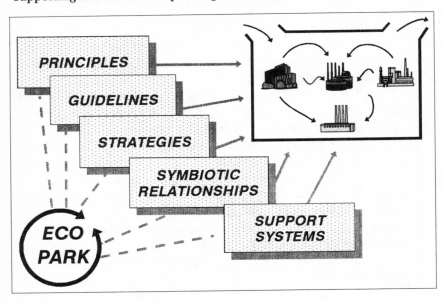

is significant in our view. Research into pollution prevention technologies for the small and medium-sized businesses will also create opportunities for exporting these technologies and consulting services. The necessary research, technology development, and information transfer might be most efficiently achieved through partnerships of industry, research institutions, and universities. One example is the recently announced Nova Scotia Management Consortium, led by the private sector, for the development and marketing of environmental technologies.

Education
Educational initiatives in support of industrial ecology have been slow but are beginning to take hold. Business associations such as the Canadian Manufacturers' Association, the Canadian Chamber of Commerce, the Canadian Federation of Independent Business, and the Canadian Chemical Producers Association have all released documents promoting waste prevention and cleaner production among their members. Somewhat surprisingly, the Canadian Federation of Independent Business, in a report titled *The Green Grassroots*, has gone further than any of the other associations in calling for an ecological approach:

The mistake of the past has been to view the environment and economy as separate cycles connected by a one-way movement of resources from nature to mankind. The ecosystem and the economy are, in fact, very similar in structure and performance. They each require elemental diversity and free-flowing circulation to function properly. Stemming the resource flow by blocking the economic cycle is not the environmental answer because it is as unnatural as trying to alter the ecosystem. Instead, the solution lies in optimizing use of natural resources and developing the return flow of resources from economic activity back to nature (Mallett 1991).

Individual companies have also mounted their own educational programs. Stora Forest Industries in Nova Scotia, for example, funded a $400,000 program to educate employees at all levels in the company, as well as contractors and spouses. Obviously the benefits will not appear immediately but the company believes that progress has already occurred. A recent court decision finding that Stora was not responsible for an oil spill suggests that educational programs are a necessary part of a due diligence defence. Other parts include an explicit environmental policy.

The federal government has run hot and cold since the creation of Environment Canada on the need to demonstrate leadership by ensuring that federal facilities demonstrate best available environmental practices. Recent initiatives appear to signal that the government is now serious. Planning within government for the *Green Plan* provided the impetus for these initiatives, and they have been supported by infusions of dollars into departmental budgets. As a result, we have seen new and strengthened initiatives in the departments of natural resources, national defence, transportation, housing, agriculture and forestry, among others. The Canadian Centre for Management Development, a training centre for senior federal civil servants, commissioned Dalhousie University to produce an environmental education strategy. The strategy recognized emerging concepts such as environmental forecasting and auditing and life cycle analysis. The centre has since offered courses consistent with the strategy.

Another component of the educational system where change is occurring more slowly than it should are the universities, where engineers, lawyers, business managers, economists, and others are being trained. Although environmental engineering and environmental law programs do exist in a few universities, progress in environmental economics and environmental management concentrations in business administration programs has been slower. Some of the exceptions in environmental business administration are the University of Western Ontario, Simon Fraser University, and Dalhousie University. The University of Ottawa and the University of British Columbia appear to have moved ahead of other universities in developing teaching and research programs in environmental or ecological economics. Making substantive and measurable progress toward the goal of sustainable development through industrial ecology will require greater efforts on the part of universities, however, and particularly the programs mentioned above, fostering interdisciplinary initiatives as well as rethinking existing business and engineering curricula to reflect ecological principles and concepts. Unfortunately this need is being recognized at a time when governments are cutting education budgets and universities are having increasing difficulty satisfying the demands on existing programs.

A Canadian Example: Turning Theory into Practice

A research project is under way in Nova Scotia to assess the potential for applying ecological principles and ecosystem concepts to the design and management of industrial parks constituted primarily of small and medium-sized businesses. The industrial park was selected to test the concept because there are a large number of parks in Nova Scotia and elsewhere. The success of these parks suggests that more will be built in the developed countries, but a large increase is also likely in developing countries as they industrialize. The industrial parks appear to provide an appropriate scale at which to apply ecosystem concepts. The thinking was that although 3M, General Motors, and Northern Telecom might be able to create an industrial ecosystem within their own corporation because of their size, diversity, and research facilities, the benefits to small and medium-sized businesses would only accrue if symbiotic relationships could be established among them.

The Burnside Industrial Park is a large area of land on the northern part of the City of Dartmouth, Nova Scotia. It comprises 480 hectares of developed land, 400 hectares of land ready for development, and a land bank of 800 hectares for future development. It is one of the largest industrial parks in Canada, constituting 80 per cent of the total commercial and industrial space in the Halifax-Dartmouth metropolitan area and 50 per cent of the multiple tenancy commercial and warehousing space in the industrial parks of the Atlantic provinces.

The park currently contains more than 1,200 businesses and a population of approximately 15,000 working people. Burnside has an extensive infrastructure of roadways and other utilities. There is a wide range of businesses in the industrial park, ranging from the one-person operation to a business that employs one hundred or more employees. The following is not a comprehensive list but is intended to provide an indication of the range of businesses located in the park: moving and storage, distribution centres, furniture manufacture, brewing, printing facilities, photo processing, restaurants, food suppliers, machine shops, general contractors, sign makers, engine maintenance, paint shops, metal plating plants, brake rebuilders, chemical suppliers, paint distributors, sales and service of electronic equipment, locksmiths, heavy equipment service, plumbing supplies, trucking, heating and air conditioning, pharmaceutical distributors, pest control services, janitorial services, manufacturers of plastic bags, makers of envelopes, office interiors, metal fabrication, and cloth products (Côté and Hall 1995).

Human settlements and industrial parks are viewed as having some things in common with natural ecosystems in terms of energy and material flows, although Odum (1993) describes them as parasites on the natural environment. By looking at an industrial park as a unit, or system, and by analyzing the pathways along which energy and materials move, we can begin to investigate how the consumptive and waste-generating activities can be reorganized and integrated with each other and with natural processes to increase the efficiency of resource use, recycling, and recovery of wasted materials and energy. This research was concerned with defining trophic levels and flows of materials and energy in cycles of varying sizes, and with analyzing the nature of the feedback loops that might be needed to encourage more efficient use of materials and energy within an industrial park. Some of the strategies and techniques that can be applied include raw material substitution, process modification, equipment upgrading, loss prevention, material handling improvements, production scheduling, energy and water conservation, heat recovery, product changes, material cascading, recovery and reuse of wastes in plant, and waste exchanges between businesses.

An industrial park ecosystem, then, is an assembly of diverse businesses and therefore of diverse materials and wastes. The design of the park should encourage mutual and commensal relationships in order to make maximum use of input, product, and waste materials. In other words, cycles should be encouraged. Industrial parks already encompass primary, secondary, and even tertiary consumers. Some scavengers and decomposers exist but more of these businesses must be established if the general objective is to be achieved. Park managers must also be in a position to identify opportunities for symbiotic relationships. A prototype of an information management system, ECOPARK, has been developed to facilitate identification of opportunities and encourage changes in practices (Figure 5.5). It is thus hoped to reduce the cumulative environmental impact of the industrial park in a manner that improves the efficiency and competitiveness of businesses.

The following benefits of operating the park as an ecosystem are expected:

- The input of materials and energy into the park will be reduced.
- New products or businesses may be established to make use of 'wastes.'
- The output of wastes will be reduced.
- The financial, ecological, and health costs of waste discharged will be reduced.
- Managers and employees of businesses in the park will be educated about opportunities to manage an industrial park in an environmentally sound manner.

Conclusion
Canada has participated in the deliberations of the World Commission on Environment and Development and the United Nations Conference on Environment and Development and continues to participate in the Organisation for Economic Cooperation and Development (OECD) and the Industry and Environment Activity Centre of the United Nations Environment Programme (IE-UNEP), among others. All of these have emphasized doing more with less, reducing waste, and making production cleaner. In some cases, Canadians have played a leadership role. For reasons that are difficult to understand, however, Canada has been very much a follower in the application of industrial ecology. No comprehensive framework of policies and programs is in place, although some components exist such as environmental impact assessment, hazard assessment, eco-labelling, and, to a lesser degree, environmental auditing and life cycle analysis.

The most effective approaches for Canada are to devote human and financial resources to learning from other countries, especially Germany, the Netherlands, Denmark, the United Kingdom, France, Japan, and the United States, and to establish partnerships among industries, universities, and government, including applied research institutes on

Figure 5.5

**ECOPARK, an information management and decision support system
to facilitate operating an industrial park as an ecosystem**

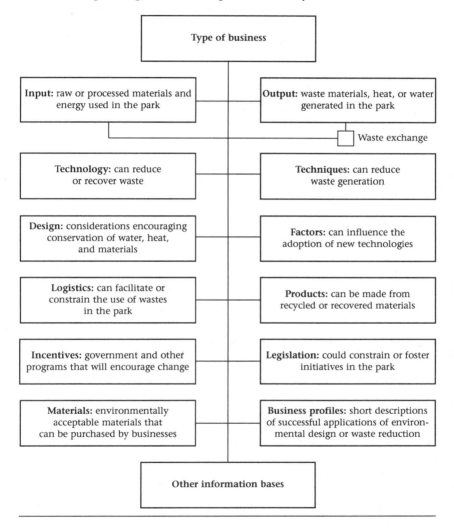

industrial ecology. Finally, industrial ecology must be adopted as the
underpinning of an industrial development policy for the year 2000
and beyond. The Netherlands provides an example of how concepts of
industrial ecology are being built into industrial development policy.
The Ministry of Economic Affairs initiated an eco-design program

aimed at modernization, competitiveness, and waste prevention in industry (Zweers 1992). In the Netherlands and other countries of the European Community, initiatives are taken by economic development agencies as well as by planning and environmental management departments.

The strategies and practices of industrial ecology are still very tentative, and with few exceptions it is only recently that attempts have been made to implement them. These practices will become more defined and numerous as the concepts take root and will become as commonplace as the concepts of safety and quality. Government has a significant role to play in encouraging industrial ecology by putting the appropriate legal framework and institutional infrastructure in place. Again, Germany's 'take back' laws for product packaging and other materials are an example.

The potential success of this new form of industrial policy and organization is evidenced by the degree to which its study is taking hold, particularly in Europe and to a lesser degree in the United States. The seeds of industrial ecology were sown by the *World Conservation Strategy* in 1981, although the World Bank had alluded to the concept as early as 1978 (World Bank 1978). The World Bank recommended that industries should be located in designated zones in such a manner that the wastes of one plant could serve as material inputs for an adjoining facility. The seeds were fertilized by the report of the World Commission on Environment and Development, which exhorted industry and industrial development strategies to do more with less. Some of the more progressive corporate leaders, especially those involved with the Business Council on Sustainable Development (Schmidheiny 1992), have begun to realize that industrial ecology may be the only way of satisfying the principles that underlie sustainable development. At least one major corporation, 3M, had been experimenting with the concept since the late 1970s, through its Pollution Prevention Pays program. The company expected by 1995 to have reduced waste by 35 per cent and energy consumption by 20 per cent from 1987 levels, with a concomitant financial savings of US$750 million (MacDougall 1993). Recent information indicates that they have achieved their goals. In the 1990s, industrial ecology appears to be gaining momentum as it is being adopted in one form or another by other Fortune 500 companies, including Volkswagen, Fiat, ABB, Dupont, and Dow.

After conceptual solutions to real problems have been developed, the solutions must be communicated to those who can implement the procedures. Allenby (1992) has issued a call to action to those now in industry and to those who will educate future industrial participants. Allenby takes a deterministic outlook, arguing that humans are responsible for their own destiny and that if we have the will, we can align our economy more closely with natural processes. He describes the need for change in real terms, though on an ethical level. Allenby states that once the ethics have been adopted, either in the workplace or in the classroom, the concepts of industrial ecology will be worked into the economy.

Beavis (1991) has edited a critical review of current industrial practices and consumer behaviour. The review offers motivation for practising sustainable development sooner rather than responding to environmental crisis later. Beavis offers many options for improvement, such as a shift in attitude to preservation and stewardship and a shift in behaviour to reduction, reuse, and recycling. In a recent article, Frenay (1995) refers to biorealism and the calls by earlier authors for the integration of nature and human design. In the final analysis, a behavioural change is required on the part of producers, consumers, and regulators if efficient and excellent production is to be achieved in all industrial sectors in Canada. When combined with a policy, economic, and legal framework and strategies for research, education, information access, and government procurement, a sustainable change in Canada's industrial development can be expected. This change should result in more efficient and higher quality production systems.

References

Allenby, B.R. 1992. Achieving Sustainable Development through Industrial Ecology. *International Environmental Affairs* 4 (1):56-68

Allenby, B.R., and A. Fullerton. 1992. Design for Environment – A New Strategy for Environmental Management. *Pollution Prevention Review* 2, 1 (Winter 1991-2):51-61

Ayres, R.U. 1989. Industrial Metabolism. In *Technology and Environment,* edited by J.H. Ausubel and H.E. Sladorich, 23-49. Washington, DC: National Academy Press

Beavis, M.A., ed. 1991. *Ethical Dimensions of Sustainable Development and Urbanization.* Occasional paper no. 23. Winnipeg: Institute of Urban Studies, University of Winnipeg

Cairncross, F. 1991. *Costing the Earth: The Challenge for Governments, the Opportunities for Business.* Boston: Harvard Business School Press

Canada. 1995a. *It's about Our Health: Towards Pollution Prevention.* Report of the House of Commons Standing Committee on Environment and Sustainable Development. Ottawa: Supply and Services Canada

–. 1995b. *Pollution Prevention: A Federal Strategy for Action.* Ottawa: Supply and Services Canada

–. 1995c. *A Guide to Green Government.* Ottawa: Supply and Services Canada

Canadian Standards Association. 1992. *Total Environmental Quality Management: The Relationship between Quality and Environmental Management Systems.* Toronto: Canadian Standards Association

Capra, F. 1991. Ecologically Conscious Management. *Environmental Law* 22:529-37

Côté, R., and J. Hall. 1995. Industrial Parks as Ecosystems. *Journal of Cleaner Production* 3 (1-2):41-6

Dethlefsen, V., T. Jackson, and P. Taylor. 1993. The Precautionary Principle: Towards Anticipatory Environmental Management. In *Clean Production Strategies: Developing Preventive Environmental Management in the Industrial Economy,* edited by T. Jackson, 41-62. Boca Raton: Lewis Publishers

Farrell, C. 1993. Survival of the Fittest Technologies. *New Scientist* 137 (1,859):35-9

Freeman, H., T. Harten, J. Springer, P. Randall, M.A. Curran, and K. Stone. 1992. Industrial Pollution Prevention: A Critical Review. *Journal of the Air and Waste Management Association* 42 (5):618-56

Frenay, R. 1995. Biorealism: Reading Nature's Blueprints. *Audubon Magazine* 97, 5 (September-October):70-106

Frosch, R.A., and N.E. Gallopoulos. 1989. Strategies for Manufacturing in Managing Planet Earth. In *Readings from Scientific American,* 144-52. New York: W.H. Freeman and Company

International Standards Organization (ISO). 1992. Developing the ISO/IEC System for International Standardization: The Strategic Advisory Group on Environment. ISO Council 6.7/1, Geneva

International Union for the Conservation of Nature (now World Conservation Union), United Nations Environment Programme, and World Wide Fund for Nature (IUCN, UNEP, and WWF). 1991. *Caring for the Earth: A Strategy for Sustainable Living.* Gland: IUCN, UNEP, WWF

Janowitz, M. 1993. Packaging Industry Proposes New Approach to Stewardship. *Nova Scotia Renews* (Fall):9-14

Knight, P. 1992. Closing the Loop. *Tomorrow* 2 (2):40-3

Kumar, R., and B. Murck. 1992. *On Common Ground: Managing Human-Plant Relationships.* Toronto: John Wiley

Lowe, E. 1992. *Discovering Industrial Ecology: An Overview and Strategies for Implementation.* Oakland: Change Management Center

MacDougall, B. 1993. An Overview of Environmental Trends and Issues for Business Enterprise. In *Business Meets the Environmental Challenge: Essays with Profiles of Nova Scotia Companies,* edited by Y. Friesen, R. Côté, and D. Patton, 1-19. Hantsport, NS: Lancelot Press

McMichael, A.J. 1993. *Planetary Overload: Global Environmental Change and the Health of the Human Species.* Cambridge: Cambridge University Press

Makower, J. 1993. *The e Factor: The Bottom Line Approach to Environmentally Responsible Business.* Toronto: Random House

Mallett, T. 1991. *The Green Grassroots: Small Business and the Environment.*

Toronto: Canadian Federation of Independent Business

Neale, R. 1993. Market-Based Environmental Strategies. In *Business Meets the Environmental Challenge: Essays with Profiles of Nova Scotia Companies,* edited by Y. Friesen, R. Côté, and D. Patton, 99-112. Hantsport, NS: Lancelot Press

Odum, E.P. 1993. *Ecology and Our Endangered Life Support Systems,* 2nd ed. Sunderland, MA: Sinauer Associates

Repetto, R., R.C. Dower, R. Jenkins, and J. Geoghegan. 1992. *Green Fees: How a Tax Shift Can Work for the Environment and the Economy.* Washington, DC: World Resources Institute

Schmidheiny, S. 1992. *Changing Course: A Global Business Perspective on Development and the Environment.* Cambridge, MA: MIT Press

Tibbs, H.B.C. 1992. Industrial Ecology: An Environmental Agenda for Industry. *Whole Earth Review* (Winter):4-19

vanWeenen, J.C., and M.C.C. Lafleur. 1993. Environmentally Responsible Development of Electronic Products. Background document for EUREKA-ECODESIGN Workshop, Interfaculty Department of Environmental Science, University of Amsterdam, Netherlands

Winsemius, P., and W. Hahn. 1992. Environmental Option Assessment. *Columbia Journal of World Business* 27 (3-4):248-66

World Bank. 1978. *Environmental Considerations for the Industrial Development Sector.* Washington, DC: World Bank

World Commission on Environment and Development (WCED). 1987. *Our Common Future – Report of the World Commission on Environment and Development.* Oxford: Oxford University Press

Young, J. 1991. Reducing Waste, Saving Materials. In *The State of the World,* edited by L.R. Brown, A. Durning, C. Flavin, H. French, J. Jacobson, N. Lenssen, M. Lowe, S. Postel, M. Renner, J. Ryan, L. Starke, and J. Young, 39-55. New York: W.W. Norton

Zweers, A. 1992. Environmental Assessment and Setting Priorities. Paper presented at First NOH-European Conference on Design for the Environment, 21-3 September, Nunspeet, Netherlands

6

Making Sustainable Development Happen: Institutional Transformation

George Francis and Sally Lerner

The Promise and the Rhetoric

It is now more than two years since the much celebrated Earth Summit, the United Nations Conference on Environment and Development of June 1992, convened some 3,500 diplomats and advisers, 700 UN officials, and 120 heads of state in Rio de Janeiro to promote sustainable development and reverse environmental degradation. Canada apparently performed well at Rio; the civil servants contributed much toward having such an event occur at all and toward having our political leaders say most of the right things for the occasion. The *Agenda 21* compilation of so much that remains to be done was offered as testimony to the benevolent intent of the nation-state system and allies among the enlightened transnational corporations.

As a creature of the nation-state system, the United Nations can confidently be predicted to call for a strengthening of government resolve and leadership to do what's right. State planning is a must. So is peacekeeping, the involvement of women, technology transfer, and a host of other iconic themes formulated in opaque UN-ese and repeated in years of UN declarations. UNCED was no exception. Some refrains have been repeated at every major UN conference since the 1972 Stockholm Conference on the Human Environment, whose twentieth anniversary UNCED served to celebrate. Consigned now to a commission that reports to the Economic and Social Council of the United Nations (ECOSOC) and disaggregated to justify a panoply of ongoing UN agency programs, has *Agenda 21* been all but forgotten? Is it simply archived testimony to the flaws and outright failures of governance within this global system?

Once the summiteers return home, other priorities take over. In Canada, the preoccupations are with the symptoms of non-sustainability: government and corporate debts, gross inequalities, unemployment and permanent job losses, collapsing resource systems, and environmental contamination. During the lead-up to Rio, our various round tables on the environment and the economy were struggling with the Brundtland messages about 'sustainable development,' especially the one that suggested that 'the real world of interlocked economic and ecological systems will not change, the policies and institutions must' (WCED 1987, 9). But how? The round tables are as stymied as the rest of us.

Dynamic Systems, Institutional Gridlock

Even die-hard optimists admit that existing Canadian institutions do not, perhaps cannot, deal effectively with the multiplying symptoms of unsustainability. The symptoms arise as the cumulative consequences of multitudes of day-to-day decisions and actions taken by institutions and individuals throughout society and, increasingly, the world. While many small local measures can deal with the symptoms of unsustainability, the larger issues must be addressed by major institutions, which appear increasingly unable to do so. The underlying causes of this institutional inadequacy tend to be an embarrassment when they are identified and examined and are largely ignored in public discourse. Both symptoms and fundamental causes deserve more attention.

When sustainability is seen as arising from the dynamic interactions of interdependent systems – ecosystems and human systems – one realizes that it is about maintaining essential ecosystemic and societal processes rather than reaching a particular end once and for all. The challenge is to understand and respond appropriately to complex systems dynamics with anticipatory and adaptive management strategies to stay the course for sustainability. These strategies, in turn, require more flexible and adaptive institutions.

Institutions, however, generally appear unable to learn, to see things in fresh perspective, or to address or adapt to the changing circumstances that the symptoms of unsustainability are signalling so clearly. Thus members of the public experience disquiet about what is happening to them, or around them, while public sector institutions experience malaise and diminished public trust. According to many corporate and political leaders, private sector energies must be mobilized under the banner of global competitiveness. This has become almost a new moral equivalent to war, the preparation for which must take precedence over all other matters in society. Competitiveness in the name of development, or vice versa, however, drives the human system in ways that destroy ecosystems and human communities. A rather vicious institutional trap appears in the making.

Dynamic Systems

Study of complex dynamic systems has been called the 'new science.' In the new science, ecological and human systems are interpreted as open, non-linear, discontinuous, largely unpredictable, and self-organizing. The new science has also introduced the concept of 'ecosystem integrity.' It is an intuitively attractive concept, given the positive connotations of wholeness, of some fully functioning entity adhering to norms, but it is also somewhat elusive. In more technical terms, ecosystem integrity has been defined as an ecosystem (humans included) that exhibits healthy components, has an inherent capacity to deal with external stresses, and can maintain its internal, self-organizational evolutionary development.

'Integrity' is a scale-dependent concept; hence perspective is everything. An apparent loss or disruption of integrity at one time and place may signal only some fluctuations over a larger scale or time that are part of the healthy functioning of a larger system. As significant parts of the world's ecosystems, humans are in a position to influence the ecosystems they depend on and to choose the components that constitute their functional integrity, but we do not have sufficient information, collective decision-making processes, or the institutional arrangements to do this.

For human systems, 'sustainability' is a societal norm, a concept analogous to integrity. Sustainability involves the maintenance of various sets of adaptive and innovative processes in society that, like markets, constitute the self-organizing capabilities rather than a given end state. It is also a scale-dependent concept and implies the need for continual human choice. Akin to ecosystem integrity, sustainability requires a healthy economic and social system, healthy people, the capacity to deal with stresses, and the ability to self-organize through adaptation and innovation. 'Management' in both ecosystems and human systems becomes a question of understanding these self-organizing capabilities and then directing human activities so that they interact synergistically with them.

Yet human systems are totally enmeshed in and dependent on non-human ecosystems; together they form interdependent, co-evolutionary systems. This poses a paradox, found within the decision-making of institutions that form a sub-set of the human system. Institutions, too, are enmeshed within the ecosystems that sustain them, but the understanding of ecosystems is also enmeshed in institutions in the form of social constructions of reality, cultural beliefs and values, and the information systems about ecosystems and human systems that inform decisionmakers.

For systems thinking, attention must be given to major components and their interrelationships at different spatial and time scales, as well as to the appropriate bounding of critical sub-systems and larger systems within which a particular system of interest is a part. An analogy with photography is apt. Panoramic views and time series shots must be complemented by close-ups of the details taken from a number of different angles. The 'boundaries' around systems, which are set within other systems, are drawn by the observer in the most appropriate ways for the purpose of some analysis. Some collective ability to focus and refocus on these interdependent systems over a wide range of spatial and temporal scales is required. It is essential for obtaining the intelligence needed for adaptive management and innovation among humans under conditions of inherent uncertainties of unknown proportions. There is some urgency in this, because the constant generation and accumulation of environmental problems signal multiple pressures from the human systems on important thresholds or limits of the integrity of the non-human ecosystems.

Institutional Gridlock
Academically, all this can be exciting, but our institutions are ill adapted for interlocking systems, especially on a global basis. Most of them developed under the myth of the world as one giant machine: it seemed sensible to deal with it in bits and pieces. For any perceived problem, take it apart, examine the parts in detail, and knowledge for management will result. Institutional arrangements reflect that viewpoint. Human-imposed boundaries divide the world spatially into jurisdictions, administrative districts, markets, and private proprietorships down to half-acre lots, corner stores, and local licensing bureaux. Intellectual boundaries create the myriad specialisms that are then grouped into multitudes of human organizations. Arrangements for governance over provinces and districts or other spatially defined regions, such as urban-centred ones or bioregions and their watersheds, in Canada consist of a rich overlay of elected political bodies, special purpose administrative agencies, corporations, and other non-government organizations. Their

collective abilities to analyze details and manage within artificial boundaries are not matched by comparable abilities to synthesize data into knowledge that extends across many of these same boundaries, as an understanding of systems requires.

Transposed onto self-organizing systems, such human boundaries just do not fit, except accidentally or for only a short while. From the perspective of self-organizing, co-evolutionary systems, the here-and-now preoccupations of the so-called practical people in government and commerce become at best myopic and at worst destructive in unanticipated ways. The boundaries are weakening, however, not only because of new communications technologies but also because of some recognition that the constraints they impose on understanding and effective action are ecologically irrelevant and crippling. This weakening is crucial for human survival but threatening because of the uncertainties that arise as a result.

Reconciling Institutions with Dynamic Systems

The image of institutional gridlock conveys a strong sense of collective dysfunctionalism for a society committed to its own sustainability. It is not that bleak. The situation has both barriers and bridges, and opportunities for essential change can be identified.

The barriers are more immediately obvious: overreliance upon hierarchical organizational structures, overspecialization at both the institutional and the individual level, and personal insecurity among organizational employees. Other fundamental problems include: the nature of the relationship between the public and private sectors; the prevailing short-term, 'bottom-line' mentality of private sector and political actors; a stubborn unwillingness to temper activities by adherence to the precautionary principle; and increasing recourse to 'mandated science,' research commissioned to support or help justify policies already adopted.

Hierarchy, a form of control over information as well as over people, works against organizational and social learning, since decisions that require a continuous flow of information can only be made by those at the top, relegating all those in lower tiers to following rules set for them. This is not the stuff of innovative adaptation. Similarly, overspecialization in postsecondary education and within organizations makes it difficult for individuals and organizational units to engage in collaborative definition of problems and their solutions. Multiple solitudes characterize the landscape of overspecialization, ensuring that communication, adaptation, and creativity are institutional rarities. A third problem underlying dysfunctional institutions is the nearly inevitable insecurity of employees in the public and private sectors. The vast majority of people who form institutions are completely dependent for their livelihood on a wage or salary. In most institutional settings, therefore, employees protect themselves by shunning innovation, risk, and change. This very human response to the inherent, and increasing, insecurity of waged employment is perhaps the major barrier to effective institutional redesign. The final section of this chapter deals with it.

How does the relationship between the public and private sectors contribute to institutional dysfunctionality? Textbooks on Canadian government portray elected officials and career civil servants as protectors of the public interest and responsible stewards of both common goods, such as air and water quality, and publicly owned resources. In reality it often appears that the public sector, for urgent reasons of political survival, serves private interests by facilitating the latter's exploitation of the public domain and by maintaining civic order during the process. In this situation, 'the public interest' and 'community values' are deemed difficult to define or protect, and what we experience as institutional dysfunctionality actually stems from institutional neglect or, in some cases, inequitable handling of competing interests. That regulators are often captured by the private interests they are supposed to regulate is not news.

The well-understood 're-election' timeline of elected officials and 'bottom-line' mentality of private sector CEOs militates against coming to terms with complex systems to ensure equitable environmental and economic sustainability. This mentality is at the root of many institutional shortcomings, including unwillingness to base actions on the precautionary principle and thus possibly prevent both economic and environmental disaster in many situations. Science cannot be certain about some serious threats to sustainability in the context of interacting systems, and to insist on certainty in order to avoid arguments based on the weight of evidence is not only a costly way to bolster policy decisions but could also damage scientific integrity and credibility over the long term.

It is important that decisionmakers identify and learn to address these problems of structure, process, politics, and habit that underlie the inability of Canadian institutions to deal effectively with urgent environmental and economic challenges. This is especially true because they, and all thoughtful people, now must begin to deal with new uncertainties about choosing institutional goals and designing strategies to reach them, uncertainties created by the emergence of a genuinely new scientific paradigm.

Tinkering and Sacrificing for the Status Quo

From a systems dynamics perspective, the essential function of institutional decision-making is to ensure that the integrity of ecosystems and the sustainability of societies are maintained. This can only be done by changing institutional arrangements and organizational behaviours in response to information about unsustainable practices and loss of integrity. Nevertheless, resistance to change arises whenever the changes under consideration cannot be shown with absolute scientific certainty to be necessary or when they conflict with the conceptions, beliefs, and values embedded within the institutions. In the latter case, maintenance of the institutions takes precedence.

Tinkering thus seems a tempting way out of gridlock, and it is frequently recommended. Conventional wisdom routinely calls for it: cleverly designed, computerized 'expert systems' to sharpen rational decision-making by government and private sector elites; more markets with fewer rules for the corporate managers; a change of personalities for needed political 'leadership'; affirmations of the sacredness of private property; and the near continuous reorganization of administrative agencies. Such actions often seem to lack widespread conviction. So do mini-sermons on changing personal behaviour, or calls for the education of the lay public, as if it were their fault that agencies and corporations cannot cope with the turbulence around them. For twenty years of the environment and development debate, all these actions have been called for and tried to some degree. Judging by the continuous production of many symptoms of non-sustainability, tinkering in the environmental and socio-economic realms is not enough, and neither is the illusion of control.

Understanding the Institutional Traps in Environmental and Socio-Economic 'Management'

The Environmental Challenge

From an environmental perspective, the collapse of resource systems such as commercial fisheries or elements of the forest industry provides examples of the sacrifice of ecosystem integrity and societal sustainability to existing institutional arrangements, belief systems, and behaviours.

These are not isolated occurrences. C.S. Holling and his colleagues have documented a pattern of events in resource management systems the world over. It generally goes like this. In the name of resource or environmental management, agencies act to control certain components or fluctuations of ecosystems in order to provide more resources for human use. They succeed, and communities develop socio-economic dependencies on the continuing supplies of these resources. Management becomes focused on the means, and considerable technical skills are developed to implement these means toward an end that before long is simply taken for granted. The ecosystems supplying the resources, however, slowly respond to these continued management measures over several decades in ways that are not detected. Elements of ecosystem integrity are undermined through the cumulative effects of management actions. Suddenly, a crisis is triggered by an extreme event of low probability that has serious consequences. Management agencies are helpless to respond except by striving harder to do more of the same things that brought on the crisis.

The result over a period of years, or even decades, is that the interactions among ecosystems, social systems, and management agencies lead to institutional rigidities within the agencies because they become very set in ways that have supposedly proven successful. The communities' socio-economic dependence on the resources provided by the management agencies is crucial to the agencies' continued well-being, but the supporting ecosystems become brittle under increasing stresses to their integrity. Ultimately, the situation becomes little more than an accident waiting to happen.

The surprise associated with these 'traps' arises in part because management agencies are not on the alert for loss of ecosystem integrity and societal sustainability and are not capable of making adaptive responses when unanticipated events do occur. Instead, agencies are committed to the institutional arrangements and management programs that they have developed and that lead to collapse. More extreme sacrifices of economies and environmental quality to the requirements of institutional arrangements have occurred in the former Communist countries, and such sacrifices are at the root of political strife elsewhere in the world. It is as if the Brundtland dilemma was interpreted backwards: the 'real world' of interlocked institutional arrangements and supporting policies will not change, so ecosystems and economies must. They do. Economic bases of communities go down, jobs are eliminated never to return, environment becomes degraded, and resource systems may collapse. Social unrest threatens to arise.

The Socio-Economic Challenge

Two self-organizing trends that began in the 1960s – economic globalization and rapid technological change toward an information society – have brought Western societies to a present that includes high and growing levels of unemployment, underemployment, and insecure employment for more and more people. Secure, adequately paid jobs are becoming the preserve of a fortunate elite. Politicians talk of training and retraining, promoting self-reliance among the poor, breaking the spiral of dependency, and mounting mega-projects to create jobs. None of the proposed solutions adequately addresses the set of problems posed by employers' declining need, and desire, for full-time, permanent, adequately waged employees. The still-employed know this and are afraid. And fearful people do not look for new ways to solve problems.

Political, administrative, and corporate officials, not to mention most citizens, are baffled by the complexity and rapidity of changes in the postindustrial world. As well, most are handicapped by dysfunctional institutional arrangements and pressured by the constant lobbying of myriad powerful interest groups. Little wonder that they find it difficult to develop a coherent understanding of the new realities of economic globalization and technological breakthrough or of effective strategies for coping. Little wonder, too, that they seem not to comprehend that ignoring these sea changes will almost certainly lead to destruction of much that is valued in Western society, through either pervasive institutional paralysis or political upheaval or, most likely, both.

Equally uncomprehended and unaddressed are the opportunities afforded by the information society's reduced requirements for paid labour. There is an abundance of 'work' to be accomplished if parenting, community service, environmental restoration, skill development, lifelong education, and other desirable activities are included in the category along with paid work. If performing work that is useful to society could be even partially uncoupled from obtaining one's essential livelihood, significant progress could be made toward freeing people to participate freely in the institutional redesign needed to ensure environmental and socio-economic sustainability.

Increasingly fewer people will be needed in industrialized societies to perform the production and service functions that were historically central to their development. Nevertheless, opinion leaders exhibit intense reluctance to re-examine traditional concepts of work, income, leisure, and community life in order to embrace, or even address, this new situation. Leaders and led in North America have been thoroughly socialized to see a paid job as nearly the sole badge of respectable personhood and lack of such a job as guaranteeing personal and family disintegration. In the existing economy, these are accurate perceptions. Perhaps the most basic tenet of our secular economic religion is that the only just distribution of income is based on paid work or on circumscribed charitable concern for those unable to perform enough paid work to live at some minimum standard.

Politicians and government officials – who are expected to confer, create consensus to the extent possible, and then implement needed change – demonstrate a seeming inability or unwillingness to understand the new information coming from the globalized, high-technology socio-economic system. Corporate executives pay scant attention to the devastating effects of downsizing, recently renamed 'right-sizing,' on employee morale, loyalty, and creativity. Tinkering with existing myths and institutions is still the order of the day in the public and private sectors. Are the ranks of the unemployed and working poor growing? We've always had to deal with the unskilled and unmotivated, and now we'll make sure they study or work in return for social assistance. Are there fewer and fewer jobs that pay a living wage? That's too bad, but governments can't create real jobs, nor is it the social responsibility of the corporate sector to do so. And private sector capital has to remain competitive to produce the highest returns for its owners and handlers. So, fewer jobs today, but certainly jobs tomorrow in unimagined new technology-linked service industries – patience, please! It should be no surprise that the survivors who now people institutions keep their heads down and opt for business as usual, no matter how dysfunctional that may be.

Redesigning for Institutional Transformation
To develop the kinds of institutions required for survival in a turbulent environment of self-organizing systems and unpredictability, it is necessary to reconceptualize the nature of organizations. To address the fundamental problems underlying contemporary institutional dysfunctionality, reconceptualization must focus attention on the need for institutional arrangements that foster a holistic, systems-aware policy perspective that includes ecology. The new vision should be of organizations – or less formal 'regimes' – that are cooperative, flexible, dynamic, adaptive, constantly learning and sharing information, and themselves more self-organizing. Development of these 'new institutions' must be understood to involve social costs.

Some new visions draw attention to the globalization of economic interdependencies and to the new technologies for communication and information management. They contrast starkly with the manufacturing machine metaphor underpinning hierarchical bureaucracies, where control over information is the key to power and crucial decisions are only to be made by elite groups of managers. These command-and-control arrangements may still have a role in contexts where repetitive tasks must be performed reliably by many employees under strict supervision of a few, but in other contexts the new technologies for automation are rapidly and permanently displacing labour.

The new institutions will require, and facilitate, more widespread and versatile participation from their incumbents. This will necessitate that as many as possible take ownership, literally or psychologically. Small, task-oriented teams formed around issues, alliances and partnerships with groups in other organizations, delegation of authority and responsibility to the front-line participants, and constant feedback to enhance individual and social learning are the requirements for effective institutional change. 'Horizontal' communication networks, multiple nodes of authority and decision-making, and rapid responses to new information coming into the system characterize these arrangements. All could be supported and enhanced by services based on modern telecommunication networks, which can span any spatial scale required. A communication and learning metaphor replaces the manufacturing machine metaphor as the perspective from which to interpret the institutional arrangements necessary for adaptation and innovation. It also meshes well with the requirements for institutions and decision-making processes set in the context of co-evolutionary self-organizing systems.

In a world steeped in both new and old uncertainties, however, moves toward effective institutional redesign can provoke resistance, as people cling to whatever promises some sense of personal security. Marshall McLuhan's global village may well be the new reality, but thanks to modern telecommunications and the media the most unpleasant aspects of it are brought daily to our attention. This may only increase personal uncertainty and concerns about security. To free creativity for innovation and adaptation, one must first free people by finding new ways to provide for their economic and socio-psychological security now that traditional secure jobs are becoming less available. The alternative is to slide into a new world of mutually hostile tribalism.

Yet perhaps we are close to winning the game and do not know it. Many jobs that have been replaced by computers – or have taken flight to regions that have low wages, minimal environmental standards, or other notable advantages for employers – are dirty, dangerous, dumb jobs that should not be missed. Arguably, to be sustainable, societies must become 'learning societies,' and this requires the ability to process incoming information in ways that transform outworn myths and models into more accurate and useful mental frames. For the individual, this translates into the need for lifelong learning, probably alternating between institutions of work and learning whose boundaries are increasingly blurred.

Western societies' conception of the natural environment has evolved over the past twenty or so years from a view of nature as the free source of resources and sink for human wastes to some acknowledgment of human dependence on our biospheric life support system and a nascent respect for its integrity. This type of societal learning is still in its rudimentary phase in Western civilization; aboriginal cultures were based much more on deep intuition of the place of humans in nature. Current belated responses to environmental concerns are recognized as reactions to the insistent messages that we began receiving from a variety of natural and human sources early in this century. There has been massive resistance to legitimizing these messages, assessing their implications, and addressing the need for basic changes in human activities. It takes hundred-year floods and ragged holes in the ozone layer to gain even limited attention from public and private sector decisionmakers who, given a choice in most situations, are likely to opt for business as usual, with perhaps a bit of cost-effective tinkering.

There are several necessary steps toward creating adaptive, innovative institutions that can promote sustainability with due regard to the integrity of ecosystems. One is to legitimize the decoupling of income security and jobs in order to free people from conformist constraints that require repetition of routines long past the point of their relevance or effectiveness and to encourage their participation in institutional critique and redesign. Another is to introduce reward structures that favour critical analysis, innovative experimentation, and constructive evaluation as core activities in institutional functioning. We should also incorporate holistic systemic understanding of social and natural phenomena into education to provide some understanding of the larger context for human striving and well-being. Finally, we need to provide much more opportunity for informed, uncoerced discourse among people to improve the feedback within and among institutions and increase the social learning necessary for innovations in response to change.

Individual Security: The Key to Revitalizing Institutions

Individual income security is key to effective organizational transformation in postindustrial societies because people in organizations must feel free to criticize, innovate, and take initiatives if they are to develop creative, adaptive institutions. A major barrier to institutional redesign in postindustrial nations is the growing polarization of employment and personal resources, leading to increasing personal insecurity. Institutions are merely patterns of social behaviours directed by rules of conformity. Dependence on paid work as a prerequisite for individual survival are the rules that securely bind, freezing institutionalized behaviour into patterns that can be dramatically unsustainable. These are the rules that must go.

As long as the great majority of people perform their work in situations where their jobs – and thus their income, social standing, and survival – depend on taking no chances and displeasing no one, institutions are unlikely to change for the better. It is generally understood that movement from a hierarchical, 'top-down' organizational structure to one that is more egalitarian, even democratic, frees workers to contribute their best efforts to an enterprise. But how are we to create work situations that genuinely reduce people's sense of dependence and constraint?

A guaranteed income framework, increasingly discussed as desirable and feasible in some form, would be one way to provide the security required for people to engage in institutional innovation. For a guaranteed income to become a political possibility, the technology-based productivity that has reduced the need for paid employees in so many spheres must be accurately identified as a product of social – that is, the public's – investment in health, education, law and order, research and development, and infrastructure, which should now begin to pay a social dividend. In this context, a basic income plan that would provide enough individual security can at least be discussed in terms of financial feasibility rather than dismissed out of hand. Also up for discussion, of necessity, are the nature and goals of education in a society where being an employee would not be a person's central role.

Once individual security has been assured and paid work distributed as evenly as possible through arrangements for shorter work weeks, annual leaves, and the like, institutional transformation through innovative change still may not occur. It can be blocked by problems such as overspecialization, inadequate and faulty feedback structures that retard social learning, organizational structures that constrain flexibility in decision-making and problem-solving, and reward and sanction structures that block innovation. The people who can respond to these problems creatively are those who have been freed from the debilitating fear of retributive removal of their only source of security. Freedom to reorganize in 'win-win' terms unleashes the healthy vitality that characterizes self-organization. In this context, unpredictability translates into change and innovation. This freedom, coupled with the appropriate institutional design changes, makes possible an arena in which ecosystem integrity and societal sustainability can be transformed from impossible ideals to feasible objectives.

Further Reading
Clark, W.C., and Munn, R.E., eds. 1986. *Sustainable Development of the Biosphere.* Cambridge: Cambridge University Press

Robertson, J. 1989. *Future Wealth: A New Economics for the 21st Century.* London: Cassell

Rosell, S.A., A. Cordell, J. Taylor, and I. Stewart. 1992. *Governing in an Information Society.* Montreal: Institute for Research on Public Policy

Schmidheiny, S. 1992. *Changing Course. A Global Business Perspective on Development and the Environment.* Cambridge, MA: MIT Press

Van Parijs, P. 1992. *Arguing for Basic Income: Ethical Foundations for a Radical Reform.* London: Verso Press

Woodley, S., J. Kay, and G. Francis. 1993. *Ecological Integrity and the Management of Ecosystems.* Delray Beach, FL: St. Lucie Press

World Commission on Environment and Development (WCED). 1987. *Our Common Future – Report of the World Commission on Environment and Development.* Oxford: Oxford University Press

7
Putting Women and the Environment First: Poverty Alleviation and Sustainable Development
Bonnie Kettel

Since the publication of *Our Common Future* in 1987, debate over the policy significance of the term 'sustainable development' has been ongoing. In the international arena, few aspects of this debate have provoked as much controversy as the issue of poverty alleviation. Poverty alleviation is a motherhood concern, with all actors and analysts in broad agreement that meeting this goal is important to the global quest for sustainable development. Nevertheless, there is surprisingly little agreement among nations and policy analysts about the meaning and incidence of poverty, the importance of poverty as a barrier to sustainable development, or the centrality of poverty alleviation to international and national agendas for a sustainable future. In my view, much of the confusion that this debate has provoked has resulted from the gendered nature of the experience of poverty, and the debate about poverty alleviation, in the international arena.

Many scholars have argued that 'sustainable livelihoods' are essential to the implementation and accomplishment of sustainable development (Chambers 1988). The defining elements in sustainable livelihoods are secure and equitable access to basic needs, appropriate technology and income, and protection or enhancement of natural resources, all over both the short and long term. Poverty, in this framework, refers to a condition of insecurity of access to the fundamentals of life in basic needs, technology, income, and a healthy environment. This approach takes us away from a simplistic view of poverty as a merely financial phenomenon or a perspective narrowly focused on material deprivation, no matter how severe. Instead the sustainable livelihoods approach highlights the importance of short- and long-term security of access to the fundamentals of life, including environmental security, as preconditions for sustainable development. This approach also helps to clarify the gendered nature of the experience of poverty in both the South and the North.

Much of the international debate surrounding poverty alleviation has proceeded on North-South lines. This debate is important for its own sake and certainly illustrates the economic tensions between North and South in the global framework. Among other important issues, however, such as the recent spread of poverty in the North (UNDP 1991, 31), it also fails to address the fact that no matter how poverty is defined, in every country in the world there are now more poor women than there are poor men. Krishna Ahooja-Patel points out that several recent international reports, including the *Human Development Report 1991* (UNDP 1991), have argued that the feminization of poverty has become 'a global economy reality' that exists 'beyond the global classification into high or medium or low income countries.' So far, however, what she refers to as the 'explosive issue' of women's disproportionate poverty – in the South and the North – has been left unaddressed at an international policy level (Ahooja-Patel 1992, 31-4).

One reason for this apparent indifference is that most of the key actors in the intergovernmental debate about poverty alleviation are men. Women's level of direct participation in this international arena is extraordinarily low. Steady reports that only 15 per cent of the official delegates and advisers at the United Nations Conference on Environment and Development (UNCED) were women, and there were only three women among the 118 heads of state in attendance (1993, 29). In the period leading up to UNCED in 1992, 93 countries out of the 159 member nations of the United Nations had no women cabinet ministers at all. Only three countries in the world – Bhutan, Dominica, and Norway – had levels of female representation in ministerial appointments higher than 20 per cent (UN 1991, 31). As a result of these gender inequities in national and international political participation, and the gender blindness and bias that so readily results from their absence, women and women's concerns have not been adequately represented or addressed in the global decision-making spheres where policy and programs for poverty alleviation are debated and determined.

This chapter examines the link between women and poverty as a gendered domain in the North-South poverty debate. It argues that viewing poverty from a gendered perspective allows us a more complete understanding of the nature of poverty, its relationship to environmental degradation, and the challenges of poverty alleviation for sustainable development. Gender bias in policy formulation and international decision-making is analyzed as a significant causal factor that, with other important factors such as racism, international debt, and structural adjustment, actually leads to women's disproportionate poverty and experience of environmental degradation and sustains their impoverishment locally, nationally, and internationally (Jacobson 1992; Steady 1993).

These issues are discussed in a global context, with particular attention to the policy avenues relevant for future action in support of women, the environment, and sustainable development at home and on the international scene. In keeping with recent efforts, the chapter identifies improving women's scientific and technological literacy and participation as a key avenue for future policy initiatives for poverty alleviation. More generally, it argues that increasing women's participation in policy formulation and decision-making in all international arenas is essential for the eradication of poverty and the promotion of sustainable development.

Gender Blindness, Gender Bias

Underneath the rhetoric of the North-South debate about poverty alleviation and sustainable development are some crucial issues concerning women and women's interests that are simply not being addressed by the world's international policymakers. *Our Common Future* offers an illustrative example of a largely gender-blind approach to policy formulation for sustainable development. The World Commission on Environment and Development report (WCED 1987) paid comparatively little attention to women and women's interests. In a text 357 pages in length, women and women's concerns with regard to food production, agricultural extension, housing, education, and family planning were indexed on only six pages, a grossly inadequate level of visibility that is common in international policy arenas. By comparison, Africa, which the report recognized as a continent 'in crisis,' was indexed over fifty times. Men, of course, are not indexed at all; the entire WCED report is addressed to the world's international policymakers, an audience that is predominately male and predominately aware of and interested in issues relevant to men's lives and well-being.

In the international debate about poverty alleviation, gender blindness has also led to distinct gender bias and the visible disparagement of women's goals and interests. The gendered nature of the North-South poverty debate was discernible in the preparatory meetings (Prep-Comms) leading up to the UNCED Earth Summit. At the final Prep-

Comm meeting in New York, the United States moved to have all references to overconsumption in the North deleted from the chapter of the UNCED platform of action dealing with poverty alleviation. In response, the Group of Seventy-Seven (G77) poor countries of the South moved to delete all references to family and population planning from the draft document. In essence what this episode involved was a group of male government representatives from the North and the South engaging in a non-collaborative political stand-off that ignored completely the disproportionate incidence of poverty among women globally and trivialized the importance of women's access to reproductive health care to their personal well-being and to sustainable development.

This episode is also revealing for the vociferous and well-organized response it provoked from the multilayered international network of women activists, policy analysts, and scholars whose origin lies in the end-of-decade World Conference on Women held in Nairobi in 1985. The abandonment of women's interests and concerns by representatives of the North and the South at the New York PrepComm was a watershed for this large and increasingly interactive network of women and women's organizations. At the Non-Governmental Organization (NGO) Forum held in association with UNCED, various key network actors – including the South-based Development Alternatives for Women for a New Era collective (DAWN), the Women's Environment and Development Organization (WEDO), and other women's organizations from around the world – collectively inserted themselves into the North-South debate through an unofficial but highly effective caucusing process led by WEDO, like 'streaks of light' on a dimly lit world stage (Ahooja-Patel 1992, 11). In the period preceding the Fourth World Conference on Women (FWCW) in Beijing, the international women's network continued to act as a powerful lobbying force for women's participation in agenda setting for sustainable and equitable development.

The North-South Poverty Debate
As Anil Agarwahl rightly suggests, on a global per capita, and therefore gender-blind, basis poverty is a largely southern issue (Agarwahl 1993). The countries of the South are disproportionately poor in comparison to the nations of the North. Seventy-three countries, all in the South, had average per capita incomes below US$1,000 a year as recently as 1987. Twenty-five per cent of people in the so-called developing countries, over 1 billion persons, presently face lives of profound material deprivation, without proper nutrition, health care, and sanitation (Carroll-

Foster 1993). If we add to these the millions of people in the southern nations whose incomes and basic needs are marginal and insecure, then the overall incidence of poverty in the South increases exponentially.

At a global level, exposure to environmental degradation is also directly linked to the experience of poverty. The poorest 20 per cent of people in the world live in ecologically vulnerable or fragile settings, especially in Latin America, Asia, and Africa (Steady 1993, 27). In the nations of the South, land degradation is widespread, with entire regions threatened by the spreading impact of deforestation, desertification, coastal and interior flooding, soil degradation, and loss of biodiversity. Deforestation alone has subjected vast regions to desertification and flooding. Lester Brown reports that the area subject to flooding in India had increased from 47 million acres in 1960 to 124 million acres, an area the size of California, by 1984 as a direct result of deforestation (1991, 149).

In the face of widespread impoverishment and environmental degradation in the South, it is difficult to comprehend the arrogance that led then American President George Bush to proclaim in response to southern complaints about resource consumption in the North that 'the American way of life is not up for negotiation' (Agarwahl 1993, 92). Poverty and environmental degradation, however, are certainly not limited to the southern countries. Poverty has increased in several industrialized countries, including the United States, Canada, and the United Kingdom, since 1980.

What 'the American way of life' really means is a poverty and near-poverty rate of 20.5 per cent, an illiteracy rate of one in five adults, and the highest infant mortality rate among the developed nations (Daly and Muirhead 1993, 10). In the United States, as in the southern countries, poverty is also associated with increased exposure to environmental hazards. Three-quarters of hazardous waste fill sites in the southeastern United States are located in low-income neighbourhoods, while toxic waste dumps can generally be found in areas occupied by African Americans and Hispanic Americans (Steady 1993, 21; Cole 1990).

In Canada recent economic decline has greatly increased the numbers of people living below the income-defined poverty-line. Some 3,129,000 people, one out of every eight Canadians, were officially 'poor' by 1989 (Carroll-Foster 1993). Meanwhile, in the United Kingdom, three out of ten households below the pensionable age level were living below or close to the poverty level by the mid-1980s (Daly and

Muirhead 1993). By 1989, there were over 400,000 homeless people, including 196,000 children, in the United Kingdom (UNDP 1991).

Given the growing incidence and intractability of poverty in the North and the clear evidence that just as in the South poverty is associated with exposure to environmental contamination and degradation, one wonders why poverty alleviation is still being debated in the international arena primarily as a North-South issue. A North-South conceptualization of the sources and incidence of poverty cannot adequately identify future policy solutions for what is increasingly a worldwide problem, albeit one still experienced to a far greater degree and with far greater intensity in the southern countries. In my view the emerging inadequacies and misperceptions of the North-South poverty debate have much to do with the gendered nature of the poverty problem and the international contexts within which poverty alleviation policies and programs are discussed and formulated.

The North-South discord surrounding the issue of poverty alleviation has centred on the relative importance of population growth in the South versus consumption of southern resources by the northern countries as the ultimate source of poverty in the South. An essentially northern perspective on this controversy was set out in *Our Common Future,* which put forward a view of the sustainable development agenda centred on economic growth. The WCED report argued that economic growth must continue in the industrialized nations of the North at a rate of 3 to 4 per cent a year, this being 'the minimum that financial institutions consider necessary if these countries are going to play a part in expanding the world economy' (WCED 1987, 51). The expressed challenge for the North was to revive growth while reducing resource consumption and improving resource efficiency.

While *Our Common Future* also encouraged economic growth in the South at even higher levels than in the North as a basis for poverty alleviation, this possibility was addressed in significant measure as a population issue as well as an economic goal. The WCED report insisted that population growth, which at its highest is also between 3 and 4 per cent per year, should be 'managed' for greater efficiency in the pursuit of economic gain, particularly in 'low-income countries, ecologically disadvantaged regions and poor households' where 'so much of the population growth is concentrated' (WCED 1987, 95).

The differences between the northern and southern viewpoints on the population issue came out clearly at the Earth Summit. The northern countries, supported by some northern environmentalists, stressed the hazardous impact of high rates of population growth in the South on the possibility of sustainable economic growth in those countries. The southern nations and NGOs responded by pointing to the detrimental effects of resource consumption and overconsumption, especially by the northern countries and north-based transnational corporations, on southern economic and environmental well-being. The southern viewpoint was vigorously put forward by Anil Agarwahl of India, who argued that the southern countries are paying the price of northern overconsumption in the form of ongoing resource extraction, national indebtedness, mass impoverishment, and increased environmental degradation (Agarwahl 1993).

In the midst of all this vibrant debate about population control and resource consumption, there was a vast silence in the official meeting at the Earth Summit – just as there was in *Our Common Future* – about *women's* disproportionate experience of poverty and the fact it is still only women who actually have babies. As van den Oever has recently pointed out, population control is 'the ultimate gender issue.' Giving birth is one of the very few aspects of social life in the human community that cannot be reversed or shared between women and men. Only women will have babies, or not have them, for the foreseeable future of humankind (van den Oever 1993, 113).

The G77 abandonment at the New York PrepComm of women's rights and interests in access to family planning information and technology indicated a profound lack of concern for women's well-being and potential contributions to sustainable development. Nor were women's rights and interests the primary issue for the northern environmental NGOs who spoke out on behalf of women's access to family planning at the Earth Summit. These groups, such as the American National Audubon Society, which organized a population program in 1979, are ultimately concerned to protect birds and other wild species against the 'threat' of human fertility. In a statement of Audubon's population policy, Patricia Waak commented that 'Audubon's mission can be stated in one key phrase: "To effect wise public policy for the environment, especially in major issues that bear on wildlife and wildlife habitat." We cannot effect that public policy without regard for the greatest threat to wildlife and wildlife habitat: Homo Sapiens' (Waak 1992, 2). As this comment indicates, at UNCED Audubon's support for women's access to family planning was ultimately, although certainly not entirely, a tactic for wilderness protection, not a human rights issue or even in the larger social and economic sense a sustainable development issue.

Reaction to the North-South poverty debate at the grassroots level in the southern countries, where local NGOs interact directly with women involved in the quest for basic needs and safe and healthy communities, has been one of considerable anger. A recent editorial published in Kampala is illustrative of the view of women-focused NGOs in the South: 'While we are aware that rapid population growth can contribute to land degradation and fragmentation, it is obvious ... that women's fertility rates cannot be the principal actors in this global environmental problem. Women must be assertive and must challenge any statements that are meant to intimidate and marginalize them' (ACFODE 1992, 2).

Following UNCED, women's potential contributions to the global quest for sustainable development have received a new level of scholarly and policy recognition. Thus it is heartening to read Anil Agarwahl – who has long been an articulate proponent of the importance of women's participation in decision-making for sustainable development – argue that 'Himalayan forests are best managed by Himalayan women, who use those forests for firewood and have a vested interest in their management' (Agarwahl 1993, 92). Meanwhile in the northern countries women-focused NGOs are attempting to address the issue of regional overconsumption. The Women, Environment, Education and Development Foundation (WEED), which is based in Toronto, has been involved recently in the Stop the Whitewash campaign (Kneipp 1994). The goal of this particular campaign is to influence women to use unbleached sanitary products in support of a cleaner, safer environment in the North. International women-focused NGOs such as WEDO are also beginning to take a hard look at the negative impact of pollution and other environmental hazards on women's health and well-being in both the North and the South (WEDO 1994a).

Within the international networks that emerged out of the 1985 Nairobi conference – where the southern, northern, and international women's NGOs were all represented – it has become very clear that women's impoverishment cannot be meaningfully addressed by a debate that conceptualizes the sources and incidence of poverty solely as the result of economic relations between the North and the South, important as these may be. Nor can they be addressed in a framework that attempts to manage women's fertility in the South as a basis for sustainable development in the North or that limits the activities of women in the North to choosing more environmentally responsible sanitary products and other forms of 'green consumerism.' Instead women worldwide must be directly involved in setting new economic, environmental, and social agendas for the alleviation of poverty and the prevention of environmental destruction locally, nationally, and internationally (Kettel 1993).

The Feminization of Poverty and Environmental Degradation

As a first step in establishing this new agenda for poverty alleviation we need to understand the incidence and sources of women's impoverishment in the global arena. Several parameters are important here, including position in the global and national economy, race and ethnicity, education and literacy, and age. Position in the global economy is certainly important, since three-quarters of the world's women live in countries where the per capita gross domestic product either declined or increased only marginally during the 1980s (Jacobson 1993, 4, 7). It is also clear, however, that women are disproportionately represented among the rural and urban poor in both the South and the North. Women worldwide at every economic level own less than men, work longer hours, and earn less income (Ahooja-Patel 1992). Women in female-headed households, which now include one-quarter to one-third of all households worldwide, are particularly vulnerable to differential impoverishment. The fundamental question that has to be addressed, therefore, is why poverty among women is far more widespread, deeper, and more difficult to overcome than it is among men (Jacobson 1993).

At a surface level it seems clear that gender blindness, and even bias, are important factors in women's disproportionate poverty. But if gender bias is, as we commonly believe, a local, cultural phenomenon then why is women's poverty a *worldwide* problem? Why are women poorer than men everywhere in the global economy? I suggest that it is simplistic to attribute the 'feminization of poverty' only to the gender bias of local cultures and traditions and that to understand and alleviate a worldwide phenomenon we must also look for a deeper and less visible explanation. We also need to come to terms with a simultaneous issue. Not only are women everywhere disproportionately poor, they are also far more likely than men to experience the daily demands and personal consequences of local environmental degradation. Thus, we also need to explain the 'feminization of environmental degradation' (cf. Newman 1992, 60; Kneipp 1994, 77).

Women who are poor in both the South and the North are also more likely to live in neighbourhoods and regions that are environmentally marginal, degraded, or polluted. As Steady reports, 'most people in rural areas who are already coping with the paucity of material resources are becoming increasingly impoverished as their physical environment is degraded' (1993, 23). Because of their role in the production of basic needs, women in the rural areas of the South are far more likely than men to bear the burden of this environmental destruction (Dankelman and Davidson 1988).

In a recent report I made the argument, based on Jacobson (1992, 19-22), that women are central to the production of basic needs in the developing world (Kettel 1995a, 29-30). They produce at least 80 per cent of all food crops in sub-Saharan Africa, 70 to 80 per cent in South Asia, and 50 per cent in Latin America and the Caribbean. As well, they provide half of the labour necessary for cash crop production, and contribute significantly to animal care and management. Women in rural areas of the developing countries are also usually the major providers of water for people and animals and fuelwood and fodder for the household. As well, they gather and process medicinal plants and oils and resins. Access to the natural environment is generally crucial for women's production of basic needs and their generation of income, especially in the informal economy. Women's needs and interests in the natural environment also have considerable importance for women in urban areas, who may continue to rely on natural resources found in both the city (especially in the form of urban agriculture) and the countryside (fuelwood and charcoal, for example) to meet their basic needs.

Nevertheless, women rarely own as much of the natural environment as men do (Kettel 1993, 41-2). Vast amounts of common property once accessible to women are now privately owned or controlled by national governments. The privatization of common property has brought the natural environment more and more under the control of male owners and absentee landlords, including transnational corporations (Jacobson 1992, 24-7). In sub-Saharan Africa, Latin America, and South Asia, land ownership is now a predominately male phenomenon, and women can acquire access to land only through their male relatives. Women have been cut off from making decisions about the healthy and sustainable management of their natural environments. Their ability to produce food, to provide water and fuelwood for household use, to acquire access to credit, to protect their own health, and to contribute to sustainable environmental management have all been seriously undermined. As a result, women have become disproportionately poor in comparison with men in their own communities.

Women who are the primary producers of basic needs, as they are in so many nations of the South, can experience extreme demands on their labour and time as the result of environmental degradation. The local environmental destruction that results from spreading deforestation and desertification generally forces women to walk very long distances, involving up to seventeen hours a week, for water gathering alone (UN 1991, 75). As the production of basic needs becomes more time consuming women commonly attempt to reduce their use of water and fuelwood by cutting down on the amount of clean water and cooked food that they serve their families. Recent research by the Women, Environment and Development Network (WEDNET) in Africa shows that women faced with environmental destruction may also use the natural environment in an increasingly unsustainable manner, violating their own environmental knowledge and interests, merely to maintain themselves and their households day to day (Kettel 1995b).

Not only are rural women in the South more likely than men to be poor and exposed to environmental degradation, they are also more likely to be denied representation in local and national planning and policy formulation (Moser 1993). Across vast regions of the South, millions of poor rural women have been denied participation in decisions involving the introduction of new technology, the transformation of local environments for economic gain, and the financial and ecological futures of their own households and communities. As a result the considerable knowledge that these women often have about sustainable use and management of local ecosystems has been ignored and undermined (Kettel 1995b).

Nor are these problems limited to women in rural areas. By the year 2025 about 60 per cent of the world's population will probably live in urban areas (Kettel 1995c; APDC 1992). In some cities in the South, such as Bombay and Calcutta, more than 50 per cent of urban dwellers presently live in slums and squatter settlements. In such settings women commonly experience inadequate shelter, water, and waste disposal services, inadequate transportation systems, overcrowding, unsafe and hazardous public spaces, pollution, and a lack of open air, trees, and parks. Environmental illnesses such as diarrhea, dysentery, hepatitis, and typhoid are major causes of death in slums and squatter settlements in the southern countries (APDC 1992). Many large cities in the South implicitly rely on women to maintain the environmental well-being of the community primarily through their informal and largely unrecognized activities as domestic cleaners and care givers. Urban sanitation and waste disposal services are simply added on to women's already heavy responsibilities.

In the countries of the North poverty also exposes women to environmental degradation and risk (Kettel 1995c). Payne found 'a powerful relationship between socio-economic status and poor health' among women in the United Kingdom (1991, 117). Poverty forces women, who spend far more time at home than men, to endure poor quality housing, inadequate heating, lack of space, damp living conditions, lack of hot water, and inadequate furnishings. Furthermore the negative impact of poverty on health is not limited to the actual dwelling. Payne argues that 'unsafe public space ... constitutes deprivation in the environment for women, as does inadequate public transport and poor public amenities' (1991, 136).

Women in the South and the North are generally denied an equitable voice, often any voice at all, in household and community decisions affecting their use and management of the so-called built environment, including their own homes and urban neighbourhoods. Women's rights to property ownership in the built environment are commonly structured by local or national legislation. The low level of participation by women in national legislatures is particularly significant with regard to the enactment of laws affecting their property rights. Some countries in the South, such as Kenya and Tanzania, have prevented women from owning even the houses they live in. As a result they are 'often denied access to loans ... and are last on the list for housing schemes. That forces them into substandard housing and unhealthy living environments for raising their children' (UN 1991, 72).

Women also lack opportunities to influence the use and management of built environments in the northern countries. Women's exclusion from the environmental decisions that affect their lives is particularly clear with regard to the production, management, and distribution of environmental contaminants in northern communities. Although, as mentioned, the WEED foundation is presently encouraging women in Toronto to avoid using bleached sanitary products (Kneipp 1994), hundreds of toxic organochlorines are being pumped into northern environments every year as the result of the use of chlorine in the manufacture of plastics, solvents, pesticides, refrigerants, and pulp and paper (Clorfene-Casten 1993). Opportunities for women in the North to affect the distribution of environmental contaminants, especially through participation in industrial decision-making or national legislative processes, are far fewer than those available to men.

At the top level of industrial decision-making women are barely represented at all. A 1989 study of 1,000 American corporations with total sales of US$3.3 trillion found only two women as chief executive officers. Fewer than 20 per cent of management and administrative positions are held by women in the commercial and industrial labour force in the developed countries. There are generally proportionately more women employed as civil servants in the public sector, but again they are most significantly represented at the lowest levels of income and decision-making. At the national legislative level women make up more than 15 per cent of parliamentary representatives in only twenty-three countries, not including Canada, the United States, or the United Kingdom (UN 1991, 31-5).

The absence of women from these decision-making arenas supports the gender blindness – and gender bias – that have led to women's differential impoverishment and risk of environmental illness and contamination across the planet. Yet it is difficult to explain the global nature of women's disproportionate experience of poverty and environmental pollution and destruction as the simple outcome of thousands of acts of gender blindness and bias at the local and national levels, or as a mere by-product of the economic inequities that exist between South and North. It is also difficult to explain these phenomena by focusing solely on the victims, on women as a social category. In order to address the policy concerns arising from the feminization of poverty and of environmental degradation, I therefore suggest that we reverse the mirror and look at the invisible issues that these phrases help to disguise.

One important factor underlying both these policy concerns is the masculinization of wealth in money (income) and in the natural environment (natural resources). If we want to alleviate poverty and halt the spread of environmental contamination and degradation then the masculinization of wealth is the invisible issue we will have to address. This cannot happen within our current policy frameworks, even within the policy frameworks for sustainable development represented by *Our Common Future* and *Agenda 21*, the global action plan adopted at UNCED in Rio de Janeiro. These documents reflect an even more fundamental dilemma, the national and international masculinization of policy and decision-making that has sustained the masculinization of wealth in income and natural resources for the past several decades. Masculinization of wealth and decision-making is the overall problem we have to overcome in the quest for poverty alleviation, sustainability, and sustainable development. So far, although some very positive and compelling attempts have been made, at an international policy level the challenge has not been met.

Recent Policy Contributions

Agenda 21, the platform of action that emerged from UNCED, devotes a whole chapter to women and environment issues. Chapter 24 represents an important step forward for international policy formulation addressed to women's participation in sustainable development. The vitality of Chapter 24 is largely due to the strenuous lobbying efforts of a few national delegations, the Canadian one prominently among them, and the efforts of the international network of women and environment activists, policy analysts, and researchers that emerged specifically in relation to UNCED. This large informal network was mobilized by WEDO, DAWN, and international NGOs such as the International Women's Tribune Center and ultimately involved a number of individual and institutional participants, including such well-known women environmentalists as Wangari Maathai of Kenya, Elizabeth May of Canada, and Vandana Shiva of India. Although the international network was, and is, characterized by considerable diversity, its collective impact was very significant.

WEDO's lobbying efforts began with the World Women's Congress for a Healthy Planet held in Miami in 1991. The congress involved over 1,500 women from eighty-three countries and was the locale for the adoption of the *Women's Action Agenda 21* (WEDO 1992), a document that has had a visionary impact on women and environment scholars, policy analysts, and activists from around the world. The *Women's Action Agenda 21* was the basis for very successful international lobbying efforts for women's participation at UNCED and their inclusion as a 'major group' in *Agenda 21.* These efforts resulted in a decision at the third PrepComm in Geneva to require that all UNCED documents should reflect the need for women's participation and the effect on women of the proposed plan of action. This decision meant that women's potential contributions to sustainable development had to be considered as a 'distinct cross-cutting issue,' rather than being 'mainstreamed' in the documentation leading to and resulting from the Earth Summit.

After the Geneva PrepComm, a team of WEDO supporters analyzed the major draft conference documents, comparing them to the *Women's Action Agenda 21.* During the five weeks of the final PrepComm in New York, WEDO organized daily caucuses of women representing government delegations and NGOs as the basis for an extensive lobbying campaign. When the North-South debate erupted, the Women's Caucus was a significant arena for protest and negotiation in response to the positions put forward by the United States and the G77. This long-term, intensive effort resulted in improved language regarding women's reproductive rights and their importance to the quest for sustainable development throughout *Agenda 21* and especially in Chapter 24.

As is commonplace for any policy document dealing with women's issues, Chapter 24 is also important for the concerns it fails to recognize or address. Few links are drawn between it and other key chapters, such as those on sustainable agriculture, the scientific and technological community, and non-government organizations (Carroll-Foster 1993). One of the most glaring omissions in Chapter 24 is its failure to recognize the links between women's poverty, environmental degradation, and women's environmental interests and action. The omission was certainly not the responsibility of the large international network of women who struggled valiantly to get women's environmental concerns and participation into *Agenda 21,* but it is, however, a symptom of the enormity of the battle that confronts anyone concerned with issues affecting women in the international and national policy formulation process.

For the international network of women activists, policy analysts, and researchers that emerged out of UNCED, the masculinization of wealth and decision-making has become a central issue for discussion and action. The North-South poverty debate has generated some anger in this international network, but the anger does not have a North-South organization. Instead, it is the anger of women, North and South, who are simply fed up with the failure of national governments, environmental activists, sustainable development policy analysts, and international policymakers to recognize that the impoverishment of women and the degradation of the natural environment are closely linked. These problems are the outcome of a world run by men for or against men but rarely for men and women and even less often for women and children first (Steady 1993).

Since UNCED there have been further contributions to gender equity in international policy formulation. The International Conference on Population and Development (ICPD), which was held in Cairo in September 1994, is central in this regard. At the ICPD, the Women's Caucus, which was again led by WEDO, provided detailed amendments to the proposed ICPD platform of action. The efforts of the caucus led to greatly improved language in the final platform concerning women's reproductive health and access to family planning and a whole new chapter dealing with women's empowerment (WEDO 1994b, 4). At the very least, the Cairo conference marked the apparent end of the policy acceptability of the top-down national management approach to 'population control' outlined in *Our Common Future* (WCED 1987).

Nevertheless, in the quest for gender equity in the international arena every significant gain appears to bring its own new hazards. The ICPD meeting also marked the beginning of a well-organized resistance to the use of the term 'gender' as a basis for women's social, economic, and political empowerment. At the April 1995 PrepComm for the Fourth World Conference on Women a coalition of delegations – including the Vatican, Guatemala, Honduras, Ecuador, Sudan, Benin, Malta, Libya, and Egypt – opposed the use of the word 'gender' in the draft platform and insisted that it be placed in parentheses, or 'bracketed,' until a definition that would accommodate their more biologically essentialist understanding of women's status and roles in society could be agreed upon (WEDO 1995, 8). The general view put forward by these delegations was that the traditional roles of men and women in the larger society and the family are not merely cultural and social, and therefore changeable, as the term 'gender' suggests, but natural and even god-given.

As a result of these interventions, 40 per cent of the FWCW draft platform had been disputed and bracketed by the end of the April PrepComm. Brackets were placed around language previously accepted at UNCED, the ICPD, and the World Summit on Social Development, which was held in Copenhagen in March 1995. The recommendations from the Social Summit, which dealt in particular with the North-South inequities of the global economy, had reaffirmed those aspects of the ICPD platform dealing with women's empowerment as a basis for poverty reduction (WEDO 1995, 1, 3). At the April PrepComm, comments and recommendations reflecting all of these significant advances were bracketed. Disputed aspects of the FWCW draft platform included women's reproductive and parental rights, their human rights, and their access to political, economic, and social empowerment as a basis for poverty reduction (WEDO 1995, 8-9). In response, the women's caucus argued that women would not be 'forced back into the "biology is destiny" concept that seeks to define, confine and reduce women and girls to the physical sexual characteristics' (WEDO 1995, 8).

As the April PrepComm clearly demonstrated, the terms 'North' and 'South,' which are used to describe the positions and well-being of nations in the global economy, are far more sacrosanct in policy formulation than the term 'gender.' Who, for instance, would even think to suggest that the current economic inequities between the nations of the North and South are natural and divinely ordained? By contrast, the antigender effort has moved international policy debate and intervention beyond gender blindness and gender bias into a whole new arena of gender denial, within which the inequities confronting women, including their disproportionate poverty, may continue to be distorted and disguised in the future.

Immediately following the April PrepComm for the FWCW, the Commission on Sustainable Development (CSD), which was set up as a result of UNCED, also met in New York. The delegates to the CSD meeting, who were mostly men, 'seemed to be unaware of agreements made ... at every UN conference since the 1992 Earth Summit on the essential role of women in sustainable development' (WEDO 1995, 7). Not surprisingly, in spite of the efforts of a small Women's Caucus, the assembled delegates refused to recommend that national delegations include gender issues, in keeping with Chapter 24 of *Agenda 21,* in their periodic reports to the CSD. As the CSD meeting makes all too clear, in spite of UNCED, the ICPD, and the Social Summit, the masculinization of wealth and decision-making, which supports and sustains women's disproportionate poverty, has by no means been adequately addressed in the international policy milieu.

The Future of Women's Participation
While women across the planet, in the North and the South, share common concerns and the experience of broadly based economic and environmental difficulties, their lives are certainly not identical from one region to another, and their particular economic and environmental dilemmas, concerns, and interests are still culturally, socially, racially, and regionally variable. For this reason there is an urgent need for women's poverty and experience of environmental degradation to be alleviated through the direct participation and involvement of women themselves.

Women are already significantly involved in environmental activism at the local level in both the North and the South. The story of the Chipko movement in India, where women 'hugged' the trees to save them from commercial exploitation and from the desires of local men to convert them into cash income, is very well known. The WEDNET research shows that women in Africa fight back against environmental destruction daily, using traditional knowledge, modern innovations, help and cooperation, careful decision-making, and collective management to maintain and protect the natural environment (Kettel 1995b). In Canada recent research has shown that environmental activists are typically women between the ages of twenty-six and forty, especially women with very young children. It was a small group of women exactly like this who forced their national government to clean up the toxic waste sites around their homes in a place called Love Canal in the United States (McIntosh 1993).

Even so, women rarely act as leaders of national or international environmental NGOs, including those based in the northern countries, in spite of the current visibility of some very well-known women environmentalists (Kneipp 1994, 49). They are also denied equitable access to the leadership of trade unions and political parties across the planet (UN 1991, 31-2). As this chapter has pointed out, they are also grossly underrepresented in public decision-making, especially at the national political level. As of 1987 an average of only 10 per cent of all parliamentarians worldwide were women. Women are still completely excluded from the four highest levels of government service, including the ministerial level, in forty-nine countries. Furthermore, men are still in almost exclusive control of those ministries most strongly dedicated to economic growth and to expenditure in the name of 'national security' – economic policy, political affairs, and defence – in all the world's regions.

As the 1995 CSD meeting reveals, all of the excellent policy directives established in the last decade have made far too little difference to the lives of women in most countries. National delegations may vote to adopt international platforms of action that support the alleviation of women's impoverishment and their greater participation as environmental and political decisionmakers, but it is easier and often more politically acceptable at home to sign a document in Nairobi or Rio de Janeiro than it is to put that document to work within national legislative and policy and planning frameworks. It is also extremely difficult to have agreements such as the *Convention on the Elimination of All Forms of Discrimination against Women,* the *Forward-Looking Strategies for the Advancement of Women,* and the *Women's Action Agenda 21* (see Kettel 1995a) taken seriously as relevant concerns within significant international arenas such as the International Monetary Fund (IMF), the General Agreement on Tariffs and Trade (GATT), and the North American Free Trade Agreement (NAFTA). Significant economic decisions that affect the lives of millions of women and children everywhere are undertaken through arenas such as the IMF, GATT, and NAFTA. Women rarely participate as key decisionmakers in these domains, and gender-based goals and interests with regard to poverty alleviation and environmental protection are rarely recognized or considered (Marsden 1992). The United Nations system is a leading example of the failure of our global institutions to address women's interests and their improved participation as key decisionmakers. Only 3.6 per cent of senior managerial appointments in the United Nations system are presently held by women (UN 1991).

In contexts such as the CSD, the IMF, GATT, and NAFTA, men in suits, and sometimes a suited woman or two, originating from all corners of the planet, establish the policies that run the world. These international bodies and the agreements they enter into act as a powerful source of continuing impoverishment and environmental degradation in the lives of women across the planet. The perspectives furthered and decisions made by these international institutions represent an ultimate dilemma for women everywhere: the masculinization of our global future.

In response to these national and international dilemmas, preparations for the FWCW in the international women's network tended to focus on specific strategic concerns for national governments to address at home and in future international agreements rather than on broadly based exhortations regarding gender equity. One of these emerging concerns was women's scientific and technological literacy and participation. From May 1992 onward women representing national, regional, and international networks and organizations met to discuss how the 1995 FWCW and particularly the Beijing NGO forum might be used to further a new 'woman-friendly' vision of science and technology for development (Kettel 1994). The institutions and networks represented in this collaborative process included the United Nations Development Fund for Women, the International Women's Tribune Center, the Third World Organization for Women in Science, the Gender, Science and Development Program of the International Federation of Institutes for Advanced Studies, the International Development Research Centre, WEDO, the Asian Alliance of Appropriate Technology Practitioners, Appropriate Technology International, the Intermediate Technology Development Group, TechnoServe, the World Women's Veterinary Association, and the World YWCA. This collaboration resulted in a planning framework for a series of activities and events centred around women, science, and technology in Beijing.

As they are presently understood and practised, science and technology are generally ill suited to the needs and interests of the southern countries in general and women in those countries in particular. In both the North and the South, women are trained in the scientific and technological professions far less often than men and are significantly underrepresented at the senior levels in the scientific and technological professions and in important national and international forums for scientific and technological policy formulation. As a result, scientific and technological research and policy formulation have tended to serve as key avenues for the feminization of poverty and environmental degradation (Kettel 1995a). The collective pursuit of a new 'woman-friendly' vision of science and technology offers an important strategic avenue for improving the impact of national and international policy formulation in support of women's interests and improved participation in the policy formulation process.

Increasing the participation of women in science and technology and their relevance to the daily lives of women are not the only answers to the worldwide masculinization of wealth and decision-making, but they offer a concrete and useful next step in policy formulation and action for the alleviation of women's poverty and the promotion of sustainable livelihoods. National governments can readily undertake specific, appropriate actions to improve women's access to vital scientific and technological training and to promote forms of scientific and technological research and application that will better support women's interests and goals. In this arena, women, and men, can put their ideas and talents to work in support of more sustainable and equitable livelihoods, and women can acquire the professional experience and visibility that will allow them better access to the policy formulation process nationally and internationally.

As the past several years and the experience of women in many countries, North and South, have made very clear, however, experience and visibility alone will not open doors to national legislatures and to international forums such as the United Nations and the IMF. The struggle to improve women's lives and alleviate their economic and environmental impoverishment can only be undertaken collectively, through collaborative concern and action on the part of women locally, regionally, and internationally. The FWCW in Beijing offered another step along that long, important road to a sustainable future for women everywhere. In spite of all efforts to the contrary, the term 'gender' was included in the Beijing platform, and so was a renewed commitment to women's empowerment and their full participation in all spheres of society on an equal footing with men. Furthermore, 'women and poverty' was identified as a 'critical area of concern' for the future.

Acknowledgment

The research on which this chapter is based was funded by research grant 410-93-1184 from the Social Sciences and Humanities Research Council.

References

Action for Development (ACFODE). 1992. Editorial. *Arise* 6 (7):2

Agarwahl, A. 1993. The Poor Pay the Price of Hypocrisy. *Ecodecision* 10:92

Ahooja-Patel, K. 1992. *Linking Women with Sustainable Development.* Vancouver: Commonwealth of Learning

Asian and Pacific Development Centre (APDC). 1992. *Asian and Pacific Women's Resource and Action Series: Environment.* Kuala Lumpur: APDC

Brown, L. 1991. Feeding Six Billion. In *The World-Watch Reader on Global Environmental Issues,* edited by. L. Brown, 147-64. New York: W.W. Norton

Carroll-Foster, T. 1993. *A Guide to* Agenda 21: *Issues, Debates and Canadian Initiatives.* Ottawa: International Development Research Centre

Chambers, R. 1988. Sustainable Rural Livelihoods: A Key Strategy for People, Environment and Nature. In *The Greening of Aid: Sustainable Livelihoods in Practice,* edited by C. Conroy and M. Litvinoff, 1-17. London: Earthscan

Clorfene-Casten, L. 1993. The Environmental Link to Breast Cancer. *Ms* 3 (6): 52-7

Cole, C. 1990. Triple Jeopardy: Race, Poverty, and Toxic Waste. *Response* 22 (4).

Daly, G., and B. Muirhead. 1993. Report on Poverty and Social Policy in Industrial Countries. Urban Poverty and Survival Strategies in Kenya Project. Faculty of Environmental Studies, York University, Toronto

Dankelman, I., and J. Davidson. 1988. *Women and Environment in the Third World: Alliance for the Future.* London: Earthscan

Jacobson, J. 1992. *Gender Bias: Roadblock to Sustainable Development.* Worldwatch paper no. 110. Washington, DC: Worldwatch Institute

–. 1993. Women's Health: The Price of Poverty. In *The Health of Women: a Global Perspective,* edited by M. Koblinsky, J. Timyan, and J. Gay, 3-31. Boulder, CO: Westview Press

Kettel, B. 1993. New Approaches to Sustainable Development. *Canadian Woman Studies* 13 (3):11-14

–. 1994. Women and the Environment: New Issues for Science and Technology. In *Human Society and the Natural World: Perspectives on Sustainable Futures,* edited by D.V.J. Bell, R. Keil, and G. Wekerle, 27-38. Toronto: Faculty of Environmental Studies, York University

–. 1995a. Key Pathways for Science and Technology for Sustainable and Equitable Development. In *Missing Links: Gender Equity in Science and Technology for Development,* edited by Gender Working Group, United Nations Commission on Science and Technology for Development, 27-53. Ottawa: International Development Research Centre

–. 1995b. Gender and Environments: Lessons from WEDNET. In *EnGENDERing Wealth and Well Being*, edited by R. Blumberg, C. Rakowski, M. Monteon, and I. Tinker, 239-59. Boulder, CO: Westview Press

–. 1995c. Women, Health and the Environment. *Social Science and Medicine*. In press

Kneipp, E.B. 1994. Ecofeminism: Theory, Practice, Praxis. MES major paper, Faculty of Environmental Studies, York University, Toronto

McIntosh, S. 1993. On the Homefront: In Defence of the Health of Our Families. *Canadian Woman Studies* 13 (3):89-93

Marsden, L. 1992. *Timing and Presence: Getting Women's Issues on the Trade Agenda*. Gender, Science and Development working paper series, 3. Toronto: International Federation of Institutes for Advanced Study

Moser, C. 1993. *Gender Planning and Development: Theory, Practice and Training*. London: Routledge

Newman, P. 1992. Killing Legally with Toxic Waste: Women and the Environment in the United States. *Development Dialogue* 1 (2):50-70

Payne, S. 1991. *Women, Health and Poverty: An Introduction*. New York: Harvester Wheatsheaf

Steady, F. 1993. Women and Children: Managers, Protectors and Victims of the Environment. In *Women and Children First: Environment, Poverty and Sustainable Development*, edited by F. Steady, 17-42. Rochester, VT: Schenkman Books

United Nations (UN). 1991. *The World's Women: Trends and Statistics 1970-1990*. New York: UNIFEM

United Nations Development Programme (UNDP). 1991. *Human Development Report 1991*. New York: UNDP

van den Oever, P. 1993. Women's Roles, Population Issues, Poverty and Environmental Degradation. In *Women and Children First: Environment, Poverty and Sustainable Development*, edited by F. Steady, 111-27. Rochester, VT: Schenkman Books

Waak, P. 1992. Population: Audubon's Policy. *Population Program Quarterly Bulletin* 4 (3):1-2

Women's Environment and Development Organization (WEDO). 1992. *Official Report: World Women's Congress for a Healthy Planet*. New York: WEDO

–. 1994a. September 7th Forum in Cairo Spotlights the Global Campaign on Environmental Links to Cancer. *News and Views* 7 (2):1, 9. New York: WEDO

–. 1994b. In Cairo, Nations Agree to Invest in Women as Alternative to Demographic Control. *News and Views* 7 (3):4. New York: WEDO

–. 1995. Women Win Praise at the Social Summit, and, Women Fight for a Role in Sustainable Development. *News and Views* 8 (1-2):1, 3, 7. New York: WEDO

World Commission on Environment and Development (WCED). 1987. *Our Common Future – Report of the World Commission on Environment and Development*. Oxford: Oxford University Press

8
Promises, Promises: Canadian Campaign Rhetoric, *Agenda 21,* and the Status of Women
Marilyn MacDonald

As an ecologist and social activist, I am most interested in systems theory sorts of questions. The components of any system may reach a point at which their interactions seem to demonstrate some form of constancy: of durability, persistence, resilience, or a number of other terms that have been used to try to capture the essence of how systems appear to be in equilibrium for an environmentally utilitarian end such as productivity or diversity. The kinds of questions that surround the concept of *stability* certainly need to be answered if we are ever to understand *sustainability.*

If stability is somehow related to an ability to bounce back from human-generated disturbances, is the community of opportunistic plants on recently bared soil more stable than a nearby forest community? Clearcutting would maintain the former and destroy the latter, so it would seem that the opportunists are a stable community as long as they are disturbed frequently. If stability is affected by the diversity of species able to live off each others' products or to stand in for each other in an ecological pinch, how stable are the forests and grasslands of Canada, which have only been here for 12,000 years or so? If stability is determined by a system's responsiveness to information about trouble spots, is the Canadian political community stagnant or stable when it resists changes required to achieve sustainability? Is stability always a desired ecosystem characteristic?

In the context of humanity's place in the biosphere, the answer to that last question is that it depends. Any system that remains stable in the sense of being closed to new information and evolutionary change is unlikely to persist. Based on the evidence of pollution, global warming, loss of biodiversity, and so on, we are badly in need of change, a move from a system based on technological fixes, progress at any cost, conspicuous consumption, and short-term bottom lines to a system based on holism, global interdependence, and long-term sustainability. Yet it appears that our political system is too stable, too closed to new possibilities, too inert to facilitate that change.

How could I illustrate this *inert stability*? First, I needed a factor that the political community had agreed was necessary for sustainability. If change was not occurring, then ignorance of the importance of the factor was not the cause. Second, I looked for a factor for which there was a relatively long history of policy development. If change was not occurring, then creating more of the same sort of policies was not the answer. Finally, I picked a factor for which there was a measurable track record. If change was not occurring, then the system interactions that produced such remarkable stability might be identified. If we wanted change, we could then make the requisite suggestions for action. The factor I picked was the inclusion of women in environmental decision-making.

Let me summarize the argument presented in this chapter. Although the majority of countries, including Canada, have agreed formally that a necessary condition for sustainability is the equal participation by women and men in its achievement, and although there is an abundance of policies to improve the status of women relative to that of men and promote equality of participation, the policies, by and large, have been ineffective against the inertia of the political status quo. They have neither sufficiently improved conditions for women nor allowed women's experience and skills in sustainability to be fully credited and used. We therefore need both concrete indicators for the improvement of the status of women and for women's active participation in the achievement of sustainability and concrete consequences for those decisionmakers who ignore, trivialize, or trade off the policies that would create that improvement.

What 'Everyone Agrees' Is Needed: Women's Equality and Sustainable Development

> Most women in the world, like most men, lead humble lives. Their daily preoccupations are with economic survival and success ... What is striking, however, is how different women's ordinary lives are from men's ordinary lives ... We do not presume a global community of women ... [but] everywhere women are worse off than men: women have less power, less autonomy, more work, less money and more responsibility (Seager and Olson 1986, 7).

In June of 1992, at the United Nations Conference on Environment and Development (UNCED), 153 member states endorsed *Agenda 21,* a non-binding plan of action for international cooperation toward a sustained and equitable development of the planet. The key threads of this agreement – revitalized and sustainable growth, efficient resource use, global and regional resource sharing, and life cycle management of chemicals and waste products – were interwoven with policies aimed at strengthening people's participation in, and responsibility for, such development.

In keeping with other UN initiatives, the empowerment of women was heralded as central to the attainment of the goals of *Agenda 21.* It was not a matter of debate that women do most of the work that maintains us and that they receive far fewer of the material benefits (UNDP 1994). In the context of a deteriorating global economy, the themes of the UN conferences on the status of women – equality, peace, development, employment, education, and health (Kerr 1993) – were agreed to be of paramount importance to the achievement of sustainability. The devaluation of women's productive and reproductive roles, the low priority for getting women into environmental decision-making, the pervasiveness of feminized poverty, the neglect of the special health needs of women, and the destructiveness of military spending and activities were condemned. It was clearly realized that women, as half of the human population, represent both a source of skills and knowledge on how to achieve sustainability and a pool of needs that, if unrecognized or not met, will overwhelm all plans that leave them out.

An Abundance of Policies

The *Agenda 21* document is a tribute to the determination, goodwill and wisdom of the many men and women who have played a part in determining the prospects of future generations. It is also a tribute to the solidarity of a global women's caucus which has played a strong role in helping to define a document which promises a world of better opportunities for women. The year 1995 marks the 50th anniversary of the United Nations and the [Fourth] World Conference on Women, and will therefore be a milestone in measuring our commitment to human development and to the goals of *Agenda 21* (UNIFEM 1993, 2).

The policies suggested to strengthen the position of women are found throughout *Agenda 21.* In essence, they are based on the not too revolutionary idea that we can achieve sustainability if, and only if, *all* members of humanity are safe, healthy, educated, and taking a meaningful part in what happens to them and to their surroundings.

Chapter 24 was devoted to objectives and activities for strengthening women's roles as planners and decisionmakers, and most of the other chapters contained specific recommendations related to women (UNIFEM 1993). In addition, specific reference in Chapter 24 to the Nairobi *Forward-Looking Strategies for the Advancement of Women,* the *Convention on the Elimination of All Forms of Discrimination against Women,* the International Labour Organization and UN Educational, Scientific, and Cultural Organization conventions on ending gender-based discrimination, and the *World Declaration/Plan for Action on the Survival, Protection and Development of Children* incorporated nearly a half century of global policy recommendations to improve the status of women into the sustainable development action plan (Rogers 1993). Listed below is an abbreviated statement of the principles contained in Chapter 24, adapted from UNIFEM (1993). The objectives can be summarized as follows:

(1) Implement the Nairobi *Forward-Looking Strategies for the Advancement of Women,* particularly with regard to women's participation in national ecosystem management and control of environmental degradation.

(2) Increase the proportion of women decisionmakers, planners, technical advisers, managers, and extension workers in environment and development fields.

(3) Develop and issue, by the year 2000, a strategy of changes to eliminate constitutional, legal, administrative, cultural, behavioural, social, and economic obstacles to women's full participation in sustainable development and in public life.

(4) Establish, by 1995, mechanisms at the national, regional, and international levels to assess the implementation and impact of development and environment policies and programs on women and to ensure their contributions and benefits.

(5) Assess, revise, and implement curricula and other educational material. Ensure access for both men and women to gender-relevant knowledge and valuation of women's roles through formal and non-formal education, training institutions, and NGOs.

(6) Make and implement clear government policies and national guidelines and plans to achieve equality in all aspects of society, including literacy, education, training, nutrition, health, and participation

in key decision-making positions and management of the environment, especially to improve women's access to resources, credit,
property rights, and food production.

(7) Ensure that women and men have access to information, education,
and means, in accordance with country-specific conditions, and the
same right to decide about family planning.

(8) Consider the adoption, strengthening, and enforcement of laws and
any necessary administrative, social, and educational measures to
end violence against women.

The activities listed in the chapter include the following:

(1) Review policies and make plans to increase the proportion of women
decisionmakers, planners, managers, scientists, and technical advisers in all stages of sustainable development programs.

(2) Strengthen women's bureaux, women's NGOs, and women's groups
to increase their capacity to contribute to sustainable development.

(3) For girls and women, eliminate illiteracy, promote universal access to
primary and secondary education, and increase education and training in sciences and technology, especially at the postsecondary level.

(4) Reduce the domestic workload of girls and women by providing
more and affordable nurseries and kindergartens, by sharing household tasks between men and women equally, and by providing environmentally sound technologies for water, fuel, and sanitation,
developed in consultation with women.

(5) Establish preventive and curative health facilities, which have
women-centred and -managed reproductive care, support women's
productive and reproductive roles, and reduce maternal and child
illness.

(6) Increase equal opportunity and pay equity, including childcare,
parental leave, and access to credit and resources.

(7) Improve agricultural credit and resource ownership for women.

(8) Increase consumer awareness and activism to switch to sustainable
consumption and production.

(9) Stop negative attitudes to and images and stereotypes of women in
media, advertising, and formal and informal education.

(10) Measure the progress in all of the above and report at the 1995
Fourth World Conference on the Status of Women in Beijing.

The following areas are also covered:

(1) Ratify and enforce relevant conventions. Strengthen the *Convention
on the Elimination of All Forms of Discrimination against Women* and
ask its signatories to strengthen those items related to environment

and development – access and entitlement to natural resources, technology, creative banking, low-cost housing, control of pollution and toxicity in the home and workplace – and to alter the country report format to include progress toward sustainable development.

(2) Develop gender-sensitive information systems and databases and participatory research and policy analyses on:
- women's knowledge of the management and conservation of natural resources
- the impact of structural adjustment programs on women, especially cutbacks in social services, education, health, and subsidies to food and fuel
- the impact of war and environmental degradation on women
- structural links between gender, environment, and development
- the integration of the value of unpaid work, including domestic, into National Accounts
- measures to include social, environmental, and gender impact analyses as an essential step in developing and monitoring all programs and policies
- environmentally sound technology transfers to women.

What sort of ideas are central to Chapter 24? Discrimination against women is defined in Chapter 24 as any impairment of women's rights and freedoms by law or by custom, and affirmative action is specifically identified as non-discriminatory (i.e., not reverse discrimination against men) and necessary. Equality for women includes the right to: vote; hold public office; obtain education, health care (including family planning), and employment equity; have fully recognized and recompensed credit for productive and reproductive labour; and take part in decision-making. There are a number of specific recommendations on this last point, to increase the proportion of women decisionmakers in the context of industry, science and technology, and national and international politics. Central to all the recommendations of Chapter 24 is the need to end violence against women, from the inherent violence of pornographic stereotypes to the indifferent violence of war.

That women were included so prominently in *Agenda 21* was due in large part to a preceding series of local, national, regional, and international meetings of women's groups, such as the Global Assembly of Women and Environment: Partners in Life and the World Women's Congress for a Healthy Planet (WEDO 1992). Women from around the world were able to reach consensus on what successful sustainable development would be and to put that consensus forward to the politicians at Rio. This process reflected three lessons that women had learned during the half century of global debates on their status (Fraser 1987). First, women must speak about, be heard on, and have direct control of issues that affect them. Men's and women's lives are different, and women cannot rely on men to understand or give priority to women's realities. Second, women must recognize the multiple sources of their marginalization and the necessity for real change to take into account race, language, ethnicity, (dis)ability, socio-economic class, sexual orientation, religion, and any other factors used to maintain systemic discrimination. Women from grassroots organizations to government bureaucracies have worked out effective ways to reach consensus and to support each other; these ways must be central rather than marginal to government activities. Third, women must claim and get a fair share of the world's human-produced resources. Economic prosperity often does not trickle down to women, in contrast to economic adversity, which seems to flood them. Too many economic models of restructuring were 'bad science' in that they left out significant factors such as volunteer and domestic labour and so failed to predict outcomes. Programs and policies have to be considered in context and in their entirety, with specified timetables and resource commitments against which their success or failure can be evaluated.

As Doern (1972) has argued, the chief test of the real commitment of governments toward any given program is the proportion of resources allocated toward it. While non-binding, the estimated expenses to carry out the recommendations contained within *Agenda 21* indicate several things. First, empowering women seems to be relatively cheap, whether it is done directly by carrying out the objectives and activities of Chapter 24 or indirectly by strengthening groups of which women are a part, such as youth, indigenous people, NGO members, farmers, local authorities, workers, business owners, and scientists, as recommended in Chapters 25 to 32. To carry out the intentions of Chapters 24 to 32, the signatories to *Agenda 21* were comfortable assigning about 0.1 per cent of the whole potential bill, the total being an uncommitted estimate of US$555 billion spent between 1993 and 2000.

Second, and the reason for this apparent parsimony, the various themes of *Agenda 21* are tightly interwoven, and what improves other aspects of human surroundings, such as attaining a just, prosperous, habitable, fertile, shared, and clean world, cuts down on the costs of empowerment. The references in Chapter 24 bring together two previously somewhat separated strands in the UN agenda. Environmental concerns had been voiced at the Conference on the Human Environment, the International Biological Program, Man [*sic*] and the Biosphere, the World Population Conference, the World Food Conference, the Conference on Environmental Education, the first and second Decades of Development and other initiatives (McCormick 1989) but had exhibited parallel rather than complementary concerns about women's equality. By the 1970s, the UN had identified the key factors for global cooperation and development – food, population, environment, human settlement, health and education – and had agreed that women's cooperation was important (WCED 1987).

Experience has taught us that women must be fully involved in all of the decision-making about sustainability or else we create more problems than we solve. What might such change involve? Picture the following scenario. First, imagine that the intent of *Agenda 21* was for real empowerment: that after women have used their share of the funds allotted for group strengthening (estimated US$0.04 billion) to get into decision-making positions, they then have about US$277.2 billion left over to solve the other problems in their lives (Table 8.1). Second, imagine that, in looking for sources of funding, the approximately US$800 billion decrease in military spending between 1992 and 2000 could be considered a peace (UNDP 1994) *and* sustainability dividend. Third, and stretching one's imagination even further, have the dividend paid out to the NGOs and to any community-based organization (CBO) that cared to apply at the 1995 Beijing forum. What might these groups accomplish with funding, when they have done so much for so long with so little?

Yet here we are, nearly midway to the year 2000, the point at which all of the goals of *Agenda 21* should be realized, and women do not seem to be leaping in droves onto the 'sustainable development' bandwagon. In fact, at a time when governments and industry are competing with each other for new and unusual ways in which to use the Rio buzzwords, many women are abandoning the concept as unworkable and appropriated. In a survey of participants at Women and Sustainable Development: Canadian Perspectives, a conference held at the University of British Columbia, 27 to 31 May 1994, nearly half of the respondents indicated that the definition of sustainable development – meeting the needs of the present without compromising the ability of future generations to meet their own needs (WCED 1987, 8) – was too vague, or ranged from placebo to oxymoron, leaving the status quo untouched by substantive action (Dale and Wright, in preparation). Why?

Table 8.1

Top ten and bottom ten issues in Agenda 21 based on total estimated required global expenditures, 1993-2000

	Estimated expenditures (US*$ billion)
Top ten	
Promoting sustainable human settlement development (7)	218.12
Fresh water (18)	54.66
Solid waste / sewage (21)	37.00
Sustainable development and rural development (14)	31.80
Combating deforestation (11)	31.25
Combating poverty (3)	30.00
Protecting the atmosphere (9)	21.23
Environmentally sound biotechnology (16)	20.01
Hazardous waste management (20)	18.50
Management of fragile ecosystems (mountains) (13)	13.05
Bottom ten	
Technology transfer (34)	0.53
Workers and trade unions (29)	0.30
Integration of environment and development in decision-making (8)	0.06
Integration of planning and management of land resources (10)	0.05
Women (24)	0.04
Science and technology community (31)	0.02
Radioisotope control (22)	0.01
Youth and children (25)	0.00
Indigenous people (26)	0.00
Local authorities (28)	0.00

Note: NGO partners (Chapter 27), business and industry (Chapter 30), and farmers (Chapter 32) have no estimate provided and are therefore not included in the table. Numerals in parentheses following chapter titles are applicable chapter numbers.
Source: Adapted from UNDPI (1993)

All Talk, No Walk: Campaign Rhetoric, Environmental Industries, and the Status of Women

Politicians are quickly becoming expert eco-bluffers ... The key to eco-political success is to avoid specifics, because you would then be called upon to make simple decisions on highly complex issues. Stick with high principle rather than practical actions (which would almost inevitably cost some of your voters money or effort). Keep talking about future generations, even though they will never vote for you ... Imply that the problems, while serious, can be fixed relatively painlessly if only we can apply more technology and efficiency to our production processes ... Try to walk the fine line between making people sufficiently alarmed to agree to action being taken and scaring them into electing somebody more reassuring ... Meet with the whole spectrum of greens, seeking advice and consensus. You don't need to worry about consensus actually being reached because most greens can't agree among themselves anyway (Wachtel and McNeely 1991, 24-6).

Running throughout the world conferences has been a growing critique of the lack of political will, from the national to the global level, to implement conference recommendations. This lack of will is central to political stability, to the resistance of political systems to change in the status quo. Let us look at Canada as an example.

According to the *Human Development Report* (see Table 8.2), Canada is the best country in which to live, unless you are a woman, in which case it ranks ninth (UNDP 1994). Gender disparity was measured by the societal gap between women's and men's well-being in terms of life expectancy, educational attainment, and real income. It is tied in with class effects as well. If one compares the best and worst off within a country, then Canada is eighth in the world in attempting to minimize that class-based gap.

Has the Canadian federal government, as one of the signatories to *Agenda 21,* made any progress in its implementation? Have the Conservatives or the Liberals undertaken new initiatives and altered old ones in order to empower women? Has the fully employed labour force participation rate for women increased? Has the gap between women's and men's earnings – for *all* women and men in Canada – narrowed? Are more women getting scientific and technical training? Are more women becoming chief executive officers or members of cabinet? Has government spending centred on military development or on environmental research, education, and preventive health care? If there were a post-Rio report card, the federal government would get a failing grade. Starting from a position of better potential than many other countries, the political response to the empowerment of women has been far from innovative. Between June 1992 and the present, the status of women in

Table 8.2

Comparison of world rankings for human development indices (HDI) of selected countries

	HDI_D	HDI_C	HDI_G
Sweden	4	2	1
Denmark	15	13	4
Finland	16	10	3
United States	6	11	12
Canada	1	8	9
Germany	11	4	13
Japan	3	1	19
Israel	19	16	–

Note: HDI_D = direct, HDI_C = income adjusted, HDI_G = gender adjusted
Source: Adapted from UNDP (1994)

Canada deteriorated due to the disproportionate burden on women of restructuring our national economy. Unemployment and underemployment, presently at about 21 per cent for both men and women; violence in both the private and public spheres; and increased demands for replacement of social programs with volunteer or unpaid work, all supported by stereotypes of the proper roles for men and women, combined to prevent the realization of Chapter 24 of *Agenda 21* (CACSW 1993, 1994; Khosla 1993; Status of Women Canada 1994).

In Canada, women are concentrated within the labour market horizontally, with 71 per cent of women workers in the five occupational groups of teachers, nurses, clerical, service, and sales, and vertically, in the lowest-paying, least secure, and least powerful positions (Armstrong and Armstrong 1984; Edmonds, Côté-O'Hara, and MacKenzie 1990; Moore 1985; Wannell 1989). There is no occupational category in which women earn more on average than men, even for full-time, full-year employment (Statistics Canada 1993). In 1993, women in full-time and all other registered work earned about 63 per cent of what men did. Women outnumbered men in the poorest segment of society (37 per cent to 24 per cent), while the opposite held true for the richest (4 per cent to 16 per cent). Women get a lower rate of financial return for education, volunteering, and domestic work; and contribute more to, and receive less benefit from, the health system (Ross 1990; Khosla 1993). All of these statistics indicate that the 'pressing need to continue to centralize women's issues and to ensure the incorporation of their collective perspectives, experiences and contributions to sustainable development' (UNIFEM 1993, 3) is not being met. What reasons might be behind the political stability of the inequitable treatment of women?

Provided below as possible answers to that question are some examples from the campaign rhetoric of the Progressive Conservatives, the party in power in Canada during the Rio Conference and up until the federal election of October 1993, and the Liberals, the party that replaced them in November 1993. Since the Conservatives promised to do more of what they'd done while in power, the most difficult exercise has been in selecting from a wide range of material. For the Liberals, still in the early days of their term at the time of writing, the examples come mostly from *Creating Opportunity: The Liberal Plan for Canada* (Liberal Party 1993). Most of this discussion is focused on the environmental industries.

The environmental industries (EIs) provide a good focus for further investigation for several reasons. First, they represent the sort of businesses that promote *Agenda 21*, the ones that make sure that environmental considerations are central to economic decisions. Second, they reflect a degree of political stability, having been supported by the Progressive Conservatives up until their election defeat and the Liberals so far (with the approval of Industry Canada/Environment Canada's 1994 *Strategy for the Canadian Environmental Industry*). Third, there is a great deal of information about the composition of EIs in terms of businesses and workforce and of government measures that will affect the growth of both.

What are the environmental industries? The Canadian federal government's definition, at its most extensive, includes:

- *goods manufacturers* of water, air, and soil pollution management equipment and monitoring or related research and development equipment
- *service providers* for such things as operations, consultation, environmental impact assessment, research and development, and natural resource conservation and preservation (Employment and Immigration Canada 1992; Industry, Science and Technology Canada 1991).

The intent for the EIs in *Agenda 21* is somewhat wider, however. In looking through the forty chapters of this agreement, one can see that such industries also involve technology transfer (including new legal, social, and political mechanisms to do so), environmental education (for all sectors of society as a lifelong process), health and family

planning, and demilitarization (Rogers 1993). Does the difference between the federal government's and the *Agenda 21* definitions make a
difference for women? The answer is yes. Using the federal definition,
most employees, almost 90 per cent, in the EIs were male (EIC 1992).
Using the *Agenda 21* definition, more women workers and more
women's work would be included.

The federal definition affected the data gathered about EI workers.
The types of jobs counted in a survey of EI companies were in male-
dominated occupations such as engineer, scientist, business administra-
tor, technician, technologist, and equipment operator (Statistics
Canada 1990), where men constituted 70 per cent or more of the workers (Edmonds, Côté-O'Hara, and MacKenzie 1990). Women who worked
in female-dominated occupations, such as clerical, for those same companies were left out. The women who are visible as 10 per cent of the
Canadian EI workforce are those in the male-dominated occupations
(Table 8.3).

The federal definition of the EIs also left out those industries that are
not male-dominated but are an integral part of developing a sustainable
relationship between humans and their environment according to
Agenda 21. Health, education, social sciences, and fine and performing
arts fit into this category. With the wider definition, the composition of
the EI workforce would be more balanced between women and men
and less technocentric in orientation.

As well, the federal definition of the EIs does not give credit to those
volunteers and activists whose time and monetary contributions promote the demand for EI goods and services (Ross 1990). The current demand for recycling was started, and is maintained, for example, by
people who went against the tide of conspicuous consumption. It is impossible to estimate the potential workforce for the environmental industry when skills acquired by volunteers and activists remain invisible.
The call in *Agenda 21* for the inclusion of unpaid labour in national accounting is based on the knowledge that strategies which ignore it are
poorly designed.

Support for the development of the EIs has involved a number of programs that have created significant opportunities, the availability of
which has been affected by the gender-bias inherent in the federal definition. These programs include the commercialization of technology
(Industry Canada, formerly Industry, Science and Technology Canada
[ISTC], working with Environment Canada), the development of the
requisite workforce (Employment and Immigration Canada or Human

Table 8.3

Occupational groups as sources for workers for environmental industries

	Women as % of occupation	Wage gap
Using the federal definition		
Management / administration	36	64
Natural science / engineering	16	70
Product fabrication	23	58
Process / machining	16	63
Materials handling	21	–
Crafts / operations	24	–
Transport	8	–
Construction	2	–
Agriculture	26	77
Other primary industries	<1	–
Additional categories *using the* Agenda 21 *definition*		
Clerical	80	69
Services	57	53
Sales	46	63
Medicine / health	79	54
Teaching	62	78
Social sciences	58	62
Artistic / recreational	44	82

Note: 1988 employment figures. Women as % of occupation = women in that occupation as a per cent of the total number of people in that occupation; wage gap = women's earnings as a per cent of men's, restricted to average annual wage for full-year, full-time workers.
Source: Adapted from Statistics Canada (1990)

Resource Development in cooperation with industry through the Canadian Council on Human Resources for the Environmental Industries), technology inflow and globalization (External Affairs and International Trade Canada), the assessment of magnitude in such things as National Accounts, employment, and entrepreneurial activity (Statistics Canada), and environmental product standards (Canadian Standards Association of Canada and Environment Canada). By 1989, the promotional effort of ISTC alone had become a $4 million Environmental Industries Sector Initiative, run by the Environmental Industries and Projects Division. Such full-scale government help was considered necessary for the environmental industries with their 'relatively undetermined financial, technical, and research strengths and capabilities, and [lack of] information on both domestic or export markets, particularly for technologies' (Brown 1992, 173). In 1993, the National Round Table on the Environment and the Economy recommended further support for the environmental industries in the form of funding for basic research and commercialization, training of managers and scientific and technical personnel, enactment of supportive pollution control and pollution prevention legislation, and a tighter focus of federal support (Fouillard 1993).

Women's inclusion in the federal strategy for the environmental industries has been negligible. It remains to be seen if the Liberal cabinet will change that status following its acceptance of the EI strategy document recently submitted by Industry Canada and Environment Canada (1994). The Liberal government's campaign promise to review the Federal Contractors Program (FCP), the Employment Equity Act (EEA), and the recommendations of the House of Commons special committee on those two items suggests that no government initiative will continue to be unrepresentative (Liberal Party 1993). The intention is to extend the FCP to include contractors with more than fifteen employees and with contracts of $100,000 or more with the federal government and to extend the EEA in full to federally regulated employers with more than seventy-five employees and in simplified form to ones with between fifteen and seventy-five employees.

Based on the federal definition, the legislation that develops a market for EIs leaves women's work out of consideration. Monitoring the effectiveness of the Workplace Hazardous Materials Information System (WHMIS) and the Hazardous Substances List could be legislated, for example, to require that a team of healthcare professionals working at a women-centred and -managed preventive healthcare facility be consulted and regularly monitor contaminant levels. For that matter, the extension of WHMIS to the domestic workplace could result in a whole new generation of well-labelled household chemicals with clear directions for their safe use and disposal.

Women who enter the EIs in male-dominated occupations face all the usual barriers that have been documented elsewhere (Ainley 1989; Cohen 1987; Cohen 1988; Davidson and Cooper 1992; Edmonds, Côté-

O'Hara, and MacKenzie 1990; Frizé 1992; Harlan and Steinberg 1989; Harriman 1985; McIlwee and Robinson 1992; Robertson 1990; Sokoloff 1992; Thompson 1993; White 1993; Witz 1992; Zuckerman and Cole 1990). Both the Conservatives and the Liberals have done little or nothing to lower those barriers.

The Conservatives, with a majority government, continued a program begun in 1984, which concentrated on deficit reduction at all costs. Fighting inflation with high interest rates, increasing exports, decreasing public social programs, and increasing productivity and efficiency have all been parts of restructuring in other countries as well as Canada; and here, as elsewhere, have resulted in distributive injustice. The people who bear the brunt of the costs of restructuring – the poor, the unpaid, the marginalized – are not the ones who get the benefits (Elson 1990).

This distributive injustice resulted from both the revenue generation and the expenditure control activities of the federal government. Unless otherwise indicated, the following information is taken from the Canadian Tax Foundation (1993), Khosla (1993), and the federal Department of Finance under Finance Minister Don Mazankowski (Canada 1993). Personal income tax and consumption taxes provide about three-quarters of the federal government revenues (Table 8.4) and over half of provincial revenues. Corporate taxes in Canada are among the lowest in the Organisation for Economic Cooperation and Development. Under such a system, the poor and the middle class bear most of the tax burden. Since 1984, taxes for people in the lowest income brackets have increased by 115 per cent, while those in the upper bracket have increased by 20 per cent. Given that more females than males are in the lowest income bracket, particularly single parents, children, and the elderly, and that about two-thirds of dual-earner families stay above the poverty line *because* both adults work in the labour force, this pattern of taxation weakens women's position (Khosla 1993).

The existing tax credit system does not support the objectives of *Agenda 21* either. Donations to political parties are fully deductible, for example, while donations to NGOs or grassroots organizations are often not deductible at all. Research and development credits can be applied toward manufacturing and industry but not toward community-based research into sustainable local economies. Neither men nor women get a meaningful message from the federal government that a new sharing, equitable, and consensual society is being created.

Expenditure control may either counteract or exacerbate the effects of revenue generation, or do both. There are several things to bear in

Table 8.4

Estimated federal government budgetary revenue from 1991-2 to 1993-4 (Cdn$ billion)

	1991-2	1992-3	1993-4
Personal income tax	61.5	63.1	64.5
Goods and services tax	16.4	18.6	20.1
UIC contributions	16.0	19.1	20.7
Sales and excise duties	10.5	11.8	11.9
Corporate income tax	8.4	9.5	11.7
Other	11.3	10.1	9.8
Total revenues	124.1	132.1	138.8

Source: Adapted from Canadian Tax Foundation (1993)

mind. First, across-the-board cuts at a set percentage have a greater impact on community groups on a shoestring budget than on groups with a surplus. Second, someone disadvantaged by one cutback may be further hurt by loss or transfer of other social services. A never-employed woman seeking shelter from a batterer, for example, may find that the local safe house has had to close or is filled to capacity and that the training that she might – barely possibly – have received under the federally funded Canada Job Strategy is not at all available to her under the current unemployment insurance-funded programs. Third, very little research has been done on these kinds of interactive double or triple jeopardies; very little exists to counteract the tendency of federal departments to plan and implement policies in isolation from one another. Fourth, and finally, the expenditures in each category are interdependent; decisions on cost assignment can give a false picture of what is really going on. Money spent on cooperative housing, for example, a program discontinued by the Conservatives, might be considered a defence expenditure if in the long run people experienced in living together have less need to resort to war.

The barriers to women's empowerment as decisionmakers can be set up at different levels. At the federal budget level, social welfare services spending (about 40 per cent of expenditures) is often presented as worsening such things as servicing the debt (about 25 per cent of expenditures) (Canadian Tax Foundation 1993). Yet that social spending includes the very items that are repeatedly agreed upon as necessary to women's equality: education and training, health protection, income security. Most of the expenditure controls undertaken by the Conservative government had a more negative effect on women than on men (CACSW 1994; Khosla 1993).

Reviews that would affect social service spending, such as Porter's critique of funding for the healthcare system (1991), and Halliwell and Bellini's concentration on prosperity through innovation (1991), suggest the return of many government services to private responsibility. Given that women are considered the primary healthcare guardians, the early childhood educators, the gender with the abnormal life cycle pattern, and the source of apparently infinite domestic labour to absorb structural adjustment, more attention needs to be paid to the effects that such changes will have on women.

The Liberal infrastructure effort is yet another example of a government initiative related to the EIs that gives men an advantage over women. This is a two-year program, to be wrapped up by March of 1997, aimed at supporting sewage, water, and road development projects at a cost to be shared with the provinces. Over 3,000 projects have been selected, for an estimated expenditure of over $3 billion. The projects are assigned priority on the basis of their contribution to health, safety, environment, economic stimulation, and, all things being equal, innovation, either as non-traditional infrastructure or in approach. Many of the projects fit with what the environmental industries should be doing, by the federal definition. Referring to Table 8.3 and bearing in mind the types of jobs likely to be involved in those projects, women's direct employment is unlikely to exceed 10 per cent. Plus ça change, plus c'est la même chose. Perhaps this is where the Liberal idea of an office of environmental auditor would be useful, to report to Parliament on the coordination and impact of government programs, particularly in light of other Liberal campaign promises concerning the Federal Contractors Program and the Employment Equity Act (Liberal Party 1993).

Overcoming Political Inert Stability
Women have outnumbered men in Canada since the mid-1970s but the economic, social, and political advantages of that numerical superiority have been slow to materialize (Statistics Canada 1990, 1991). The gap between the Canada of the haves and of the have-nots is increasing, and all too often women are in the latter group. There is less need now for committee reports and reviews and more for political will to improve the status of women. The policies and programs that were tried by the Conservatives are ample evidence of what doesn't work well. It

remains to be seen if the Liberals, operating in a polarized Parliament and within the context of free trade and globalization, can do better.

As argued throughout this chapter, the delay in equity for women is not due to ignorance on the part of politicians about the importance of the connection between women's empowerment and the achievement of sustainability; nor is it due to an absence of policy recommendations by which politicians might be guided to take action. Rather it seems to be rooted in a lack of political will to change, in an inertia within the political community that resists the ever-increasing evidence that 'unless we do something radical today, we will be unable to do anything tomorrow' (J. Cousteau quoted in Rogers 1993, 19).

Studies of cooperative situations have found that three of the most important factors favouring cooperation are communication, duration, and retaliation. My only additions to the already policy-rich area of strengthening women's status in order to achieve sustainability are these:

- Establish better communication between grassroots women's organizations and the political community. A political system with poor information flow among its departments and with its constituency may be stable in the short run but not the long run.
- Work toward a decentralized political system, in which decisionmakers have to live with the direct consequences of their decisions and the environment that they 'develop' is the environment in which they live.
- Develop a more equitable political system, in which the gap between the poorest and highest paid worker is no greater than 100 per cent (to pick a figure that rewards achievement but not greed), and in which the fulfilment of campaign promises is monitored and compensated.
- If you, as a decisionmaker about the health of your family and the value that you add to the world by your daily work, believe that your contribution to sustainability – through taxes, appropriation of volunteer, unpaid, or underpaid work, and so on – is being invested poorly, then find some way to reinvest it.

References
Ainley, M. 1989. *Despite the Odds: Canadian Women and Science*. Montreal: Vehicule Press

Armstrong, P., and H. Armstrong. 1984. *Double Ghetto: Canadian Women and Their Segregated Work*. Toronto: McClelland and Stewart

Brown, P. 1992. Target or Participant? The Hatching of Environmental Industry Policy. In *Canadian Environmental Policy: Ecosystems, Politics and Process,* edited by R. Boardman. Don Mills, ON: Oxford University Press

Canada, Department of Finance. 1993. *The Budget, 1993.* Ottawa: Department of Finance

Canadian Advisory Council on the Status of Women (CACSW). 1993. *Work in Progress: Tracking Women's Equality in Canada.* Ottawa: CACSW

–. 1994. *Building the 'Platform for Action': CACSW Proposals.* Ottawa: CACSW

Canadian Tax Foundation. 1993. *The National Finances 1992.* Toronto: Canadian Tax Foundation

Cohen, G. 1988. *Enterprising Canadians: The Self-Employed in Canada: Labour and Household Survey Analysis.* Ottawa: Statistics Canada

Cohen, M. 1987. *Free Trade and the Future of Women's Work: Manufacturing and Service Industries.* Toronto: Canadian Centre for Policy Alternatives and Garamond Press

Dale, A., and P. Wright. In preparation. Women, Environment and Sustainability: Perspectives of Activists. In *As Canadian as Possible under the Circumstances: Women and the Environment in Canada,* edited by M. MacDonald, R. Raglan, and M. Hessing

Davidson, M., and C. Cooper. 1992. *Shattering the Glass Ceiling: The Woman Manager.* London: Paul Chapman

Doern, B. 1972. *Science and Politics in Canada.* Montreal: McGill-Queen's University Press

Edmonds, J., J. Côté-O'Hara, and E. MacKenzie. 1990. *Beneath the Veneer: The Report of the Task Force on Barriers to Women in the Public Service.* Ottawa: Supply and Services Canada

Elson, D., ed. 1990. *Male Bias in the Development Process.* Manchester: Manchester University Press

Employment and Immigration Canada (EIC). 1992. *Human Resources in the Environment Industry: Summary Report.* Ottawa: Steering Committee of the Environment Industry, Employment and Immigration Canada

Fouillard, A. 1993. *Emerging Trends and Issues in Canada's Environmental Industry.* Ottawa: National Round Table on the Environment and the Economy

Fraser, A. 1987. *The U.N. Decade for Women: Documents and Dialogue.* Westview Special Studies on Women in Contemporary Society. Boulder, CO: Westview Press

Frizé, M. 1992. *More Than Just Numbers: Report of the Canadian Committee on Women in Engineering.* Fredericton, NB: University of New Brunswick

Halliwell, J., and F. Bellini. 1991. *Prosperity through Innovation.* Background report, Task Force on Challenges in Science, Technology and Related Skills. Ottawa: National Advisory Board on Science and Technology

Harlan, S., and R. Steinberg, eds. 1989. *Job Training for Women: The Promise and Limits of Public Policies.* Philadelphia: Temple University Press

Harriman, A. 1985. *Women/Men/Management.* New York: Praeger Press

Industry Canada and Environment Canada. 1994. *A Strategy for the Canadian Environmental Industry.* Ottawa: Supply and Services Canada

Industry, Science and Technology Canada. 1991. *Industry and the Environment:*

Directory of Manufacturers of Environmental Products (and) Directory of Canadian Environmental Services Firms. Ottawa: Supply and Services Canada

Kerr, J. 1993. Background Documentation for Fourth World Conference on Women in Beijing 1995. Collection provided by the Sustainable Development Research Institute, University of British Columbia, Vancouver

Khosla, P. 1993. *Review of the Situation of Women in Canada.* Ottawa: National Action Committee on the Status of Women

Liberal Party. 1993. *Creating Opportunity: The Liberal Plan for Canada.* Ottawa: Liberal Party

McCormick, J. 1989. *Reclaiming Paradise: The Global Environmental Movement.* Bloomington: Indiana University Press

McIlwee, J., and G. Robinson. 1992. *Women in Engineering: Gender, Power, and Workplace Culture.* Albany: SUNY Press

Moore, G. 1985. *Horizontal and Vertical – The Dimensions of Occupational Segregation by Gender in Canada.* Ottawa: Canadian Research Institute for the Advancement of Women

Porter, R. 1991. *The Health Care System in Canada and Its Funding: No Easy Solutions.* Standing Committee on Health and Welfare, Social Affairs, Seniors and Status of Women. Ottawa: Supply and Services Canada

Robertson, H.-J. 1990. *A Cappella: The Realities, Concerns, Expectations and Barriers Experienced by Adolescent Women in Canada.* Toronto: Canadian Teachers' Federation

Rogers, A. 1993. *The Earth Summit: A Planetary Reckoning.* Los Angeles: Global View Press

Ross, D. 1990. *The Economic Dimensions of Volunteer Work in Canada.* Ottawa: Secretary of State

Seager, J., and A. Olson. 1986. *Women in the World: An International Atlas.* London: Pan Books

Sokoloff, N. 1992. *Black Women and White Women in the Professions: Occupational Segregation by Race and Gender, 1960-1980.* New York: Routledge

Statistics Canada. 1990. *Women in Canada: A Statistical Report.* Ottawa: Supply and Services Canada

–. 1991. *125th Anniversary Year Book: 1992.* Ottawa: Ministry of Industry, Science and Technology and Statistics Canada

–. 1993. *Employment Income by Occupation: The Nation '91 Census.* Cat. no. 93-332. Ottawa: Ministry of Industry, Science and Technology

Status of Women Canada. 1994. *Canada's National Report for the UN Secretariat of the Fourth World Conference on Women.* Ottawa: Status of Women Canada

Thompson, S. 1993. *Winning with Women in Trades, Technology, Science and Engineering.* Ottawa: National Advisory Board on Science and Technology

UNIFEM. 1993. *Agenda 21: An Easy Reference to the Specific Recommendations on Women.* New York: UN Development Fund for Women

United Nations Department of Public Information (UNDPI). 1993. *Agenda 21: Programme of Action for Sustainable Development, Rio Declaration on Environment and Development; Statement of Forest Principles.* Final text of agreements negotiated by governments at the United Nations Conference on Environment and

Development (UNCED), 3-14 June, 1992. New York: UN Department of Public Information

United Nations Development Programme (UNDP). 1994. *Human Development Report.* New York: Oxford University Press

Wachtel, P., and J. McNeely. 1991. *Eco-bluff Your Way to Greenism: The Guide to Instant Environmental Credibility.* Chicago: Bonus Books

Wannell, T. 1989. *The Persistent Gap: Exploring the Earnings Differential between Recent Male and Female Post Secondary Graduates.* Business and Labour Market Analysis Group Report no. 26. Ottawa: Statistics Canada

White, J. 1993. *Sisters and Solidarity: Women and Unions in Canada.* Toronto: Thompson Educational

Witz, A. 1992. *Professions and Patriarchy.* London: Routledge

Women's Environment and Development Organization (WEDO). 1992. *Official Report: World Women's Congress for a Healthy Planet.* New York: Women's Environment and Development Organization

World Commission on Environment and Development (WCED). 1987. *Our Common Future – Report of the World Commission on Environment and Development.* Oxford: Oxford University Press

Zuckerman, H., and J. Cole. 1990. *The Outer Circle: Women and Science.* New York: Pergamon Press

9
Aboriginal Peoples: The Basis for Policy-Making toward Sustainable Development
Fikret Berkes and Helen Fast

Estimates vary but there are approximately 200 million indigenous peoples in the world, the inhabitants of vast landscapes in remote parts of every continent. According to international criteria, four characteristics distinguish indigenous peoples from others. They are descendants of groups inhabiting an area prior to the arrival of another population; they are politically not dominant; they are culturally different from the dominant population; and they identify themselves as indigenous (ICIHI 1987, 6). The Brundtland report suggested that the Western world could learn about sustainable development from indigenous peoples: 'These communities are the repositories of vast accumulations of traditional knowledge and experience that link humanity with its ancient origins' (WCED 1987, 114).

Agenda 21 of the Rio Conference extends the Brundtland argument that these peoples have unique historical ties to their lands and seeks policies and actions to implement sustainability. Chapter 26 of *Agenda 21* is about recognizing and strengthening the role of indigenous peoples and their communities on the grounds that there is a close relationship between sustainable development and the well-being of indigenous peoples. Chapter 26 sets out some general principles and objectives: empowerment of indigenous peoples and their communities through the recognition of their traditional knowledge, values, and priorities; active participation of indigenous peoples in formulation of national policies; and involvement of indigenous peoples in resource management and conservation strategies.

These are not easy objectives to meet. For most groups of indigenous peoples, participation in national policies could only be a distant objective. All too often, their struggles centre around mere survival. A number of observers have pointed out that the loss of indigenous cultures, or cultural diversity, is comparable to loss of biological diversity. As Durning (1993, 83) puts it, 'worldwide, the loss of cultural diversity is keeping pace with the global loss of biodiversity.' Both kinds of losses have to do with policies that have an unsustainable outcome. Brascoupé (1992) argues that Western models of development, with their emphasis on the efficient extraction of resources, have been particularly damaging to indigenous peoples through colonization and economic marginalization.

The report of the Independent Commission on International Humanitarian Issues (ICIHI) paints a dismal picture of the state of indigenous peoples almost everywhere. They tend to be landless or squeezed into marginal lands, to have high unemployment rates, to be poorer than their neighbours, to suffer from comparatively ill health and high mortality rates, to have low levels of education, and to be discriminated against in courts of law and in other government institutions (ICIHI 1987). Many of these generalizations hold for Canada's indigenous peoples as well. One can well add to the list high rates of suicide, substance abuse, and addiction.

Despite all these problems, however, in some countries indigenous peoples have been gaining a stronger voice and stronger legal rights. In Canada, this comes at a time when policy alternatives for northern development are being debated vigorously. The policies of the 1950s to integrate Native people into Canadian mainstream society and to open up the North have largely failed. As well, the 'mega-project' decade of the 1970s resulted in altered landscapes over vast areas of the North without bringing the expected social and economic development for the people who live there. As Canada approaches the twenty-first century, new visions are being sought for northern economic development, land use, and Native self-government. One reflection of this concern is the attention directed to the concept of sustainable development and its application. What is the prospect and potential of sustainable development for the North?

As it is coming to be interpreted in Canada, sustainable development involves more than ecological sustainability; it also includes economic and socio-cultural sustainability. Thus sustainable development planning for the North involves multiple objectives, including those pertaining to economic development, the land and resource base, and environment-culture relationships (NMEDC 1993; Chance 1993; Huskey and Morehouse 1992; Duerden 1992).

The aim of this chapter is to evaluate progress made in Canada in meeting *Agenda 21* objectives with respect to indigenous peoples of the

North. The chapter traces the evolution of northern development policies that impinge upon aboriginal peoples and provides an understanding of changes over the years as a foundation for policy-making leading
toward sustainable development. The chapter first reviews some of the
outcomes of northern development of the last few decades and offers an
overview of 'homeland' versus 'frontier' economics in the North. It then
covers the basis of policy-making, focusing on three substantive areas:
traditional ecological knowledge (TEK), indigenous land and resource
use, and subsistence economies. We consider these three interrelated
areas to be the key in meeting *Agenda 21* objectives and achieving sustainability. The local traditional economy needs to have a land resource
base, and the use of land and resources depends on local knowledge,
management systems, and institutions. The discussion then deals with
policies for sustainability and summarizes the arguments in the chapter
into seven principles. *Cultural sustainability* is a key issue when sustainable development planning involves indigenous peoples; the support of
subsistence economies is particularly important in this regard. *Traditional
ecological knowledge* of indigenous peoples has to be recognized and
used, especially in the *co-management* of land and resources. In turn, *in-
stitution-building* is important for co-management, empowering Native
groups to become partners in resource management rather than poach-
ers on their own land. *Property-rights* issues underlie aboriginal land use
and resource management institutions; the unique Native system of
communal property rights needs to be recognized in order to reverse the
processes of disempowerment. Finally, *cumulative impact assessment* is
needed for conservation planning because assessing impact project by
project has not been adequate to protect the land resource base.

For the purposes of this chapter, the words indigenous, aboriginal,
and Native will be used interchangeably although they have somewhat
different technical meanings (ICIHI 1987; Durning 1993). The term Indian will be used only when referring to Indian status under the Indian
Act. The terms TEK and indigenous knowledge (IK) will be used interchangeably, TEK being the more popular term in the literature and IK
being the preferred term for some scholars. TEK will be defined as 'a cumulative body of knowledge and beliefs, handed down through generations by cultural transmission, about the relationship of living beings
(including humans) with one another and with their environment'
(Berkes 1993, 3). TEK is an attribute of societies with historical continuity in resource use practices. Many of these societies are indigenous or
tribal and include Canada's northern Native groups.

The dictionary definition of the term subsistence, as 'what one lives on,' accurately describes the northern Native concept, even though there is no word for it in languages such as Cree. We use the term subsistence not merely as an economic concept but one that denotes important societal relationships and cultural characteristics of indigenous societies (Freeman 1993; Wenzel 1991; Usher 1987).

The term harvesting, which describes the activity of subsistence, does have Native language equivalents. In eastern James Bay Cree usage, for example, the word *nituuhun* refers collectively to all hunting, fishing, and trapping activities (Berkes 1988a). Accordingly, in this chapter, harvesting refers primarily to hunting, fishing, and trapping (e.g., James Bay and Northern Québec Native Harvesting Research Committee [JB&NQNHRC] 1982).

The phrase subsistence economy is used to indicate non-market values of goods and services from the bush. The phrase traditional economy – used interchangeably in this chapter with bush sector and land-based sector – denotes subsistence plus fur and fish production. Land use refers, in this study, to activities pertaining to harvesting wildlife and gathering other products of the land. The study of land use includes transportation routes and camp sites, as well as aspects of traditional occupation that the Native people themselves consider important, such as burial grounds and other culturally significant areas.

The Hudson Bay Bioregion
Indigenous peoples live in almost all parts of Canada. For the geographic scope of this chapter, we have chosen the arctic and subarctic parts of the Hudson Bay bioregion (Figure 9.1). The bioregion no doubt has its own unique characteristics, but in many ways it also typifies the Canadian North. Most discussions of indigenous peoples of the Canadian North focus on political subdivisions of the landscape. We focus on an ecological unit, albeit a very large one. The Hudson Bay bioregion shows evidence of ecosystem-wide contamination and large-scale effects of development projects. Thus it has been chosen as the site of a long-term project on indigenous knowledge, cumulative impact assessment, and sustainable development called the Hudson Bay Program (Sly 1994).

The Hudson Bay bioregion, the drainage basin of Hudson-James Bay, covers almost 40 per cent of Canada's land mass and is inhabited by some 4 million people, most of whom live in the agricultural area in the southwest part of the basin. The arctic and subarctic zones of the

Figure 9.1

Hudson Bay bioregion (drainage basin)

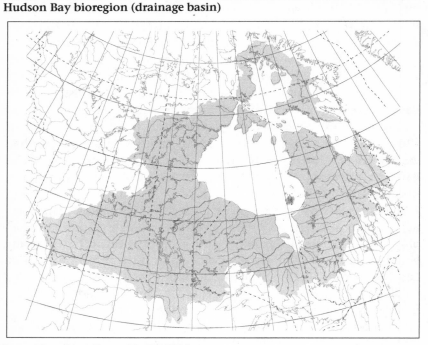

Source: Adapted from Fast and Berkes (1994)

bioregion are among the last remaining large wilderness areas in the world, but it is a wilderness extensively used by people. The population density is very low; there are only about 32,000 people around the entire Hudson-James Bay system, mostly Inuit and Cree Indian people.

The chapter will focus on the non-agricultural part of the bioregion, where indigenous peoples predominate. The northern part of the bioregion, above the treeline, is home to the Inuit. The treeline often serves as a demarcation between the arctic and the subarctic regions, but it is an indented and gradual boundary, not a sharp one. Immediately to the south of the limit of trees is a transition zone, tundra-open woodland, sometimes called the taiga. Further to the south is the boreal forest.

The Cree live in the tundra-open woodland and the boreal forest zones. The Naskapi live in tundra-open woodland in the eastern part of the bioregion in Québec, along the Labrador border. The Algonquian live in the southern edge of the bioregion in Québec. The Ojibwa (Nishnabwe) live in Ontario and Manitoba to the south of the Cree, in the boreal forest. In north central Ontario and east central Manitoba, the term Oji-Cree is applied to people living in the transition area between the Ojibwa and the Cree. In the western part of the bioregion, the Chipewyan (Dene) live in the tundra-open woodland in Manitoba and Saskatchewan, between the Cree and Inuit areas. Cree, Ojibwa, Naskapi, and Algonkin languages all belong to the Algonkian language family. Chipewyan is of the Dene (Athapascan) language family. All Inuit speak variations of what McMillan (1988) calls Eskimoan or Inuktitut language (Figure 9.2).

Extensive aboriginal occupation and use of the area, leaving few if any 'blanks' on maps, is well documented (Freeman 1976; Riewe 1992). Yet many conservationists see the arctic and subarctic zones of the area as a vast, untouched wilderness to be preserved (Rosenthal and Beyea 1989). Many politicians and developers, on the other hand, see it as a treasure chest of riches to be exploited (e.g., Bourassa 1985). The area is by no means an untouched wilderness but nor is it economically

Figure 9.2

Seventeenth-century aboriginal language families of the Hudson Bay bioregion

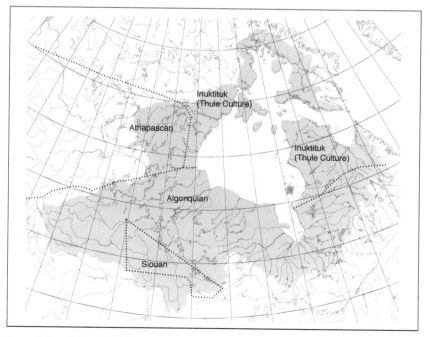

Source: Adapted from McMillan (1988)

developed. There is mining and forestry throughout the region, and the area is strongly affected by hydro-electric development in the three provinces that ring the southern part of Hudson-James Bay: Manitoba, Ontario, and Québec (Berkes 1988b; Waldram 1988).

Northern Development Policies: The Problematique

The Canadian North has traditionally been viewed by the South as 'frontier' to be developed for the benefit of the South (Dacks 1981; Page 1986). The aboriginal inhabitants see the North differently, as land that links them to a past shared by people who have always lived there. They consider the land and resources to be theirs, god-given and inalienable. This view of the North as 'homeland,' was first popularized in the South by the report of the Mackenzie Valley Pipeline Inquiry (Berger 1977). It is not generally accepted by governments and developers but is asserting itself through land claims agreements and other self-government negotiations, and through the increasing political control being exercised by aboriginal groups over the future of their land and people.

With the strengthening of the indigenous vision, the two views, homeland versus frontier, entered a collision course in the 1970s. The fundamental reason for the incompatibility of the two views is the dual economy in the North: one economy for indigenous people and another for Euro-Canadians. The Euro-Canadian economy is based on resource extraction. It produces primary products for export out of the North and requires large capital investments for economies of scale. It is dominated by crown corporations, especially in hydro-electricity production, and by multinational companies in mining, forestry, and fossil fuel development. Demands for raw materials and energy integrates the northern resource extraction economy with global markets. Globalization can only be expected to accelerate under free trade agreements.

The indigenous economy in the arctic and subarctic zones of the bioregion evolved from a subsistence hunting-gathering economy. It has been partially based on trade for at least three centuries (Francis and Morantz 1983). In the bioregion, as elsewhere in the Canadian North, there are no societies of pure hunters; all indigenous economies may be characterized as a mix of transfer payments, wage employment based mainly on service sector jobs, and a traditional sector based on land (George and Preston 1987). It is important to note that indigenous people have not to any extent participated in the resource extraction economy (Salisbury 1986). One exception may be the Naskapi and Montagnais (Innu) of Schefferville, who were integrated into the mining economy in the 1960s and 1970s until the iron ore mine closed in the late 1970s

The land-based sector has a number of components. Trapping provided substantial cash income until the 1940s; since the mid-1980s, it has accounted for very little (Wenzel 1991). In some regions, commercial fisheries and logging also provide cash income, as do wild rice and berry picking on a smaller scale. Recreational industries based on land, guiding for hunting and fishing, provide seasonal employment. Ecotourism is just emerging. Land is the source of raw materials for handicrafts, which are a significant source of cash income throughout the area. Soapstone, the raw material for an important cash income source for some Inuit communities, is locally mined. Wood fuel and a variety of materials for local needs also come from the land. By far the most important produce of the indigenous economy is locally used bush food, or country food, from hunting and fishing.

The indigenous economy is deeply rooted in Native cultural values and reflects indigenous aspirations and values. Similarly, the resource extraction economy reflects the values and beliefs of the Euro-Canadians of the North, that it is a frontier to be exploited for raw materials needed by the industrial economy. There are very few Euro-Canadians in the arctic and subarctic parts of the Hudson Bay bioregion with a sense of belonging and commitment. This is reflected in the presence of only three small non-Native communities around Hudson-James Bay: Radisson in Québec, Moosonee in Ontario, and Churchill in Manitoba. The first is the nerve centre for the James Bay hydro project and the other two are railheads. The Euro-Canadian populations in the northern parts of the bioregion have been small and impermanent. There is little dialogue between the two groups of people and the two economies. The gap between them has if anything widened since the time of the fur trader who lived in everyday contact with the indigenous people.

The earliest development policies in the North involved indigenous northerners as labour for the fur trade, which started with the Hudson Bay Company (HBC) in 1670. In the subarctic and later the arctic zones of the Hudson Bay bioregion, the HBC controlled the fur trade, the only industry, but did not attempt to establish colonies. The only permanent settlements were fur trade posts, and the only Europeans living there were HBC employees involved in the fur trade (Ray 1974). Initially, the way of life of indigenous northerners did not change much, except that they started to use trade goods and European technology. The James

Bay Cree who worked for the fur trade posts, for example, were using muzzle-loading guns as early as the seventeenth century. Some indigenous groups started to include European food in their diets shortly after the start of the fur trade, but it was not until the turn of the twentieth century that the 'bush Cree,' those who were not living at the trading posts, became dependent on non-Native foods such as flour and lard (Francis and Morantz 1983).

With depletion of the beaver throughout the subarctic region in the 1920s, followed by the crash of fur markets in the 1940s, many subsistence economies entered a period of collapse (Ray 1990). The results of health surveys in the 1940s were bleak (Vivian et al. 1948; Moore et al. 1946). Moore and colleagues showed, for example, that the diet of bush Indians at Norway House in northern Manitoba significantly deteriorated in the first half of the twentieth century. In 1941 the Native people were taking about eight times as much non-Native food into the bush as they did at the turn of the century, probably as a result of game depletion. In that same year, purchased food in Norway House was calculated to provide over half of the caloric requirements. No less than 85 per cent of the total was supplied by white flour, lard, sugar, and jam, all of them practically devoid of vitamins and minerals.

A famine in the Keewatin region in the late 1940s and early 1950s, popularized by Farley Mowat's two books, *The People of the Deer* (1951) and *The Desperate People* (1959), contributed to the development of public opinion in the South that Native peoples were destitute and that the hunting way of life, an anachronism, was impossible to sustain. The late 1940s saw the federal government introduce policies that provided family allowance cheques and allocated rations to Native peoples (Kerr 1950; Honigmann 1961). Centralized health, educational, and social services were extended, and central administrative structures were established. Massive cultural changes were precipitated by the influence of southern institutions, values, and technologies (Stenbaek 1987). Dacks explains the logic and dynamics of these policy changes:

> Ottawa's southern values led it to interpret the native lifestyle as so unrewarding as to be dead, incapable of resuscitation. Accordingly, the special characteristics that differentiated northern natives from other 'poor Canadians' were ignored and it was decided that the northern native people should have applied to them the politics of welfare state generally applied to its less-advantaged members. This policy meant concentrating the native people into settlements where medical and

educational programs could be economically provided. Ultimately, native people who were healthier and better educated (in white terms) would be able to assume a position alongside the other elements of the Canadian population. While this goal was assimilationist and highly judgemental, it was not necessarily malicious in its intent, for it was based on the individualistic and materialistic view that no alternative to 'poverty' existed for northern natives (1981, 29).

As aboriginal people moved off the land and into permanent settlements, the South started to develop a greater interest in the development of this 'empty' land, especially in the Diefenbaker years of the late 1950s. 'In appealing to the myth of the North,' Page states, 'Diefenbaker brilliantly caught the mood of the day and secured the largest electoral majority in the history of the country ... Canadians ... responded to this idealism of the frontier spirit and of developing the North for Canada's future greatness' (1986, 19). His 'Northern Vision' was a concept of development that would open the North by improving transportation and communications and by developing power sources.

The mega-project decade of the 1970s was no doubt influenced by the Northern Vision of the 1950s and the 'Mid-Canada Corridor' concept of the 1960s (Page 1986). One of the first major developments was the Churchill Falls hydro-electric project in Labrador, which started in 1967 and is located to the southeast of the bioregion. Two of the largest projects were within the bioregion, the James Bay and Churchill-Nelson developments. There were smaller developments as well, and many others that were planned but never built.

Policy Implications

Many of the development projects in the Hudson Bay basin have come into direct conflict with the interests of local northern communities. A sampling of projects from the Northwest Territories (Page 1986), Manitoba (Waldram 1988; Wagner 1984), Ontario (George, Berkes, and Preston 1995), and Québec (Salisbury 1986; McCutcheon 1991) vividly demonstrates the problematique of the dual economy in the North. The Euro-Canadian resource extraction economy has been driven by export markets rather than by sustainability concerns, and the southern urban centres have benefited most from these development projects by exporting resources. The resource extraction economy has almost never been open to the participation of indigenous peoples. Everywhere it has conflicted with the indigenous economy and damaged it. Because the subsistence economy is dependent on a pristine environment, it is vulnerable to the impact of development. In fact, the indigenous economy is vulnerable even to certain types of industrial activity occurring far from the bioregion. The long-range transport of atmospheric pollutants are suspected in the contamination of Hudson Bay, Foxe Basin, and Arctic Ocean food chains. The accumulation of certain PCBs and other toxic organics have been documented in the larger marine mammals (Kinloch and Kuhnlein 1988; Cameron and Weiss 1993).

Throughout the Hudson Bay bioregion, policies that were in effect from the 1950s onwards have not been successful in integrating indigenous peoples into the Euro-Canadian economy (Dyck and Waldram 1993). They have resulted in the settlement of people into centralized communities to which health and social services can be brought and have fostered dependence, with huge costs to the Canadian public. As well, churches, Euro-Canadian legal and other institutions, and 'innovations' such as the residential school system were the policy mechanisms to integrate aboriginal people into mainstream society. From an *Agenda 21* point of view, these policies have disempowered indigenous peoples and dispossessed them of their land and resources. Policy mechanisms to counter disempowerment and dispossession would therefore need to include measures to build and strengthen indigenous social institutions, to recognize indigenous communal property rights for land and resources, and to assess the cumulative impact of development projects.

Paradoxically, in the process of dispossession, many indigenous groups have learned to fight for their rights. Some groups have become experts in the use of legal processes, the media, and international politics, as with the James Bay Cree (McCutcheon 1991; Barker and Soyez 1994). They have been able to block some projects and conclude agreements to help strengthen their own economies. They have started to articulate their own unique views of the environment, their use of land and resources, and their community-based economies. In the quest for sustainability, these three areas can serve as the basis for action. Each is further elaborated in the following three sections to provide the basis for policy development.

Traditional Ecological Knowledge

There is a considerable technical literature from the bioregion about indigenous knowledge pertaining to the use of natural resources in the local economy. This literature is based on the accounts of non-Native researchers. As Brightman (1993) put it, we only hope that someday indigenous authors will come along and offer a more complete summary of indigenous ecological knowledge than what we are able to provide. This section will offer a sampling of cases to argue that the indigenous views of the environment are distinct from Western scientific concepts of the environment and offer potential for implementing sustainability.

The best known kind of traditional ecological knowledge (TEK) is aboriginal local information of animals and land, as documented mainly by biologists and anthropologists. A large literature going back many decades shows that Inuit and Cree hunters, trappers, and fishers have detailed information on the natural history of the animals they hunted and their biophysical environment (Berkes and Freeman 1986). Among these studies, for example, is Freeman's (1979) summary of the importance of the knowledge of harp seal behaviour for a successful hunt. Similarly, Feit (1987a) and Berkes (1977) showed the importance of the use of environmental and natural history knowledge by the Cree in moose hunting and fishing respectively. Detailed maps of animal locations, seasonal movements, and natural habitat, as known by the Inuit of the Hudson Bay area, have been documented by Freeman (1976) and Riewe (1992).

Interest in TEK as a means of resource *management* is relatively more recent than interest in TEK as a source of biological and ecological *information*. One of the earliest studies suggesting that aboriginal management systems were different from scientific management and yet ecologically viable comes from Freeman (1979). When the NWT Game Management Service started to explore the possibility of reopening the musk-ox hunt in the mid-1960s, the plan was to allow a small number of old bulls, on a fixed quota, to be taken by trophy hunters. Only reproductively inactive, biologically superfluous, solitary males would be killed, scientific data would be gathered from the animals harvested, and appreciable economic benefits would accrue to the local Inuit. Nevertheless, the local Inuit community strongly opposed this plan. They argued that old solitary males were useless as trophy animals; the best trophy animals were in fact the prime bulls in the herds and these older bulls were important for the social organization of the herd, playing a dominant role in maintaining the integrity of the group and in defence. The Inuit argued that, given the importance of social organization for the survival of the small number of herds and the variable reproductive success of a herd from year to year, management by a fixed quota on older bulls was a most unsound management plan, and surplus yield calculations on a geographic basis did not make sense.

Berkes (1977; 1979) investigated Cree subsistence fisheries, which are not regulated by government, in Chisasibi and compared the Cree fishing system with biologically based fishery management systems elsewhere in the subarctic region. Government regulations normally include restrictions on kinds of gear and mesh size and prohibitions on fishing at certain times and places where fish are congregated and vulnerable to overexploitation. By contrast, Cree fishermen used the most effective gear available to them and the mesh sizes that gave them the highest return in a given season and location. The Cree concentrated their fishing effort on aggregations of fish that were most efficiently exploitable, rotating fishing areas according to season and to signals from changes in the catch per unit effort. Restraints on the fishing effort were supplied by social controls: restrictions by family hunting-fishing territories, prohibitions against wastage, and the idea that the harvest be keyed to the consumption needs of the family and kin. Any short-term surplus was, in any case, given away to others; hence there was no incentive to fish harder than necessary for livelihood. Comparing the biological prescriptions with indigenous practice, the Cree fishery practice violated nearly every biologically oriented, indirect control measure in the repertoire of scientific fisheries management. Yet the overall Chisasibi Cree fishery, based on social and ethical controls, appeared to be sustainable, with evidence of some overfishing only on one local stock of one species (Berkes 1979; 1987).

Feit (1986a) studied the beaver hunting of the Waswanipi Cree. Three hunting strategies were used: looking for beaver at dawn and dusk when beavers were active; trapping by setting traps underwater so the animals would drown with a minimum of suffering; and 'waking the beaver,' which involved rousing beavers during the day and driving them from their lodges, thereby making them easy to capture. Waking the beaver was more productive than trapping, but it was used only when there was a pressing need for food. Trapping was the preferred method because it provided controlled harvests, allowing the trapper to exercise selectivity in harvest. Further evidence that the Waswanipi managed beaver populations was their practice of rotating subdivisions of their hunting territories, thereby resting parts of their land so that animals would replenish themselves. Feit demonstrated a statistically significant difference in productivity between territories hunted during the previous year and those that had not been hunted for two or more years. He observed that beaver colony densities and beaver harvests were stable from 1968-9 to 1972-6, providing evidence of the viability of the beaver management practices of the Waswanipi.

Goose hunting practices of Cree hunters along the coast of James Bay have been studied by Scott (1986; 1989) and Berkes (1982). This activity was observed to have a very important communal aspect because coordination of all hunters was necessary for continued good hunting. Overseeing the hunt was a 'goose boss,' a senior hunter from a family with traditional hunting rights in a given area. The main hunting strategy was to minimize disturbance to the main flocks of feeding and resting geese and to kill small groups of geese at the periphery of main flocks quietly and efficiently. To achieve this, elaborate rules of group cooperation and a code of hunting practices had been developed, as overseen by the goose boss. A hunter never shot unless there was wind to muffle the sound; a hunter never shot after sunset or before sunrise because the flare frightened the geese; no open fires were built; and colourful objects were hidden, blood spots were covered, and all animal remains cleaned up. Since geese would not return to an area that had been hunted frequently, sites were rotated and 'rested.' Ideally no site was visited on two consecutive days, and all hunters were expected to cooperate with the goose boss's choice of hunting area in a given territory on a particular day. The hunts were not regulated by government-established seasons or bag limits but only by traditional social practice.

Resource Use Institutions and Ethics

Each of the traditional management systems summarized above requires an organizational basis; the word institution is used here to refer to such organization, basically a system of rules. Among the indigenous groups of the bioregion, all resource management institutions are of the communal property type: land and resources are not owned by individuals but are used for the benefit of all community members (Berkes 1989). This lack of private ownership was interpreted by colonialists as lack of property and used to justify dispossession of indigenous groups (Richardson 1993).

Common property institutions include, for example, the system of James Bay Cree family hunting territories. The use of these territories is overseen by a family head, steward, 'beaver tallyman,' or 'goose boss,' who is responsible for ensuring that the resources are shared equitably and optimally and that they are harvested in a proper manner. Appropriate harvesting practices include the rotation of hunting and trapping areas, as in the beaver management case study above. The practice is common at least in the Cree parts of the bioregion. Omushkego Cree trappers of western James Bay, for example, consider rotation as part of traditional management. In 1990, it was found that two-thirds of Omushkego hunter-trappers rotated parts of their land, and more than one-third joined other trappers in some years, which has the same effect of allowing animal populations to recover between pulsed harvests; some used both techniques (Table 9.1).

Table 9.1

Number of hunter-trappers who rotate their trapping areas or join other trappers, 1990, Omushkego Cree

Communities	Rotating		Joining others	
	Yes	No	Yes	No
Moose Factory	26	43	19	41
Moosonee	2	43	0	43
New Post	2	3	0	5
Fort Albany	3	1	0	5
Kashechewan	138	5	65	61
Peawanuck	20	0	9	7
Fort Severn	15	3	11	6
Total	206	98	104	168

The Inuit associate specific family groups with specific hunting or fishing sites, and place names are socially significant (Müller-Wille 1992). This is similar to the practice among the Cree and other subarctic groups, but among the Inuit access to resources is not restricted to these groups or individuals, and many hunting activities are performed cooperatively under the guidance of the local group leader. Inuit inhabitants of various areas are known by names that describe their geographic location. The suffix -*miut* means 'inhabitant of.' In Arctic Québec, for example, the inhabitants of Belcher Island are called Qikirktamiut, that is, the people of the Belcher Islands. Areas defined by the suffix are variable in size, and they frequently overlap. The -*miut* designation is not merely a geographical identification but a moral and ethical statement signifying one's sense of place and belonging (Graburn 1969).

Just as sense of place in the Native culture is different from Euro-Canadian notions, the concept of property is also fundamentally different. According to Scott (1988), the traditional Cree understanding of 'property' cannot be interpreted as ownership of 'things' but as a set of relationships between people. The fundamental relationship was that among members of a household, a self-sustaining group; the second level was the collective relationship dictating that members of a household should consider the needs of the larger community in their use of resources; and the third level was the relationship of the household and community with others. Territory stewards or goose bosses, for example, were required to exercise their authority over land access wisely and for the benefit of all. It was the steward's responsibility to ensure that the sacred relationship between humans, as well as between humans and the land and other living creatures, was maintained. Hunting groups were formed by the steward and included those with long-term rights of access to the territory as well as those without such rights who were invited to join a hunting group. The invitation to join a hunting group was indicative of the importance of social relations to hunting practices in the society. It was in fact a gift of food (Feit 1991).

Freeman (1979; 1989) described the traditional aboriginal hunter's understanding of the natural environment as being more complex than that allowed by deterministic models of nature used in ecology and resource management. Ecosystems were perceived as circular, complex, interrelated, dynamic, and fluctuating. Relations between humans, animals, and their environment were so important because they had to do with establishing an individual's identity in the world. A sense of place as a basic human need was symbolized for the hunter by the land on which hunting was carried out. The relationship between the hunter and the hunted involved more than the economics associated with procuring food; it extended to encompass social relations between individuals, families, and communities. Detailed studies elsewhere in the bioregion, including northwestern Manitoba (Brightman 1993), Rupert House (Waskaganish) (Preston 1975), and northern Mistassini (Tanner 1979) all indicate that social relations have their parallels in hunter-animal relations, and humans are part of a larger web of environmental relationships based on respect. This world view of humans as part of nature is fundamentally different from the world view of humans as above nature prevalent in Western societies.

Just as there is a dual economy in the North, there is a dual resource management system. Indigenous and Euro-Canadian systems are organized in fundamentally different ways (Berkes 1981; Usher 1987). In contrast to the Euro-Canadian system, which is driven by science, centralized, and based on the technical expertise of government resource managers, the indigenous system is based on the moral and ethical leadership of experienced hunters who act as stewards on behalf of their social group. The two systems are based on distinctly different ideas of how the universe works. TEK systems may be characterized as ethnoscience (Feit 1987b), but they are not scientific in the Western sense. Many have therefore questioned if indigenous systems are oriented for 'conservation' in the sense of Western resource management (Brightman 1993).

The conservation that arises from indigenous knowledge and management systems has little to do with conventional Western conservation, with its concern over population dynamics and externally imposed restrictive harvest measures. Rather, it has to do with the basic design of the common property system, which creates incentives for long-term wise use, or ecological sustainability. Such systems are found in many traditional societies (Berkes, Folke, and Gadgil 1995). Almost all indigenous property rights systems in the arctic and subarctic parts of the bioregion are of the communal property type, in which the community controls access to resources and makes rules for their use (Berkes 1987; Berkes et al. 1989). Properly functioning communal property systems and common property institutions create a stake in conservation. Self-interest, including the interest of one's community and one's descendants, is the key to sustainability.

Policy Implications
Indigenous knowledge, as a field of research, has become 'respectable' only since the 1980s. It is just beginning to be used as a basis for sustainable development planning but remains unproven. In the Hudson Bay Program, TEK has been used for assessing cumulative impacts to supplement Western science, which so far seems inadequate to deal with combinations and interactions of a multitude of deleterious effects on the environment (McDonald 1993; McDonald, Arrangutainaq, and Novalinga 1995). Using indigenous knowledge may well be the key to the involvement of indigenous peoples in resource management and conservation strategies. Resource co-management is not merely a matter of adding Native participants to committees but also of taking into account their ecological insights. TEK is more than local environmental knowledge; it is a complex system of knowledge, practice, and belief that reflects indigenous world views (Gadgil, Berkes, and Folke 1993).

In the indigenous communities of the Hudson Bay bioregion, TEK systems still exist, complete with social institutions such as hunting territory systems and with world views that constitute the ethical basis of these systems. For many hunters, 'respect' for the land and animals is still important. As many indigenous leaders point out, however, elders' knowledge is being lost. Younger generations no longer have the same level of intimate contact with the land. Some traditional environmental ethics, with the associated practices and rituals that reminded people of their obligations to nature, have fallen into disuse, and traditional institutions that govern indigenous management systems have been weakened. A study by Ohmagari (1995) among the Omushkego Cree of northern Ontario found that only about half of ninety-three elements of women's bush skills and indigenous knowledge were being transmitted. Erosion of TEK is an important issue, but it should be considered in context: 'Cultural change is not the same thing as cultural *loss*. And "tradition" in all societies is perpetually reinvented in association with changes in custom and practice' (C. Scott, personal communication)

In the past TEK was not used in mainstream environmental management partly because local management was marginalized by state management. The use of TEK therefore cannot be contemplated in isolation, as a supplement to conventional management practice, but only as a part of an empowerment process involving institution building, social and cultural sustainability, self-government, and resource co-management. The use of TEK affects power relationships, and it will thus be much harder to combine with scientific knowledge than many assume.

Integral to a comprehensive view of sustainable development is the understanding of cultural change. Much export-oriented northern development has not been sustainable from the point of view of Native cultures. An appropriate policy objective might be culturally sustainable development, defined as 'development that meets the material needs of the present without compromising the ability of future generations to retain their cultural identity, social relationships and values, and to allow for change recognized and guided in ways that are consistent with existing cultural principles of a people' (Berkes et al. 1994, 358). Development of policies for culturally sustainable development requires strategies by which TEK is not only 'collected' but actually used in decision-making. Perhaps 'the key point is that TEK is not just about *knowledge*, but about management, social organization and governance' (J. Robinson, personal communication).

Land and Resource Use

Since the 1970s, a large number of aboriginal land use studies have been undertaken in Canada, many to document Native land claims (e.g., Freeman 1976; Riewe 1992), some to assess environmental impact (e.g., Kayahna Tribal Council 1985), and one for regional planning and resource co-management (Berkes et al. 1995). Sixteen of them include parts of the bioregion. Table 9.2 summarizes these studies by location, period, objective, coverage, and method, and Figure 9.3 depicts the areas covered. They include Freeman's land use maps from 1976, Riewe's Nunavut area maps, the comprehensive traditional environmental knowledge study of the Hudson Bay bioregion (McDonald, Arrangutainaq, and Novalinga 1995), the TASO study of northern Ontario, and a number of land use studies of more limited geographical coverage, including Weinstein's (1976) map for Fort George (Chisasibi) and studies in Manitoba by researchers at the Natural Resources Institute, University of Manitoba, and Manitoba Keewatinowi Okimakanak. Not shown in Table 9.2 and Figure 9.3 are many other studies in progress or not available for review. These include Grande-Baleine (Québec), Cross Lake and Split Lake (Manitoba), and land use studies in the Treaty 3 area of Ontario.

These studies permit some generalizations about aboriginal land use in the region. The extent of changes in Inuit land use in west Hudson Bay may be assessed by comparing maps in Freeman (1976) and Riewe (1992). Freeman (1976) sought to identify land use patterns of the Inuit residents of thirty-three communities in the Northwest Territories for three specific periods in living memory, including the period of sedentarization (post-1955-67). Riewe (1992) mapped Inuit land use in 1986-7, with details of the species harvested. Both Freeman's and Riewe's land use maps show a good deal of overlap in land use between neighbouring communities and very little land on which harvesting does not take place.

In a study of the traditional harvesting activities of the Chipewyan-Denesuline Bands in the Northwest Territories, Usher (1990) noted that land use activities have continued to be an important aspect of life. Land use studies covering parts of the Northwest Territories, Saskatchewan, and Manitoba show that the earlier land occupation of the Dene, which had been based on the search for caribou, have been modified with the establishment of permanent settlements in the southern part of their ancestral territory, near former fur trade posts to which the Dene typically travelled in the summer to trade and collect treaty monies (Usher 1990; MKO 1993).

Table 9.2

Aboriginal land use studies in the Hudson Bay bioregion

Location	Year(s)	Objective	Coverage	Method	Reference
NWT	Pre-1925-35 1925(35)-55(67) 1955(67)-74	To document native land claims	Land use over time, including habitation	Map biographies and interviews	Freeman (1976)
Nunavut region of the NWT	1986-7	To document native land claims	Land use and intensity and wildlife	Previously published information, map biographies, and interviews	Riewe (1992)
Hudson Bay bioregion	1992-3	To document traditional environmental knowledge and to assess cumulative impacts of development	Traditional knowledge of marine, freshwater, and land environment	Workshops conducted with elders, hunters, and trappers, followed by verification	McDonald et al. (1995)
Tadoule Lake and Lac Brochet	1990-1	To document native land claims	Land use, including travel routes and habitation	Map biographies and stratified random sampling	MKO (1993)
Use of NWT by the Fond du Lac, Black Lake, and Hatchet Lake bands	1989-90	To document native land claims	Land use, including travel routes and habitation	Map biographies	Usher (1990)

(continued on next page)

Table 9.2 (continued)

Aboriginal land use studies in the Hudson Bay bioregion

Location	Year(s)	Objective	Coverage	Method	Reference
Inuit communities in northern Québec	1973-80	To document native land claims	Land use based on distance from the community	Questionnaires and statistical sampling	JB&NQNHRC (1988)
Cree communities in northern Québec	1974-9	To document native land claims	Cree wildlife harvests of thirty-two species	Diary/calendars and questionnaire/ interviews	JB&NQNHRC (1982)
Chisasibi	1972-4	To document native land claims	Harvests; family and household composition, including incomes and subsistence activities	Map biographies and interviews	Weinstein (1976)
Moosonee	1981-3	To document harvesting areas	Hunting and wildlife areas for major species	Questionnaires	Thompson and Hutchison (1989)
Mushkegowuk region	1989-91	To facilitate regional planning and resource co-management	Distribution and intensity of land use by community, by hunter type, and by species	Questionnaires and computerized regional database	Berkes et al. (1995)

Location	Date	Purpose	Data	Source
North central Ontario	1920-81	To assess environmental impacts	Land use and intensity over time	Map biographies, questionnaires, and genealogies	Kayahna (1985)
South Indian Lake	Pre-1946-90	To document land use activities over time	Land use pre- and post-flooding, including travel routes and habitation	Map biographies and interviews	Hrenchuk (1991)
Fox Lake First Nation	1957-92	To document land use activities over time	Travel routes and habitation	Map biographies and interviews	Hill (1993)
Churchill and Reindeer rivers	1977	To assess environmental impacts	Land use, including travel routes and habitation	Map biographies and interviews	Begrand (1978)
Grande-Baleine	1990	To fulfill environmental impact assessment requirements	Hunting and wildlife areas	Not available	Hydro-Québec (1993)
Waterhen	1991-2	To document land use activities over time	Land use	Map biographies and interviews	Stock (1996)

Figure 9.3

Land use studies in the Hudson Bay bioregion

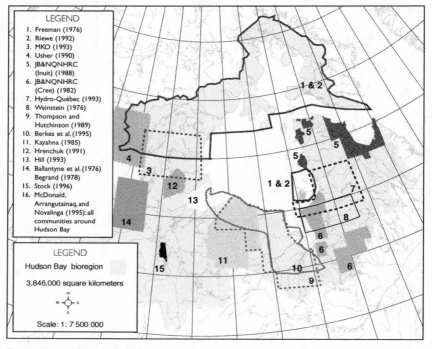

Source: Adapted from Fast and Berkes (1994)

Extensive contemporary use of the land by north central Ontario Ojibwa was described in the *Kayahna Region Land Utilization and Occupancy Study* (1985). The authors reported that not only land use patterns but also the social organization of the Nishnabwe was enduring despite strong external influences. Traditional social organization was evident in communal hunting lands, the areas used by families related through the male line, and the shared living areas of two or three households, co-residential units, which continued to be the land-controlling group. The extent of the area used had changed relatively little.

Similarly, the actual harvesting area used by the Omushkego Cree of western James-Hudson Bay in 1990 bears a close resemblance to their nineteenth-century land use area (Honigmann 1981), as shown in Figure 9.4. Contemporary land use is based on a one-year 'snapshot' and accounts for a sample of 56 per cent of all hunters (Berkes et al. 1995). Even though the geographic extent of harvesting areas may not have changed much over the decades, lifestyles and activity patterns of harvesters have changed a great deal. Once living on the land in scattered hunting groups and getting together only in summer in trading post communities, the Omushkego Cree of 1990 carry out much of their harvesting on the basis of day trips and overnight or weekend outings (Berkes et al. 1994).

This contemporary hunting pattern is the outcome of the policy of centralizing indigenous populations, a policy motivated by the belief that the hunting lifestyle was dead and that indigenous peoples should be integrated into the mainstream society. The resource extraction economy, unlike the earlier fur trade economy, had little need for the skills of

Figure 9.4

Traditional territory of the West Main (Omushkego) Cree

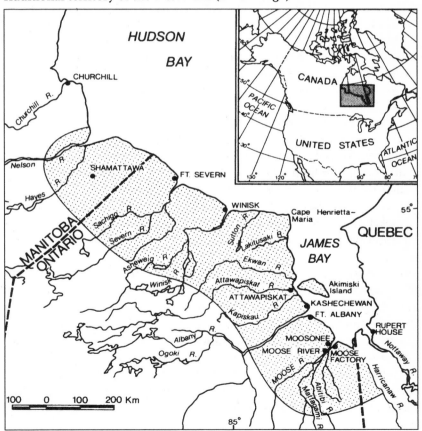

Source: George and Preston (1987) after Honigmann (1981)

hunters. In the new economy of the North, indigenous peoples were dispensable; their hunting culture and relaxed way of life were utterly ill adapted for employment in resource extraction industries. Many Native communities were caught in a bind. Settled far from game, they were unable to hunt but at the same time they could not find an alternative livelihood either. The cycle of economic dependency closely followed from this pattern. The conventional wisdom of the day regarded these difficulties as a necessary transition phase toward a modern economic order. Usher explains this view and how it subsequently changed:

> The views I held on the traditional economy in the 1960s were essentially those held by the great majority of administrators and social scientists at that time. The collapse of the traditional fur trade in the late 1940s and early 1950s, the subsequent massive intervention of government throughout the North in the fields of health, education and economic development, and the rapid urbanization of native people, had indeed created an economic and social crisis in the North. By the time these processes were largely complete, in the late 1950s and early 1960s, native society was in profound retreat, disorganization and demoralization at every level ...
>
> Since then, however, both the objective situation, and many peoples' perception of it, have changed. Native people have accommodated themselves to community living in many respects, and with the aid of either or both increased employment and fur prices, as well as such technological innovations as the snowmobile, have readjusted their land and resource use practices so that the areas used, and in some cases the harvests obtained, are as great or greater than they were a generation ago (Usher 1978, 91).

By and large, Native people did not abandon settled communities to go back to the bush. Some communities did leave the larger settlements to go back to *smaller* communities, however, near good hunting areas. Examples include the Tadoule Lake Dene who were resettled in 1956 in Churchill but returned to the land in 1973-7 (Bruemmer 1977; Brandson 1981); the Nemaska Cree who left Waskaganish and Mistassini in 1979-82 (Preston 1982); the Chibougamau Cree who left Mistassini for Ouje-Bougoumou; the Naskapi who left Schefferville for Kawawachikamach; and the Great Whale Inuit who left Kuujjuarapik for Umiujaq, all in the 1980s.

Although indigenous societies adapted themselves to community living, they appear to have decided not to accept the future that the policymakers of the 1950s and the 1960s had in mind for them. They certainly found that the promised jobs in the resource extraction economy did not exist for them. As well, even those individuals who had some wage income decided that obtaining their meat from the land was culturally and psychologically more satisfying. The rediscovery of the importance of the land and the rejection of cultural and economic integration – even if such integration were possible – fuelled the growth of Native political organizations. As Usher (1978) and others have pointed out, the growth of the land claims movement attests to this fact.

Native Land Claims and Agreements

All parts of the bioregion are covered either by recent agreements or by older treaties (Figure 9.5). The three modern comprehensive land claims agreements – the James Bay and Northern Québec Agreement (JB&NQA), the Northeastern Québec Agreement for the Naskapi, and the Nunavut Agreement – are negotiated legal documents that spell out rights to land and resources in some detail. The JB&NQA, 455 pages long, and the Nunavut Agreement, 229 pages, also include chapters on local and regional government powers, health, social development, education, justice, environmental assessment of future development projects in the region, social and economic development, and compensation.

By contrast, the older treaties are short, unnegotiated documents deficient in detail on land and resource use rights. Some of them spell out the indigenous right to hunt and fish on unoccupied crown lands, and some are simply silent on the issue. McMillan (1988, 296) writes:

Indians received very little for their surrender of nearly half of Canada's land surface. What is more, it appears that there were great differences between what the Indians were told they were signing and the actual written words of the treaties ... A widespread grievance is the abrogation of treaty-promised hunting and fishing rights. Various commissioners remarked that without assurances of such rights the Indians could never have been persuaded to sign the treaties.

The first major challenge to indigenous hunting rights under treaty came in the 1920s. As railways were making parts of the North accessible, large numbers of non-Native trappers were attracted by high fur prices. Many outsiders started to enter areas previously controlled by indigenous peoples in the boreal-subarctic regions of Québec (Feit 1979; 1986b; Scott 1988), Ontario (Ray 1990; George, Berkes, and Preston 1995), and Manitoba (Brightman 1993).

Figure 9.5

Native land claim agreements and treaties

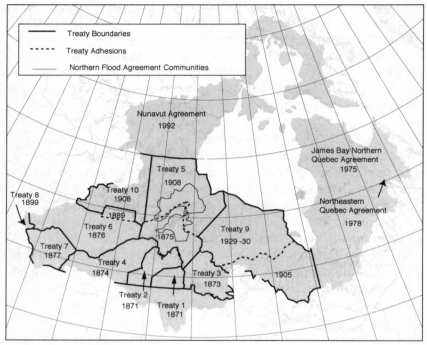

Source: *National Atlas of Canada,* 5th ed. (1991)

Beaver stocks throughout much of the North were depleted by outsiders overhunting and local hunters reacting by trapping the animals
out first. Only after many Native groups that had depended on trapping
faced extreme hardships did the provincial governments decide to recognize and enforce exclusive aboriginal trapping rights, both for the
welfare of Native people and for conservation of fur resources. This had
the effect of restoring indigenous land tenure systems. Beaver preserves
were established in the 1930s and Native hunting territories recognized
as 'registered traplines,' with indigenous stewards, called 'tallymen,'
who were paid an honorarium to count annually the number of active
beaver lodges in a territory (Feit 1986b). The federal government's perspective was that it retained ownership of all lands except private, allowing Natives only the right to hunt on unoccupied Crown lands. As
beaver populations regenerated, traplines were mapped jointly by federal and provincial government representatives and formal trapline
areas established, based on existing territorial systems. In Ontario's

James Bay region, for example, the mapping took place in the 1940s, and the management system was taken over by the province's resource management agency in 1948 (George, Berkes, and Preston 1995).

Exclusive *trapping* rights of the northern indigenous groups were thus secured, but hunting and fishing rights still came under pressure from non-Native populations who followed the new access routes opened up by development and from the impact of development on fish and wildlife habitat. As well, indigenous hunting started to come under government regulation. Feit (1986a), for example, writes that when he started work in the Waswanipi area in the late 1960s, conservation officers were trying to enforce a directive that the Cree not hunt moose within ten miles of roads and towns: areas where the sport hunt was concentrated. In some cases, government game management was carried out with an eagerness that disregarded Native welfare. There is strong evidence that the removal of Duck Lake Sayisi Dene to Churchill in 1956 was in part motivated by the alleged overhunting of caribou at a time when caribou were erroneously thought to be in terminal decline (Brandson 1981; MKO 1993).

Frustration and resentment over government game management dates back decades in Native communities throughout the Canadian North. Over the years, but especially since the 1970s, indigenous groups have posed increasingly serious legal challenges to government jurisdiction over Native hunting and fishing rights, culminating in the Sparrow decision of 1990. The decision has been considered a landmark 'on the nature of aboriginal fishing rights and on the constitutional protection afforded them. The court confirmed and advanced other recent judgments that the aboriginal right to fish cannot be extinguished by the Fisheries Act but only regulated by it' (Usher 1991, 20). The decision put the onus on governments to justify regulations affecting Native harvesting and set forth a number of tests, thus exposing policies and practices of fish and wildlife management to closer public scrutiny and debate.

The impact of development on wildlife habitat and thus on the indigenous economy was first brought to public scrutiny and debate by the James Bay court case that led to the JB&NQA (Malouf 1973). The court debate over indigenous rights and the impact of development had a major role in shaping government policy. In Manitoba, the effects of Churchill-Nelson hydro development were addressed after the fact by the Northern Flood Agreement (NFA) of 1977, which sought to establish guidelines for compensation to the communities affected by the project (Figure 9.5). A flawed agreement, the NFA has proved very difficult to implement and has resulted in a patchwork of court cases and settlements. These have solved neither local grievances nor environmental problems but have nevertheless been very costly.

The JB&NQA was more successful in dealing with the effects of the James Bay I development of the late 1970s and early 1980s (Feit 1986b) but inadequate to deal with the potential impact of the proposed James Bay II hydro development, starting with the Grande-Baleine (Dwyer 1992; Fenge 1992). Although there are mining and forestry developments throughout the bioregion, hydro-electric projects have had by far the most profound impact. Figure 9.6 provides a summary of existing and proposed hydro-electric developments in the three provinces that ring the southern part of the bioregion. The figure helps to illustrate the idea that assessing effects project by project may not be adequate to measure cumulative impact. There appears to be a convergence of views among scientists (Sly 1994) and indigenous peoples (TEKMS 1994) that the overall impact of these projects may be greater than the sum of their individual effects.

Policy Implications

As with traditional ecological knowledge, the extent and persistence of aboriginal land use in the North has only recently been recognized and appreciated. As studies in the Northwest Territories and Mushkegowuk region show, land use by settlement-based hunters continues to be extensive. Indigenous adaptations have included mechanized rapid transport and commitment of considerable amounts of cash income from wage employment and transfer payments to the pursuit of harvesting. In the *Agenda 21* sense, these adaptations may be considered self-empowerment. The same can be said about the Native rejection of policymakers' integration visions of the 1950s and 1960s, but it is still a matter of debate whether the current way of life of northern aboriginal people is sustainable or whether the current mixed economy is simply a longer route to eventual social and economic integration (Boldt 1993; Berkes et al. 1994).

Land claims have redistributed income and political power in the North since the 1970s. There remains a huge gap, however, between the three modern comprehensive agreements in the bioregion and the older treaties with their unspecified land and resource use rights. On the one hand, the treaties allow almost no protection of aboriginal rights outside reserves. Yet groups such as the Omushkego Cree depend on land that extends well beyond reserve boundaries. In the Mushkegowuk region, the combined area of the reserves is about 900 square kilometres; the area enclosed by the outer boundary of harvest areas (Figure 9.7) is about

Figure 9.6

Hydro-electric development projects in the Hudson Bay bioregion

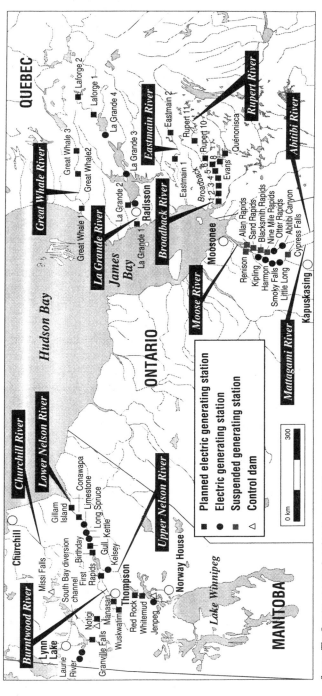

Source: The Gazette, as reproduced in Fenge (1992)

250,000 square kilometres (Berkes et al. 1995). Thus, the area legally controlled by the Omushkego Cree is less than 0.5 per cent of the land used!

On the other hand, a series of court cases, including the Sparrow decision, has just about paralyzed the ability of federal and provincial fish and wildlife management agencies to enforce regulations on Native groups. The severe threat to the wildlife of the North in areas covered by the older treaties is that there is a resource management vacuum. Governments are reluctant to enforce regulations, but many of the Native groups are not in a position to exercise self-management either. As H. Payne puts it, 'the resource managers of the future will never be able to ignore aboriginal rights' (personal communication). Yet rights and responsibilities go together. The sustainable use of a common property resource requires that both rights and responsibilities be specified (e.g., Berkes 1989). Recognizing indigenous property rights will therefore be a key element of a new northern land use policy. To implement such a policy would require that government resource management agencies share control of access to resources with local northern communities and that rights and responsibilities for their use be established.

There is more at stake than merely compensation for the earlier land surrenders by treaty. The larger policy issues include the development of appropriate mechanisms for self-government and co-management. Access to land and resources has become a vital issue for many aboriginal communities, especially in the southern parts of the bioregion threatened by further development (George, Berkes, and Preston 1995). Natural resources are needed to develop local and regional economies, yet the resource base is being constricted by policies favouring competing land uses from hydro-electric development, large-scale forestry, and mining. New policies are needed to tip the balance in favour of recognizing the priority of local land and resource use over export-oriented resource development.

The Subsistence Economy

Usher (1989) compared the northern Native village economy to the rural economy in southern Canada, one sustained by wildlife and the other by agriculture. He defined the term 'domestic economy' to include harvesting as well as processing activities for the provision of food, fuel, and other material household needs. This domestic economy provided

> a net self-sufficiency in protein for the Native population of the NWT (and probably much of the rest of northern Canada), not only on a re-

Figure 9.7

Harvesting areas in the Mushkegowuk region, 1990

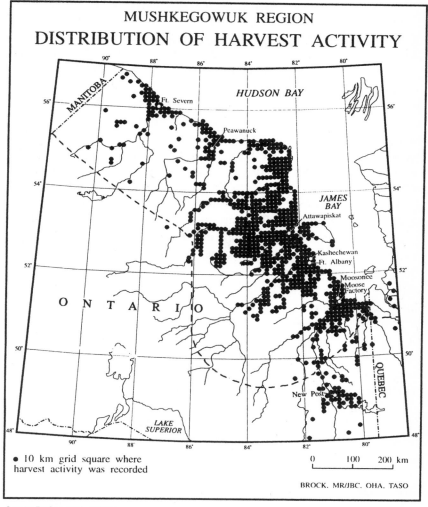

Source: Berkes et al. (1995)

gional basis, but also largely, village by village. This is of no small importance in a region in which there is virtually no agricultural production ... Wildlife is thus the nutritional basis of health and well-being
for most Native northerners, and remains today the foundation of a
distinctive Native economy' (Usher 1987, 4).

In the Northwest Territories in 1987, domestic production added about 10 per cent to total labour income and an estimated 80 per cent of Native households participated in the domestic economy, for a total of 4,000 Native households and 5,500 active harvesters. As well, several thousand women prepared the meat for consumption. Even though harvesting was done part time, Usher (1989) estimated that the average arctic hunter took 1,000 to 1,500 kilograms of meat and fish annually with an imputed value of $10,000 to $15,000. Imputed values are calculated using the Berger Commission approach, in which the harvest of bush food is converted into dollar values by calculating the cost of a comparable kind of meat in the local store (Usher 1976; Berger 1977). Harvested waterfowl, for example, is valued by comparing it to the local store cost of chicken, and big and small game is compared to local red meat prices.

In the Hudson Bay bioregion, the major harvest of the land for the aboriginal populations is meat from hunting, fishing, and trapping. Table 9.3 summarizes wildlife harvest studies by region; it does not include studies based on actual consumption or nutritional surveys. The review shows that most of the values fall in the range from 50 to 350 kilograms of potential edible meat per capita (man, woman, and child) per year. The more northerly Inuit communities ranged between 200 and 400 kilograms per capita per year. Québec Cree communities fell between 100 and 150 kilograms per capita per year in the 1970s, and the Ontario Cree (Mushkegowuk region) averaged 106 kilograms per capita per year in 1990. By contrast, the figure for the northern Manitoba Cree, 52 kilograms per capita per year, is lower and should be treated with caution, given that some of the communities heavily dependent on local resources are not represented in the sample (M. Anderson, personal communication). There are no detailed regional studies for the Saskatchewan Cree or for the Dene of Manitoba and Saskatchewan. There are some studies on the fish harvests in Saskatchewan but not on total wildlife harvest, and they are similar to the Ontario and Québec values (Berkes 1990).

Table 9.3 provides little evidence that wildlife harvests have been declining in recent years. One might expect a decline in per capita harvests, if not in the total community harvest. Such a hypothesis is not supported by the data for Keewatin and Hudson Bay Lowlands-Mushkegowuk region. It may be supported, however, for the data for northern Québec, keeping in mind that the James Bay I hydro-electric project was under construction in the 1970s. Other analyses of quantitative changes in harvesting over time indicated that there is evidence

Table 9.3

Wildlife harvest studies by region

Region	Year	Potential edible weight (kg)[1]	Population	Per capita (kg/year)	Reference
Baffin region[2]	1984	924,635	2,689	344	Pattimore (1985)
Keewatin[3]	1981-2	829,440	3,769[4]	220	Gamble (1984, 1987)
	1982-3	793,003	3,882	204	Gamble (1984, 1987)
	1984-5	895,298	3,999	224	Gamble (1984, 1987)
Northern Québec Inuit[5]	1976	1,403,846	3,427[6]	410	JB&NQNHRC (1988)
	1977	1,181,159	3,530	335	JB&NQNHRC (1988)
	1978	852,432	3,636	234	JB&NQNHRC (1988)
	1979	1,096,408	3,745	293	JB&NQNHRC (1988)
	1980	1,100,179	3,857	285	JB&NQNHRC (1988)
Northern Québec Cree[7]	1974-5	918,182	6,267	147	JB&NQNHRC (1982)
	1975-6	783,909	6,462	121	JB&NQNHRC (1982)
	1976-7	876,954	6,626	132	JB&NQNHRC (1982)
	1977-8	766,964	6,870	112	JB&NQNHRC (1982)
	1978-9	809,181	7,022	115	JB&NQNHRC (1982)

(continued on next page)

Table 9.3 (continued)

Wildlife harvest studies by region

Region	Year	Potential edible weight (kg)[1]	Population	Per capita (kg/year)	Reference
Hudson Bay lowlands[8]	1981-2	350,147[9]	4,700[10]	75	Thompson and Hutchison (1989)
	1982-3	351,595	4,700	75	
Mushkegowuk[11]	1990	686,713	6,470	106	Berkes et al. (1994)
Northern Manitoba[12]	1983-4	355,529	6,808	52	Wagner (1985)

Notes:

1 Calculated by converting the number of animals harvested into food weights. Does not include berries, wild rice, or wildfowl eggs.

2 Foxe Basin only. Includes Cape Dorset, Hall Beach, Igloolik, Lake Harbour, and Sanikiluaq.

3 Includes Baker Lake, Chesterfield Inlet, Coral Harbour, Eskimo Point, Rankin Inlet, Repulse Bay, and Whale Cove.

4 Population given only for 1983. Other years estimated on the basis of 3 per cent per year adjustments.

5 Includes Kuujjuarapik, Inukjuak, Akulivik, Salluit, Kangiqsujuaq, Quaqtac, Kangirsuk, Aupaluk, Tasiujaq, Kuujjuaq, Kangiqsualujjuaq, Killiniq, and Chisasibi.

6 Population given only for 1976. Subsequent years are estimated on the basis of 3 per cent per year increase.

7 Includes Great Whale, Fort George, Paint Hills, Eastmain, Rupert House, Nemaska, Mistassini, and Waswanipi.

8 Includes Moose Factory, Moosonee, Winisk (Peawanuck), Fort Severn, Attawapiskat, Kashechewan, Fort Albany, and Moose River Crossing. Some communities did not participate in the study and their harvests were estimated on the basis of adjacent communities.

9 Beaver, muskrat, and sturgeon (considered commercial species) were not included in the questionnaire.

10 Resident Native population (Indian status) (OMNR 1985).

11 Includes Moose Factory, Moosonee, New Post, Fort Albany, Attawapiskat, Kashechewan, Peawanuck, and Fort Severn.

12 Includes the communities of Berens River, Cross Lake, Hollow Water, Mathias Caalomb (at Pukatawagan), Split Lake, and The Pas. Excludes agricultural communities. Wagner's harvest numbers were converted into potential edible weights using conversions in Berkes et al. (1994).

of both declines *and* increases in different communities in per capita subsistence fish harvests, as shown by Berkes (1990).

Table 9.4 provides a summary of the imputed value per household of subsistence bush meat in the study area. Regional studies in Table 9.3 are also listed in Table 9.4 if the author provided replacement values for bush food. In fact, any harvest value reported in Table 9.3 could be converted into imputed food values if store prices were known. Table 9.4 includes three additional community studies, Sanikiluaq (NWT), Pinehouse (Saskatchewan), and Wemindji (Québec). Table 9.4 shows that most values fell in the range of $5,000 to $20,000 per household. Québec Cree communities were in the $8,000 range and Ontario Cree in the $7,000 range. The inclusion of values for fuelwood, berries, and fur added about another $1,000 per household per year in the case of Mushkegowuk Cree (Berkes et al. 1994).

Offsetting the value of country food are the cash costs incurred in conducting harvesting activities using modern rapid transport such as snowmobiles, canoes with outboard motors, charter aircraft, trucks where roads are available, and all-terrain vehicles. Usher (1989) estimated that the capital and operating costs ranged from $5,000 to $10,000 annually in the Northwest Territories. For the eastern James Bay Cree, Scott and Feit (1992, 135) cited a figure of $4,583 for 1976-7 as the annual cash costs of all harvesting activities.

A significant part of the cash income of households is used to support country food production. Quigley and McBride (1987) pointed out that hunting was possible only following certain capital expenditures for equipment and transport. These costs can be considerable but necessary; since hunters no longer live on the land year round but operate from communities, they are dependent on rapid transport to do any hunting at all. Support for hunters is a controversial subject, with some experts holding the view that expenditures for subsistence harvesting often exceed the replacement value of the food produced. The evidence indicates, however, that expenditures for items such as snowmobiles and canoes equipped with outboards cannot be entirely attributed to harvesting. The communities of Fort Albany and Kashechewan had similar populations, for example, but a very different harvesting activity profile in 1990, with a total of 11,386 person-days of harvesting in Kashechewan (one of the highest in the Mushkegowuk region) compared to 1,780 person-days in Fort Albany (one of the lowest). The percentage of equipment – motorized canoes and snowmobiles – owned by heads of households in the two communities was almost identical (Berkes et al. 1994).

Table 9.4

Imputed value of subsistence bush meat

| Region | Year | Potential edible weight (kg)[1] | Imputed value ($)[2] | No. of households[3] | Value per household per year | | Reference |
					Current $ (year of study)	Constant $ (1991)[4]	
Sanikiluaq[5]	1984	289,750	2,917,515	79	36,930	50,594	Quigley and McBride (1987)
Keewatin[6]	1981-2	829,440	7,879,680	665	11,849	17,892	Gamble (1984, 1987)
	1982-3	793,003	7,533,529	685[7]	10,998	15,727	Gamble (1984, 1987)
	1984-5	895,298	8,505,331	705	12,064	15,925	Gamble (1984, 1987)
Mushkegowuk[8]	1990	686,713	7,846,155	1,116	7,031	7,453	Berkes et al. (1984)
Pinehouse	1983-4	84,455	451,307	98	4,605	6,290	NVP (1987), Tobias and Kay (1994)
Wemindji	1975-6	67,636	372,000	117	3,180	8,459	Scott (1982)
	1976-7	79,272	436,000	121	3,603	8,863	Scott (1982)

| Northern Manitoba[9] | 1983-4 | 355,529 | 1,462,931 | 1,238 | 1,167 | 1,594 | Wagner (1985) |

Notes:

1 Calculated by converting the number of animals harvested into food weights. Does not include berries, wild rice, or wildfowl eggs.
2 The average price of the replacement value of store meat was applied to the harvest value to estimate imputed value.
3 If the number of households is not provided, it is estimated assuming 5.5 people per household.
4 Conversions have been made to current dollars using the Consumer Price Index.
5 The figures for Sanikiluaq should be used with caution as the community considers the harvest figure to be inflated (Lucassie Arragutainaq, personal communication).
6 Includes Baker Lake, Chesterfield Inlet, Coral Harbour, Eskimo Point, Rankin Inlet, Repulse Bay, and Whale Cove.
7 Figure given only for 1983. Other years are estimated on the basis of 3 per cent per year adjustments.
8 Includes Moose Factory, Moosonee, New Post, Fort Albany, Attawapiskat, Kashechewan, Peawanuck, and Fort Severn.
9 See Table 9.3 n. 12.

The Bush Sector in the Overall Economy

Table 9.5 provides a summary of studies of the bush sector compared to the overall cash economy of Hudson Bay bioregion communities and areas. The Sanikiluaq study collected data on income and expenditure flows to quantify the economic significance of the traditional sector in one Inuit community. In the Mushkegowuk study, Farley (1992) estimated average household income of $25,500 for 1990-1, including $10,000 in wages (formal employment), $13,000 in income support (including transfer payments), and $2,500 'other.' The table also includes data from northern Manitoba, Waswanipi and Wemindji (Québec), and Pinehouse (Saskatchewan).

The comparison of imputed values with cash incomes is controversial. Some authors have expressed the value of the traditional sector as a percentage of the overall economy (e.g., Quigley and McBride 1987). Others think that the cash economy and imputed values for the subsistence economy should not be combined (F. Hill, personal communication). In Table 9.5 we have chosen to express the magnitude of the imputed values of the harvest not as a percentage of the total economy but as a ratio of the cash economy to the bush economy. These ratios ranged from a high of 1:1.37 in Sanikiluaq, where the community has questioned the numbers used in the subsistence study as too high (L. Arrangutainaq, personal communication), to a low of 1:0.13 in northern Manitoba. Most of the ratios fell in the range of 1:0.33 to 1:0.66 for the more recent studies, but Table 9.5 does not include any other Inuit area, where the ratios would have been higher.

Available literature on the role of bush economy in the overall economy is fragmentary, and the references in Table 9.5 fall short of providing historical depth or even recent trends. Clearly, if one goes back in time, the bush sector *was* the overall economy. The first appearance of the wage sector is difficult to gauge, but transfer payments started with the institution of universal family allowances in Canada in 1945 (George and Preston 1987). In what must have been one of the earliest studies of a Native economy, Honigmann (1961) found that the Attawapiskat Cree had a cash income of $763 per household per year, as averaged over three years from 1945 to 1948. Most of this income (54 per cent) still came from trapping; family allowance and food relief together accounted for 35 per cent and wage income for 7 per cent. Honigmann (1961) also conducted a harvest survey, but imputed values could not be calculated because fresh meat was not available at the store in Attawapiskat at that time.

Table 9.5

The bush sector in the overall economy

Region	Year (year of study)	Total cash economy per year		Imputed value of Native traditional activities[1]		Cash economy to traditional economy	Reference
		Current $ (year of study)	Constant $ (1991)	Current $ (year of study)	Constant $ (1991)		
Sanikiluaq	1984	2,155,000	2,952,350	2,946,515	4,036,726	1:1.37	Quigley and McBride (1987)
Mushkegowuk[2]	1990	25,370,880	26,893,133	8,372,400	8,874,744	1:0.33	Berkes et al. (1994), Farley (1992)
Northern Manitoba	1985	178,827,600	236,052,430	22,367,500[3]	29,525,100	1:0.13	NMEDC (1992)
Waswanipi[4]	1968-70	251,315	774,050	209,665	645,768	1:0.83	Feit (1991)
	1982	1,814,451[5]	2,739,821	684,667	1,033,847	1:0.38	Feit (1991)
Wemindji	1975-6	625,000	1,687,500	531,000	1,433,700	1:0.85	Scott (1982)
	1977-8	1,184,000	2,960,000	732,000	1,830,000	1:0.62	Scott (1982)
Pinehouse	1983-4	2,101,289	2,878,766	1,135,281[6]	1,555,335	1:0.54	Tobias and Kay (1994)

Notes:
1 Includes all bush products for which data are available. These include meat, fur, fuelwood, berries, and wild rice.
2 Includes Moose Factory, Moosonee, New Post, Fort Albany, Attawapiskat, Kashechewan, and Peawanuck. Excludes Fort Severn, which was not included in the Mushkegowuk region cash economy data.
3 Edible meat only. Comparable data for fish, fur, and fuel not available.
4 Excludes fuelwood, berries; includes fur, handicrafts, sales-tourism.
5 Includes payments of $915,851 under the Income Security Programme (ISP). There was no ISP in 1968-70.
6 Of this value, $451,307 is for bush meat, $108,307 is for other income-in-kind, and $575,667 is for commercial fisheries, fur, wild rice, and other commodities.

In the 1980s and early 1990s, a number of background studies were undertaken on the feasibility of subsidizing the traditional sector through hunters' income support programs: in the Mushkegowuk region, the Nishnabwe-Aski area, and the Northwest Territories (e.g., Usher 1989). As of 1996, however, there was only one regional program. Under the JB&NQA, the Cree Hunters and Trappers Income Security Programme (ISP) was introduced in 1976 (Scott and Feit 1992). Hunters and trappers who meet eligibility criteria receive payments for days that they and their families spend outside the settlement in harvesting activities. The impact of this program on access to lands and to social exchanges was analyzed by Scott (1982), Feit (1989; 1991), Salisbury (1986), and Scott and Feit (1992). There was an initial increase in the number of active hunters and trappers as well as in the amount of time they spent in the bush, but the demand levelled off over the years. The program encouraged more family-level bush activity, reversing the trend of women staying in the settlement, and in some communities the number of children going into the bush increased as well, thus improving opportunities for the transmission of traditional knowledge and skills (Ohmagari 1995). The ISP contributed to making bush life viable again in the perception of hunters and trappers. It had a positive cultural impact also by supporting the traditional Cree values of self-reliance, cooperation, reciprocity, and sharing. Over half the hunting groups harvested more than they could use and shared the surplus with others in the community.

In Waswanipi, ISP benefits accounted for almost half the cash income. Many wage earners were part-time hunters and the transition from full-time hunter to full-time wage earner and back again was common. Most extended families had members in each group, and full-time community residents got country food from relatives and friends who harvested game, in exchange for money or favours. The use of charter airplanes and trucks in getting to the bush allowed more frequent trips and enabled hunters to take more supplies and to bring back more food. Increased mobility also spread hunting activity over a wider area and enabled access to the more remote, infrequently used regions. The result was an enhanced relationship of interdependence and cooperation rather than of competition (Feit 1991).

Despite the increased number of hunters, access to hunting territories continued to be controlled by hunting stewards. The hunting territory system appeared to remain effective for managing wildlife despite intensification of hunting effort. Following an initial increase in the moose hunting effort after 1976, for example, the Waswanipi reduced annual harvests to the earlier, presumably more sustainable levels. Figure 9.8 shows a summary of the eighteen years of experience with the ISP. The resident Native population of the region has been increasing and per cent participation in ISP has been declining, but the actual number of ISP participants has remained relatively steady, providing a healthy base for the mixed economy. This trend suggests that economic and cultural sustainability fostered by the ISP has not been compromised by loss of ecological sustainability. Despite increasing population, the land tenure system and common property institutions of the eastern James Bay Cree have limited the number of hunters on the land and thus the hunting pressure.

Also in Québec's James Bay, Salisbury's (1986) analysis showed that from 1971 to 1981, the real income per capita increased 83 per cent, and the income per household, including the imputed value of bush meat, reached $14,366 in 1981 terms – within the range of Southern Canadian families. Much of this increase came from ISP payments, which accounted for 21 per cent of all income in 1981. Welfare declined from 11 per cent of total income in 1971 to 3 per cent in 1981 (Salisbury 1986, 94). The major increase in wage income was in professional, managerial, and white-collar jobs brought about by the self-government provisions of the JB&NQA, not in hydro-electric jobs related to development!

Policy Implications

In the mixed economy of northern Native peoples, the bush sector is no longer the entire economy. Fur income has declined to become a minor item in the overall economy, but the imputed value of meat and other products from the land is comparable to the total cash income from all sources in the more remote regions. In the less remote boreal-subarctic parts of the bioregion, the imputed value of the bush sector is about half of the total cash income. Yet government statistics do not even include the value of subsistence harvests, and they categorize self-sufficient hunters as 'unemployed.' Thus, on the one hand, the values of subsistence are dismissed, but on the other, imputed values of bush food are overstated by not taking into account the production cost and the opportunity cost of time spent in the bush.

The development of appropriate new policies requires baseline information for the calculation of future losses from development projects. Lack of baseline data on subsistence harvests is a major problem and has impeded the calculation of compensation payments for northern Manitoba groups affected by hydro-electric development (Usher and Weinstein 1991). Similar issues have come up elsewhere, including the Moose River basin. Compensation is, in any case, not a satisfactory social

Figure 9.8

Eastern James Bay Cree participation in the Income Security Programme

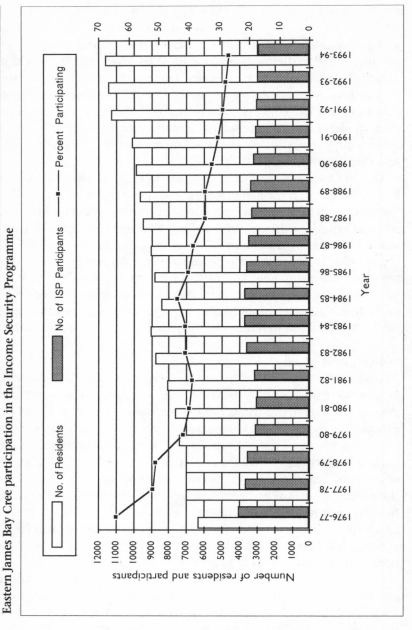

Source: Annual Reports, Cree Hunters and Trappers Income Security Board

solution. Better policy mechanisms need to be developed to calculate present values and future potential losses *before* development occurs.

The question of carrying capacity is crucial for sustainable development planning in the North. The assessment of biological productivity of the land and resource base is needed, in relation to current and projected aboriginal populations and their land use. Such work would not be on carrying capacity in the classical biological sense of a constant and deterministic limit but in a dynamic sense, with multiple equilibria corresponding to different options of institutional, social, and economic organization (Gunderson, Holling, and Light 1995). As well, information on carrying capacity would help the evaluation of the planned and potential impact of development.

Analysis of the role of the bush economy in the overall economy needs an historical dimension to follow trends and their likely causes, 'for making these studies more comparable from one community or region to another, and for providing longitudinal data through re-studies of the same communities/regions at consistent intervals' (C. Scott, personal communication). Policies are needed in support of subsistence economies. Social and economic programs such as hunters' income support can then be formulated to remedy the loss of land and resources. Social health and culture need to be integrated into planning for such programs, since loss of subsistence resources has ramifications beyond the merely economic. As a major agenda for policy development, the larger Canadian society would need to know the cost of maintaining self-sufficient, viable northern mixed economies, as opposed to the costs of dealing with social pathologies of Native populations migrating into urban centres following the collapse of local northern economies. In effect, what is needed is sustainable development information that allows decisionmakers to assess the real trade-offs.

Policies for Sustainability

'Yukon elders were asked to define development. After some deliberation, they said that development was "spirituality" ... They were then asked to examine the meaning of economic development and again, after some deliberation, they concluded that it was "respect." A development model based on exploitation had little use for respect' (Brascoupé 1992, 8).

Aboriginal groups of the Hudson Bay area have been adapting to development brought about by European contact since 1670 (Francis and Morantz 1983). The real issue is not *whether* there should be development but the *kind* of development. George and Preston (1987), who studied the work patterns of the Omushkego (West Main) Cree, observed that the Cree adapted to European technology and institutions such as those associated with the fur trade without cultural disintegration. To the extent that the fur trade fitted well with the seasonal round of activities of the aboriginal groups and relied on skills that they possessed and readily perfected, the argument could be made that fur trading was culturally sustainable development.

As income from trapping declined, wage employment opportunities became important in making settlement life attractive (George and Preston 1987). Yet a large proportion of the cash income was being used to support hunting, fishing, and trapping, partly because these activities were essential to indigenous cultural identity and partly because they provided high-quality food. For indigenous communities to become more self-reliant and pursue a culturally sustainable lifestyle, George and Preston recommended flexible work periods and employment schemes in which wage work could be seasonally rotated to allow continuation of traditional harvesting activities.

Policies for sustainable development in the North need to address questions such as the extent to which wage employment is an appropriate part of a mixed economy and whether employment creation through larger power, forestry, and mining developments has a role to play. The opposition of the Cree to the proposed Moose River basin development in 1991-2 and of the Québec Cree to James Bay II in 1992-4 indicated that these aboriginal groups considered the costs of large-scale development to be greater than the benefits. The cultural component of these costs was overwhelmingly important. There is a widespread feeling among aboriginal groups of the bioregion that northern economic development policies of the past have not brought benefits but merely undermined aboriginal economies (R. Matthew, personal communication; TEKMS 1994).

Development projects have thus triggered a renewed struggle for control of the land and resources and stimulated the revitalization of indigenous cultures. This can be said of developments such as James Bay, Churchill-Nelson, and the Moose River basin, all of which have helped focus attention not only on environmental degradation but also on the consequences for the culture of indigenous peoples. This phenomenon applies equally well to the whole polar basin (Chance 1993).

Subsistence, Aboriginal Cultures, Traditional Knowledge
Continued Native dependence on subsistence has been a crucial factor in aboriginal response to development. 'Subsistence is generally thought of as a material or economic aspect of a people's lifeway, whereas in reality ... it is perhaps most important in today's mixed economy northern

communities in sustaining very important social relationships and distinctive cultural characteristics in that society' (M.M.R. Freeman, personal communication). Subsistence helps maintain social and cultural identity and provides a source of social values. Indigenous knowledge, ethical values, and cultural identity are transferred to succeeding generations through the annual, cyclical repetition of subsistence activities (Freeman 1993). The loss of subsistence resources would dismantle 'the social relations of production,' which include 'the socialization of children, mutual aid and sharing, and the reinforcement of stewardship and use arrangements with respect to land and resources' (Usher 1981, 61).

Although many observers have played down the role of the traditional land-based economy, characterized it as an anachronism, and predicted its demise, the fact of the matter is that it has not disappeared. There are very few wage income opportunities in northern communities; people need food; the major produce of these non-agricultural areas is wild meat; and wildlife harvesting is a biologically and culturally appropriate way of obtaining food. As Usher (1976) put it, 'the North may well be the only place where a poor man's table is laden with meat'.

Even in the most recent studies, in the Mushkegowuk region, northern Ontario, the bush harvest was 106 kilograms per person per year (Berkes et al. 1994), which is comparable to the value (100 kilograms per person per year) given for 1975 in the Mackenzie Valley region (Berger 1977). A case can be made that the extensive use of land and the harvest of bush food may actually have increased in the last two decades because of revival of interest and increase in the availability of disposable cash for the purchase of mechanized transport for hunters who operate from permanent communities (Usher 1987; Berkes 1990). Such a pattern would not be biophysically sustainable if it were not that aboriginal land use institutions appear to limit the number of hunters in a given area. The sustainable development of the North as 'homeland' may do well to start with the assumption that strengthening the bush economy would substantially improve the quality of life of aboriginal peoples (Hill 1986). The link between cultural sustainability and subsistence is real and has to do with the identification of indigenous peoples with the land (Freeman 1993). The traditional economy warrants support if sustainable development policies consider a wider range of socio-economic benefits than do conventional economic development policies.

In retrospect, the development policies of the 1950s and 1960s appear to have overestimated the capacity of the resource extraction economy to absorb the indigenous labour force. It was little appreciated that this 'labour force' was in fact not mobile and not predisposed, for cultural reasons, to the kind of work offered by the resource economy. The social planners' wisdom also appears to have underestimated Native attachment to the land and to related cultural values. Thus, the vision of integrating indigenous people into the resource extraction economy of the North was built on poor premises. Indigenous peoples in fact had little choice but to return to hunting; there was not much else for them to live on.

Can sustainable development policies for the North be based on aboriginal aspirations? There is no uniform, single Native vision for the future of land-based activities. In northern Manitoba, for example, it seems that there is a strong desire by many indigenous groups to participate in the resource economy and to share benefits with Euro-Canadians (NMEDC 1993; T. Henley, personal communication). One of the impediments to such aspirations is that resource extraction industries and one-industry towns tend to be relatively short-lived. The Naskapi spent the years between the mid-1950s and the late 1970s as urbanized wage-earners in Schefferville, one of the largest subarctic cities in Canada at that time. When the iron ore mine closed down and the city of Schefferville was reduced to a settlement of less than 1,000, the Naskapi were stranded, having spent twenty-five years off the land (P. Wilkinson, personal communication). A good part of the Northeastern Québec Agreement, which surrenders traditional Naskapi land, deals with social and economic development to resurrect Native land use and bring back the hunting economy.

Behind economic and cultural sustainability is Native indigenous knowledge of land and animals, which constitutes a distinctive ethnoscientific tradition. So far, TEK has not been brought to bear on the real issues, and this is only partly because its study is a relatively new area. Collecting information about TEK is in itself 'no guarantee of the preservation of this knowledge in any form relevant to resource management and sustainable development,' as C. Scott (personal communication) observed. Further,

> TEK has not been used in mainstream natural resource management despite its demonstrated efficacy in various indigenous contexts; and it has yet to be brought to bear in environmental review in decisive ways – this, no doubt, has as much to do with the politics of development as with the applicability of indigenous knowledge to the intellectual issues of environmental assessment. Indigenous knowledge is, after all, valid in precisely those social contexts that development projects put at risk, and it is difficult to accept the validity of local expertise without accepting the validity of the society-land relationship that sustains it (C. Scott, personal communication).

Much the same can be said for the use of TEK in resource management. The management of northern resources by government agencies has marginalized local resource management systems (Usher 1987; Berkes, George, and Preston 1991). Real participation of Native peoples in the management of resources that affect their welfare requires the use of indigenous knowledge systems. Thus, TEK should be considered the basis of co-management, not lower order co-management but co-management that involves partnership in decision-making and the delegation of management responsibility (Figure 9.9). There are quite a few co-management agreements in the bioregion. In Manitoba alone, Haugh (1994) has identified sixteen. A sampling of these, with an additional three examples from Osherenko (1988), is summarized in Table 9.6. Perhaps the most robust cases among the eight in the table are those mandated by the JB&NQA and the Nunavut Agreement, both of which have legislative bases. Some, such as the Beverly and Kaminuriak case, have been operating successfully for a long time (Osherenko 1988). Others, such as the Northern Flood Agreement, have not worked well (Haugh 1994).

Figure 9.9

Levels of co-management

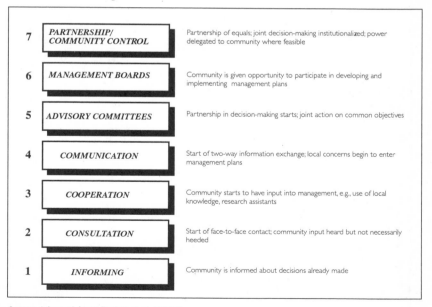

7	*PARTNERSHIP/ COMMUNITY CONTROL*	Partnership of equals; joint decision-making institutionalized; power delegated to community where feasible
6	*MANAGEMENT BOARDS*	Community is given opportunity to participate in developing and implementing management plans
5	*ADVISORY COMMITTEES*	Partnership in decision-making starts; joint action on common objectives
4	*COMMUNICATION*	Start of two-way information exchange; local concerns begin to enter management plans
3	*COOPERATION*	Community starts to have input into management, e.g., use of local knowledge, research assistants
2	*CONSULTATION*	Start of face-to-face contact; community input heard but not necessarily heeded
1	*INFORMING*	Community is informed about decisions already made

Source: Adapted from Berkes et al. (1991)

Table 9.6

Examples of co-management agreements

Number	Regime	Year created	Resources covered	Location	Participants
1	James Bay and Northern Québec hunting, fishing, and trapping regime	1975	All marine and terrestrial species	James Bay and Northern Québec	Province of Québec (4),[1] Government of Canada (4), Inuit (3), Cree (3), Naskapi (2)
2	Nunavut Wildlife Management Board	1992	All marine and terrestrial species	Nunavut Settlement Area (eastern Arctic)	Designated Inuit organizations (4), governor in council (3), commissioner in executive council (1), chair appointed by governor in council from nominations from the board
3	Beverly and Kaminuriak cariboo management regime	1982	Beverly and Kaminuriak cariboo herds	Central Arctic/ west Hudson Bay	INAC (1), Environment Canada (1), MNDR (1), SDP (1), NWTRR (1); members from user communities, NWT Inuit (2), Manitoba Dene (2), Sask. (2), NWT Dene (2)
4	Beluga management regime	1986	Belugas of eastern James Bay, Hudson Strait, and Ungava Bay	Northern Québec	DFO, Anguvigaq (regional wildlife organization), Anguvigapiks (local wildlife committees)
5	Northern Flood Agreement Wildlife Advisory and Planning Board	1979	All aquatic and terrestrial species	Resource areas of the Cross Lake, Norway House, Nelson House and York Landing FNs	Community representatives from Agreement areas, INAC, DNR, MDNA, Environment Canada[2]

6	Nelson River Sturgeon Management Agreement	1992	Sturgeon	Nelson River and tributary sturgeon spawning streams	Norway House, Cross Lake, Split Lake, York Factory, Fox Lake, War Lake FNs (6), Wabowden, Thicket Portage, Ilford and Pikwitonei (4), MKO, MMF, MH (3 ex-officio members)
7	Split Lake Cree Resource Management Board	1992	All aquatic and terrestrial species	Resource area corresponding to the registered trap-line district of the Split Lake Cree Nation	Split Lake Cree Nation-York Factory and Fox Lake FNs invited to participate in deliberations affecting their resource use interests (5), INAC, MDNR, MDNA, MDE, Gillam (5)
8	Whiteshell Wild Rice Management Agreement	1983	Wild rice	Whiteshell Provincial Park (southeast Manitoba)	Native Advisory Committee: Interlake Tribal Council, SE Resource Development Council, Sagkeeng FN, Communities of Black River, Scanterbury, Manitoba Sectoral Committee (8), MDNR, INAC (6), RCMP Whitemouth (1)

Acronyms:

DFO	Department of Fisheries and Oceans	MH	Manitoba Hydro
FN	First Nations	MKO	Manitoba Keewatinowi Okimakanak
INAC	Indian and Northern Affairs Canada	MMF	Manitoba Métis Federation
MDE	Manitoba Department of Environment	NWTRR	NWT Renewable Resources Department
MDNA	Manitoba Department of Northern Affairs	SDP	Saskatchewan Department of Parks
MDNR	Manitoba Department of Natural Resources		

Notes:

1 Numbers in parentheses indicate the number of votes each party has on the management board.

2 There is no board membership. Department staff act as advisers and ministers approve board recommendations only.

Sources: Osherenko (1988), Haugh (1994), and R. Riewe (personal communication) on the basis of the Nunavut Agreement.

Some Principles for Policy Development

Several principles can be derived from experience in the Hudson Bay bioregion. Many are applicable to other parts of the Canadian North, and probably to lands inhabited by indigenous peoples elsewhere, and can guide policy priorities:

(1) *Culturally sustainable planning development.* Sustainable development in the bioregion needs to take into account indigenous cultures, which remain different and distinct from the dominant Euro-Canadian culture. To be culturally sustainable, development should reinforce cultural values such as self-reliance, cooperation, sharing, reciprocity, and respect. As the indigenous concept of respect applies equally well to people and nature, cultural sustainability reinforces ecological sustainability.

(2) *Support of subsistence economies.* For aboriginal people, subsistence is part of a mixed economy that assures self-reliance and cultural sustainability. Yet development in the North has often operated to the detriment of subsistence economies. A new balance can be achieved by including socio-economic objectives in development planning and reorienting investment policies from resource extraction to community-based development. An essential component of such a policy change would be to seek development opportunities that are consistent with subsistence activities and the maintenance of environmental quality, again reinforcing ecological sustainability.

(3) *Recognition and use of traditional ecological knowledge.* Recognizing the value of TEK is relatively easy, but using it in resource management, impact assessment, and development planning is not because that would require reassessment of some of the basic values and policies behind each of these activities. TEK is not value free. As a complex system of knowledge, practice, and belief, it embodies indigenous cultural values, world views, and institutions. Sustainable development policy for the North needs to design processes that incorporate TEK from the very beginning.

(4) *Co-management of land and resources.* A key role for TEK is in the joint management of resources by government experts and indigenous resource users. Without TEK, there is no co-management but merely tokenism or the co-opting of local users into a government management process. Real co-management is attractive to both parties for its potential in lowering management costs, improving enforcement, assuring compliance, improving the quality of information, and

providing rapid information feedback. All of these facilitate more sustainable outcomes.

(5) *Building and strengthening of indigenous social institutions.* Many indigenous social institutions, including those important for resource management, have been weakened over the years. Successful co-management requires empowerment of Native communities to help strengthen these institutions, especially in areas covered by the older treaties, where a management vacuum has now developed. In such areas, resource co-management will become an essential and major component of self-government. The general policy direction needed is the legal recognition of aboriginal self-governance.

(6) *Recognition of communal property rights of indigenous groups.* Ownership of resources is the overriding determinant of success in co-management and self-government. Indigenous people have a stake in conservation if, and only if, they have property rights. The traditional property rights regime for control of land and resources in northern Hudson-James Bay is communal property. This regime still persists but requires legal recognition. The community should therefore control access to resources and establish rights and responsibil-ities for their use. The 'unoccupied Crown land' under Canadian law is often 'communal land' under traditional land tenure, as in the Mushkegowuk region.

(7) *Assessment of the cumulative impact of development projects.* There is an emerging consensus among scientists and indigenous groups that the overall impact of hydro-electric projects in Hudson-James Bay may be greater than the sum of their individual effects. This applies to both environmental and cultural impact, which indigenous peoples are often the first to experience. Although there are some legal provisions for public participation in impact assessment in various northern regions, assessment of cumulative effects has only recently started (McDonald, Arrangutainaq, and Novalinga 1995).

Conclusion

Indigenous peoples of the world mostly inhabit marginal lands onto which the industrialized world has been encroaching. Chapter 26 of *Agenda 21* argues that indigenous people hold the key for the sustainable development of these lands and urges their enrolment in a partnership for conservation and development planning, starting with measures to protect their land rights and culture. The *Agenda 21* initiative coincides with movements of cultural revival and rediscovery of tradition in aboriginal and tribal groups in many parts of the world (ICIHI 1987), including India, the Philippines, Scandinavia, Australia, New Zealand, Hawaii, and Brazil.

In Canada, much of the discussion about aboriginal peoples has centred on the question of self-government, consistent with the *Agenda 21* objective of empowering indigenous peoples by recognizing their traditional knowledge and values, enabling them to participate in national policies and in sustainable development planning. The Royal Commission on Aboriginal Peoples, also addressing questions related to self-government, has not filed its report at the time of writing. The analysis in this chapter suggests that self-government consisting merely of local powers would not suffice. It would also have to include some degree of control over land and resources used by the various groups. As in the Mushkegowuk example, reserve land may be less than 0.5 per cent of the land actually used.

Recognition of communal property rights to land and resources fosters good stewardship of resources; open access policies do not. In the experience of aboriginal groups in the bioregion, central governments have always allowed open access to their land, permitting mining, forestry, and power projects without even consulting with the people of the area (TEKMS 1994). Establishing legally backed rights and responsibilities and building appropriate institutions to bring indigenous peoples up to speed for the task helps make aboriginal groups equal partners in resource management. Traditional ecological knowledge is not merely information on the local biophysical environment but is a complex system of knowledge, practice, and belief. It can be brought to the service of sustainable development through co-management arrangements that foster joint decision-making and power sharing.

The current view of the North as a development frontier has not led to policies that can be considered successful from either a northern or a southern perspective (Chance 1993). Development has not been sustainable for the most part; local economies have more cash flow than before, but the social and economic problems of development and social change have been very costly. The future of the northern economy and the roles of Native land use, indigenous knowledge, and subsistence are being debated in government, university, NGO, and indigenous peoples' circles. Policies for northern economic development, land use and control, and self-government are all in a period of rapid change. The failure of many of the past policies has, in effect, forced an assessment of development alternatives that are more sustainable environmentally, culturally, and economically.

Acknowledgments

This chapter is partly based on a technical report prepared for the Hudson Bay Program. We thank Ann Dale and John Robinson for their comments on the chapter. Michael Anderson (Manitoba Keewatinowi Okimakinak), Milton Freeman (University of Alberta), Peter George (McMaster), Fred Hill (Indian and Northern Affairs Canada), Peter Sly (Rawson Academy), and Colin Scott (McGill) provided helpful comments and criticisms on an earlier draft. We have benefited from the comments and information provided by Glen Okrainetz (CARC), Thomas Henley (University of Manitoba), Georg Lithman (Stockholm University), Robbie Matthew (Chisasibi), Harvey Payne (Waterhen), Dick Preston (McMaster), Rick Riewe (University of Manitoba), Paul Wilkinson (P.W. and Associates), and David Young (Symbion). A digitized base map was provided courtesy of Natural Resources Canada, and technical support in producing the final maps was provided by David Mosscrop (University of Manitoba). Fikret Berkes's work has been supported by the Social Sciences and Humanities Research Council of Canada (SSHRC). Helen Fast's HBP technical report was supported by the Hudson Bay Program.

References

Ballantyne, P., P. Brook, P. Burns et al. 1976. Aski-Puko – The Land Alone: A Report on the Expected Effects of the Proposed Hydroelectric Installations at Wintego Rapids upon the Cree of the Peter Ballantyne and Lac La Ronge Bands. Prepared for the Federation of Saskatchewan Indians

Barker, M.L., and D. Soyez. 1994. Think Locally, Act Globally? *Environment* 36 (5):12-20, 32-6

Begrand, R. 1978. *Report Accompanying the Traditional Land Use Atlas of the Churchill and Reindeer Rivers.* Saskatoon, SK: Institute for Northern Studies

Berger, T.R. 1977. *Northern Frontier Northern Homeland: The Report of the Mackenzie Valley Pipeline Inquiry.* 2 vols. Ottawa: Supply and Services Canada

Berkes, F. 1977. Fishery Resource Use in a Subarctic Indian Community. *Human Ecology* 5:289-307

–. 1979. An Investigation of Cree Indian Domestic Fisheries in Northern Quebec. *Arctic* 32:46-70

–. 1981. The Role of Self-Regulation in Living Resources Management in the North. In *Renewable Resources and the Economy of the North,* edited by M.M.R. Freeman, 166-78. Ottawa: Association of Canadian Universities for Northern Studies and Canada Man and Biosphere Programme

–. 1982. Waterfowl Management and Northern Native Peoples with Reference to Cree Hunters of James Bay. *Musk-Ox* 30:23-35

–. 1987. Common Property Resource Management and Cree Indian Fisheries in Subarctic Canada. In *The Question of the Commons,* edited by B.J. McCay and J.M. Acheson, 66-91. Tucson: University of Arizona Press

–. 1988a. Subsistence Fishing in Canada: A Note on Terminology. *Arctic* 41:319-20

–. 1988b. The Intrinsic Difficulty of Predicting Impacts: Lessons from the James Bay Hydro Project. *Environmental Impact Assessment Review* 8:201-20

–. 1990. Native Subsistence Fisheries: A Synthesis of Harvest Studies in Canada. *Arctic* 43:35-42

–. 1993. Traditional Ecological Knowledge in Perspective. In *Traditional Ecological Knowledge: Concepts and Cases,* edited by J.T. Inglis, 1-9. Ottawa: Canadian Museum of Nature and International Development Research Centre

–, ed. 1989. Common Property Resources. Ecology and Community-Based Sustainable Development. London: Belhaven

Berkes, F., D. Feeny, B.J. McCay, and J.M. Acheson. 1989. The Benefits of the Commons. *Nature* 340:91-3

Berkes, F., C. Folke, and M. Gadgil. 1995. Traditional Ecological Knowledge, Biodiversity, Resilience and Sustainability. In *Biodiversity Conservation,* edited by C.A. Perrings, K.-G. Maler, C. Folke, C.S. Holling, and B.O. Jansson, 281-99. Dordrecht: Kluwer

Berkes, F., and M.M.R. Freeman. 1986. Human Ecology and Resource Use. In *Canadian Inland Seas,* edited by I.P. Martini, 425-55. New York: Elsevier Press

Berkes, F., P. George, and R.J. Preston. 1991. Co-management. *Alternatives: Perspectives on Society, Technology and Environment* 18 (2):12-18

Berkes, F., P.J. George, R.J. Preston, A. Hughes, J. Turner, and B.D. Cummins. 1994. Wildlife Harvesting and Sustainable Regional Native Economy in the Hudson and James Bay Lowland, Ontario. *Arctic* 47:350-60

Berkes, F., A. Hughes, P.J. George, R.J. Preston, B.D. Cummins, and J. Turner. 1995. The Persistence of Aboriginal Land Use: Fish and Wildlife Harvest Areas in the Hudson and James Bay Lowland, Ontario. *Arctic* 48:81-93

Boldt, M. 1993. *Surviving as Indians. The Challenge of Self-Government.* Toronto: University of Toronto Press

Bourassa, R. 1985. *Power from the North.* Scarborough, ON: Prentice-Hall

Brandson, L.E. 1981. *From Tundra to Forest. A Chipewyan Resource Manual.* Winnipeg: Manitoba Museum of Man and Nature

Brascoupé, S. 1992. Indigenous Perspectives on International Development. *Akwe:kon Journal* 9 (2):6-17

Brightman, R.A. 1993. *Grateful Prey: Rock Cree Human-Animal Relationships.* Berkeley: University of California Press

Bruemmer, F. 1977. Life after Degradation: Imposed Civilization Killed Some Manitoba Chipewyans – The Survivors Are Going Home. *Winnipeg Free Press Weekend Magazine* 27 (2):4-7

Cameron, M., and I.M. Weiss. 1993. Organochlorine Contaminants in the Country Food Diet of the Belcher Island Inuit, Northwest Territories, Canada. *Arctic* 46:42-8

Chance, N. 1993. Commentary: Sustainable Utilization of the Arctic's Natural Resources. *Arctic* 46:iii-iv

Dacks, G. 1981. *A Choice of Futures. Politics in the Canadian North.* Toronto: Methuen

Duerden, F. 1992. A Critical Look at Sustainable Development in the Canadian North. *Arctic* 45:219-25

Durning, A.T. 1993. Supporting Indigenous Peoples. In *State of the World 1993*, edited by L.R. Brown, 80-100. New York and London: Worldwatch Institute and W.W. Norton

Dwyer, A. 1992. The Trouble at Great Whale. *Equinox* 61:29-41

Dyck, N., and J.B. Waldram, eds. 1993. *Anthropology, Public Policy and Native Peoples in Canada*. Montreal and Kingston: McGill-Queen's University Press

Farley, R.M. 1992. The Mushkegowuk Economy: 1992 Summary Report. Mushkegowuk Council, Moose Factory, Ontario

Fast, H., and F. Berkes. 1994. Native Land Use, Traditional Knowledge and the Subsistence Economy in the Hudson Bay Bioregion. Technical paper prepared for the Hudson Bay Programme. Canadian Arctic Resources Committee; Environmental Committee, Municipality of Sanikiluaq and Rawson Academy of Aquatic Science

Feit, H.A. 1979. Political Articulations of Hunters to the State: Means of Resisting Threats to Subsistence Production in the James Bay and Northern Quebec Agreement. *Études/Inuit/Studies* 3 (2):37-52

–. 1986a. James Bay Cree Indian Management and Moral Considerations of Fur-Bearers. In *Native People and Resource Management*, 49-65. Edmonton: Alberta Society of Professional Biologists

–. 1986b. Hunting and the Quest for Power: The James Bay Cree and Whitemen in the Twentieth Century. In *Native Peoples: The Canadian Experience*, edited by R.B. Morrison and C.R. Wilson, 75-91. Ottawa: Carleton University Press

–. 1987a. North American Native Hunting and Management of Moose Populations. *Swedish Wildlife Research Vitlrevy Supplement* 1:25-42

–. 1987b. Waswanipi Cree Management of Land and Wildlife: Cree Cultural Ecology. In *Native Peoples: Native Lands*, edited by B. Cox, 75-91. Ottawa: Carleton University Press

–. 1989. James Bay Cree Self-Governance and Land Management. In *We Are Here: Politics of Aboriginal Land Tenure*, edited by E.N. Wilmsen, 68-98. Berkeley: University of California Press

–. 1991. Gifts of the Land: Hunting Territories, Guaranteed Incomes and the Construction of Social Relations in James Bay Cree Society. *Senri Ethnological Studies* 30:223-68

Fenge, T. 1992. Hydroelectric Power on the Great Whale River. *Northern Perspectives* 20 (2):n.p.

Francis, D., and T. Morantz. 1983. *Partners in Furs: A History of the Fur Trade in Eastern James Bay 1600-1870*. Kingston and Montreal: McGill-Queen's University Press

Freeman, M.M.R. 1979. Traditional Land Users as a Legitimate Source of Environmental Expertise. In *The Canadian National Parks: Today and Tomorrow*, edited by J.G. Nelson et al., 345-69. Waterloo, ON: University of Waterloo

–. 1989. Graphs and Gaffs: A Cautionary Tale in the Common-Property Resources Debate. In *Common Property Resources: Ecology and Community-Based Sustainable Development*, edited by F. Berkes, 92-109. London: Belhaven Press

–. 1993. The International Whaling Commission, Small-Type Whaling, and Coming to Terms with Subsistence. *Human Organization* 52 (3):243-51

–, ed. 1976. *Report of the Inuit Land Use and Occupancy Project.* 3 vols. Ottawa: Department of Indian and Northern Affairs

Gadgil, M., F. Berkes, and C. Folke. 1993. Indigenous Knowledge for Biodiversity Conservation. *Ambio* 22:151-6

Gamble, R.L. 1984. A Preliminary Study of the Native Harvest of Wildlife in the Keewatin Region, Northwest Territories. *Canadian Technical Report of Fisheries and Aquatic Sciences* no. 1282

–. 1987. Native Harvest of Wildlife in the Keewatin Region, Northwest Territories for the Period October 1984 to September 1985. *Canadian Technical Report of Fisheries and Aquatic Sciences* no. 1544

George, P.J., F. Berkes, and R.J. Preston. 1995. Aboriginal Harvesting in the Moose River Basin: A Historical and Contemporary Analysis. *Canadian Review of Sociology and Anthropology* 32:69-90

George, P.J., and R.J. Preston. 1987. Going in Between: The Impact of European Technology on the Work Patterns of the West Main Cree of Northern Ontario. *Journal of Economic History* 47:447-60

Graburn, N.H.H. 1969. *Eskimos without Igloos: Social and Economic Development in Sugluk.* Toronto: Little, Brown

Gunderson, L.H., C.S. Holling, and S.S. Light, eds. 1995. *Barriers and Bridges to the Renewal of Ecosystems and Institutions.* New York: Columbia University Press

Haugh, A. 1994. Balancing Rights, Powers and Privileges: A Survey and Evaluation of Natural Resource Co-management Agreements Reached by the Government and First Nations of Manitoba. Practicum, Natural Resources Institute, University of Manitoba, Winnipeg

Hill, F.I. 1986. Commentary on 'Prospects for the North Canadian Native Economy.' *Polar Record* 23 (142):91-4

Hill, S. 1993. Fox Lake First Nation Land Use and Occupancy: Living Memory of the Fox Lake Cree. Practicum, Natural Resources Institute, University of Manitoba, Winnipeg

Honigmann, J.J. 1961. *Foodways in a Muskeg Community: An Anthropological Report on the Attawapiskat Indians.* Ottawa: Northern Co-ordination and Research Centre, Department of Northern Affairs and National Resources

–. 1981. West Main Cree. In *Subarctic.* vol. 6 of *Handbook of North American Indians,* edited by J. Helm, 217-30. Washington, DC: Smithsonian Institution

Hrenchuk, C. 1991. South Indian Lake Land Use and Occupancy: Kayas Akwa Wapahki. Practicum, Natural Resources Institute, University of Manitoba, Winnipeg

Huskey, L., and T.A. Morehouse. 1992. Development in Remote Regions: What Do We Know? *Arctic* 45:128-37

Hydro-Québec 1993. *Grande-Baleine Complex, Feasibility Study: Summary.* Montreal: Hydro-Québec

Independent Commission on International Humanitarian Issues (ICIHI). 1987. *Indigenous Peoples: A Global Quest for Justice.* Reading, GB: Cox and Wyman

James Bay and Northern Québec Native Harvesting Research Committee (JB&NQNHRC). 1982. *The Wealth of the Land: Wildlife Harvests by the James Bay Cree, 1972-73 to 1978-79*. Québec City: JB&NQNHRC

–. 1988. *Final Report: Research to Establish Present Levels of Harvesting for the Inuit of Northern Québec 1976-1980*. Québec City: JB&NQNHRC

Kayahna Tribal Council. 1985. *The Kayahna Region Land Utilization and Occupancy Study*. Toronto: University of Toronto Press and Kayahna Tribal Area Council

Kerr, A.J. 1950. Subsistence and Social Organization in a Fur Trade Community. Anthropological report on the Ruperts House Indians presented to National Committee for Community Health Studies, Ottawa

Kinloch, D., and H.V. Kuhnlein. 1988. Assessment of PCBs in Arctic Foods and Diets. *Arctic Medical Research* 47, supplement 1:159-62

McCutcheon, S. 1991. *Electric Rivers: The Story of the James Bay Project*. Montreal: Black Rose Books

McDonald, M. 1993. An Aboriginal Understanding of the Area. Special issue: Focus on the Hudson Bay Bioregion. *Canadian Water Watch* 6 (7-8):5-6

McDonald, M., L. Arrangutainaq, and Z. Novalinga. 1995. *A TEKMS Overview for Assessment of Cumulative Impacts in Hudson Bay, Parts 1 and II*. Environmental Committee of Sanikiluaq, Municipality of Sanikiluaq, Hudson Bay Programme. Ottawa: Canadian Arctic Resources Committee

McMillan, A.D. 1988. *Native Peoples and Cultures of Canada*. Winkler, MB: D.W. Friesen

Malouf, A.H. 1973. *Le Baie James indienne. Texte intégral du jugement du juge Albert Malouf*. Montréal: Editions du jour

Manitoba Keewatinowi Okimakanak (MKO). 1993. *Denesuliné Néné and Nunavut, A Boundary Dispute: A Study of Manitoba Denesuline Land Use, Occupancy and Habitation*. Thompson, MB: MKO

Moore, P.E., H.D. Kruse, F.F. Tisdall, and R.S.C. Corrigan. 1946. Medical Survey of Nutrition among the Northern Manitoba Indians. *Canadian Medical Association Journal* 54:223-33

Müller-Wille, L. 1992. Nunavik: Land and People, Places and Names. In *Wrapped in the Colours of the Earth*, 89-103. Cultural Heritage of the First Nations. Montreal: McCord Museum of Canadian History

National Atlas of Canada, 5th ed. 1991. *Canadian Indian Treaties*. Ottawa: Geographical Services Division, Canada Centre for Mapping, Energy, Mines and Resources Canada

Northern Manitoba Economic Development Commission (NMEDC). 1992. *Northern Manitoba: A Benchmark Report*. Winnipeg: Manitoba Department of Northern Affairs

–. 1993. *Sustainable Economic Development: A Plan for Action for Northern Manitoba*. Winnipeg: Manitoba Department of Northern Affairs

Northern Village of Pinehouse (NVP). 1987. Pinehouse Planning Project Technical Appendix 1: Bush Harvest Surveys. Pinehouse, Saskatchewan

Ohmagari, K. 1995. Transmission of Indigenous Knowledge among Cree Indian Women of Northern Canada. *Indigenous Knowledge and Development Monitor* 3 (1):27

Ontario Ministry of Natural Resources (OMNR). 1985. Moosonee District background information document. Ministry of Natural Resources, Moosonee

Osherenko, G. 1988. Wildlife Management in the North American Arctic: The Case for Co-management. In *Traditional Knowledge and Renewable Resource Management in Northern Regions,* edited by M.R. Freeman and L.N. Carbyn, 92-104. Edmonton: Boreal Institute for Northern Studies

Page, R. 1986. *Northern Development. The Canadian Dilemma.* Toronto: McClelland and Stewart

Pattimore, J.H. 1985. *Inuit Wildlife Harvest for 1984 in the Baffin Region.* Frobisher Bay, NWT: Baffin Region Inuit Association

Preston, R.J. 1975. *Cree Narrative: Expressing the Personal Meanings of Events.* Mercury Series, Canadian Ethnology Service Papers, 30. Ottawa: National Museum of Man

–. 1982. The Politics of Community Relocation: An Eastern Cree Example. *Culture* 2 (3):37-49

Quigley, N.C., and N.J. McBride 1987. The Structure of an Arctic Microeconomy: The Traditional Sector in Community Economic Development. *Arctic* 40:204-10

Ray, A.J. 1974. *Indians in the Fur Trade: Their Role as Hunters, Trappers and Middlemen in the Lands Southwest of Hudson Bay, 1660-1870.* Toronto: University of Toronto Press

–. 1990. *The Canadian Fur Trade in the Industrial Age.* Toronto: University of Toronto Press

Richardson, B. 1993. *People of Terra Nullius. Betrayal and Rebirth in Aboriginal Canada.* Vancouver and Toronto: Douglas and McIntyre

Riewe, R., ed. 1992. *Nunavut Atlas.* Edmonton: Canadian Circumpolar Institute and the Tungavik Federation of Nunavut

Rosenthal, J., and J. Beyea. 1989. *Long-Term Threats to Canada's James Bay from Human Development.* New York: National Audubon Society

Salisbury, R.F. 1986. *A Homeland for the Cree: Regional Development in James Bay, 1971-1981.* Montreal and Kingston: McGill-Queen's University Press

Scott, C. 1982. Production and Exchange among Wemindji Cree: Egalitarian Ideology and Economic Base. *Culture* 2 (3):51-64

–. 1986. Hunting Territories, Hunting Bosses and Communal Production among Coastal James Bay Cree. *Anthropologica* 28 (1-2):163-73

–. 1988. Property, Practice and Aboriginal Rights among Quebec Cree Hunters. In *Hunters and Gatherers 2: Property, Power and Ideology,* edited by T. Ingold et al., 35-51. New York: St. Martin's Press

–. 1989. Knowledge Construction among Cree Hunters: Metaphors and Literal Understanding. *Journal de la Société des Américanistes* 75:193-208

Scott, C., and H.A. Feit. 1992. *Income Security for Cree Hunters: Ecological, Social and Economic Effects.* Montreal: McGill Programme in the Anthropology of Development

Sly, P.G. 1994. *Human Impacts on the Hudson Bay Region, Its Present State and Future Environmental Concerns.* Ottawa: Canadian Arctic Resources Committee

Stenbaek, M. 1987. Forty Years of Cultural Change among the Inuit in Alaska, Canada and Greenland: Some Reflections. *Arctic* 40:300-9

Stock, K. 1996. Mapping the Traditional Land Use of the Waterhen First Nation. University of Manitoba, Winnipeg. Typescript

Tanner, A. 1979. *Bringing Home Animals*. London: Hurst

Thompson, J.E., and W.A. Hutchison. 1989. *Resource Use by Native and Non-Native Hunters of the Ontario Hudson Bay Lowland*. Moosonee: Ontario Ministry of Natural Resources

Tobias, T.N., and J.J. Kay. 1994. The Bush Harvest in Pinehouse, Saskatchewan, Canada. *Arctic* 47:207-21

Traditional Ecological Knowledge Management Systems (TEKMS). 1994. *Hudson Bay Traditional Ecological Knowledge and Management Systems Study*. Proceedings of the second workshop, February, Hull, Québec

Usher, P.J. 1976. The Evaluation of Country Food in the Northern Native Economy. *Arctic* 29:105-20

–. 1978. A Reply to J.C. Stabler's Critique of the Report of the Mackenzie Valley Pipeline Inquiry. *Musk-Ox* 21:90-1

–. 1981. Sustenance or Recreation? The Future of Native Wildlife Harvesting in Northern Canada. In *Renewable Resources and the Economy of the North*, edited by M.M.R. Freeman, 56-71. Ottawa: Association of Canadian Universities for Northern Studies and Canada Man and the Biosphere Programme

–. 1987. Indigenous Management Systems and the Conservation of Wildlife in the Canadian North. *Alternatives: Perspectives on Society, Technology and Environment* 14 (1):3-9

–. 1989. Towards a Strategy for Supporting the Domestic Economy of the Northwest Territories. Background study prepared for the NWT Legislative Assembly's Special Committee on the Northern Economy, Yellowknife

–. 1990. Recent and Current Land Use and Occupancy in the Northwest Territories by Chipewyan-Denesoline Bands (Saskatchewan Athabasca Region). Report, Office of the Prince Albert Tribal Council

–. 1991. Some Implications of the *Sparrow* Judgment for Resource Conservation and Management. *Alternatives: Perspectives on Society, Technology and Environment* 18 (2):20-1

Usher, P.J., and M.S. Weinstein. 1991. Towards Assessing the Effects of Lake Winnipeg Regulation and Churchill River Diversion on Resource Harvesting in Native Communities in Northern Manitoba. *Canadian Technical Report of Fisheries and Aquatic Sciences* no. 1794

Vivian, R.P., C. McMillan, P.E. Moore, E.C. Robertson, W.H. Sebrell, F.F. Tisdall, and W.G. McIntosh. 1948. The Nutrition and Health of the James Bay Indian. *Canadian Medical Association Journal* 59 (6):505-18

Wagner, M.W. 1984. Postimpoundment Change in the Financial Performance of the Southern Indian Lake Commercial Fishing. *Canadian Journal of Fisheries and Aquatic Sciences* 41:715-19

–. 1985. *TARR Centre Domestic Harvesting Survey*. Winnipeg: Treaty and Aboriginal Rights Research Centre of Manitoba

Waldram, J.B. 1988. *As Long as the Rivers Run: Hydroelectric Development and Native Communities in Western Canada*. Winnipeg: University of Manitoba Press

Weinstein, M.S. 1976. *What the Land Provides*. Montreal: Grand Council of the Crees (of Québec)

Wenzel, G. 1991. *Animal Rights, Human Rights: Ecology, Economy and Ideology in the Canadian Arctic.* London and Toronto: Belhaven Press and University of Toronto Press

World Commission on Environment and Development (WCED). 1987. *Our Common Future – Report of the World Commission on Environment and Development.* Oxford: Oxford University Press

Assessing Progress

10

A Systemic Approach to Assessing Progress toward Sustainability

R.A. (Tony) Hodge

This chapter describes a systemic framework that can serve as an organizing template for assessing and reporting on progress toward sustainability. With such a framework indicators emerge naturally, appropriately honed to the needs of a given locale or a given set of decisionmakers. In the absence of such a framework, choice of key indicators among the many possible occurs in a vacuum and the results are ad hoc, reactive to current concerns, and potentially an impediment to anticipatory thinking. The adjective 'systemic' denotes 'of or concerning a system as a whole.' Over the past several decades, there has been a marked shift in systems thinking from optimization of ideal systems with well-defined objectives to emphasis on systemic processes of learning related to problems or issues with ill-defined objectives. This shift has facilitated the use of systems thinking in analysis of complex, ill-defined, real situations. (See Checkland and Scholes 1990 and Goldberg 1989 for interesting discussions of this topic). The difficult issue of assessing progress toward sustainability falls well within the bounds of this latter category of problems. At the core of the challenge lies the need to go beyond reaction to today's concerns in a way that anticipates and deals with issues before they becomes crises.

The chapter begins by identifying the purposes of assessing and reporting on progress toward sustainability. Seven building blocks are offered to guide development of the proposed approach. The discussion then addresses various topics that provide a transition from theory to practice. The debate over the feasibility of identifying a short list of key indicators in the form of a report card is examined next. Lastly, a generic table of contents for assessing progress toward sustainability is listed. The chapter draws heavily on Hodge (1993; 1994; 1995) and NRTEE (1993).

The Purpose of the Proposed Reporting System

The purposes of a system of reporting on progress toward sustainability are captured in a general goal and five objectives. The goal is to improve the way that decisions are made: to support informed and responsible decision-making and decision-making processes. The objectives are:

(1) to communicate key signals to targeted decisionmakers, in particular to give early warning signals for required policy, institutional, and behavioural change
(2) to ensure accountability
(3) to encourage initiative by giving credit where credit is due
(4) to identify knowledge gaps and to facilitate setting priorities for filling these gaps
(5) to provide a systemic framework for designing and staffing research in support of assessment of progress toward sustainability and ultimately for determining the organization and content of the final assessment report.

Building Blocks

Seven necessary building blocks provide the foundation for the proposed system. Ultimately it is most important that the subject of each building block be explicitly addressed, not that the particular descriptions offered here are taken as written in stone. Changes in any one of these will cause a change in the final system design. The seven are: definition of terms, a value base, an overall goal, a set of principles, a conceptual framework, strategic reporting elements, and the linkage of the goal to the framework.

Definitions

Working definitions of sustainability and sustainable development are required. In this work, sustainability is defined as the persistence over an apparently indefinite future of certain necessary and desired characteristics of both the ecosystem and the human sub-system within (modified from Robinson et al. 1990). It is a normative concept. Thus, the choice and the degree to which specific characteristics are to be sustained will depend on the operating set of values.

Sustainable development is the human and most importantly, the *action* part of this set of ideas; it covers what people do and how they do it. People should take actions leading to development that meets the needs of the present without compromising the ability of future generations to meet their own needs (WCED 1987, 8). Conversely, actions that reduce the ability of future generations to meet their own needs should be eliminated. The term development is taken to mean the expansion or realization of potentialities, bringing something – whether an individual, a corporation, a community, or a country – gradually to a fuller, greater, or better state (Daly 1989, 4). It has both qualitative and quantitative characteristics and is to be differentiated from growth, which applies to a quantitative increase in the physical dimensions of the subject (NRTEE 1993, 10).

Strictly speaking, it would be possible to differentiate a system of reporting on sustainable development from a system of reporting on sustainability. Because people are part of the ecosystem, however, it makes little sense to do so.

Value Base
An operating value base should be explicitly described. In this work, the value base is best described as concern and respect for the ecosystem and the people within: not for one or the other, not for one more than the other, but for both together.

Overall Goal
With the value base in place, an overall goal for achieving progress toward sustainability can be articulated: to maintain or improve human and ecosystem well-being. The form of this goal is chosen to provide internal consistency with the statement of underlying values as well as the system description that governs the conceptual framework.

Principles or Value-driven Design Criteria
To bring the above general concepts from theory to practice, a set of operating principles emerges for governing policy development, decision-making, and in particular monitoring, assessing, and reporting on progress. These are as follows:
- *Time horizon.* A time horizon should be used that captures both human (short-term) and ecosystem (short- and long-term) time scales.
- *Space.* A spatial frame of reference should be used for assessing actions and decisions that includes the full extent of affected ecosystems.
- *Whole system.* Individual ecosystem components such as air, groundwater, surface water, soil, fauna, flora, and so on should be considered not only independently but also within the context of the connected ecosystem.
- *Imposed stress.* The complete range of chemical, physical, and biologi-

cal stress on the ecosystem should be addressed, including naturally occurring stress and that imposed by human activities.

- *Valuation of human activity.* All aspects of the value of human activity should be considered.
- *Anticipation.* An anticipatory perspective should be adopted that might include predicting implications for the very short term, building scenarios to extend options for dealing with uncertainty, and backcasting.
- *Uncertainty.* Uncertainty should be accepted as inevitable and considered in decision-making.
- *Values.* The existence of alternative and changing values should be recognized with implications for both setting standards and evaluating progress.
- *Distribution of costs, benefits, and participation in decision-making.* Central to policy development and decision-making should be the distribution among different social groups of environmental, economic, social, and cultural costs and benefits, and participation in decision-making that affects their lives.
- *Quantitative and qualitative measures.* Quantitative and qualitative measures should be used, drawing on both objective and subjective information. Intuitive understanding based on experience of everyday life, including experience gained from subsistence and traditional lifestyles, is included in the latter (modified from Hodge 1995, 75; NRTEE 1993, 14).

Conceptual Framework
The conceptual framework proposed in this chapter reflects the underlying value base, is consistent with systems theory, and draws on insights from state-of-environment reporting, macro-economics, and roughly thirty theoretical treatments of the human-ecosystem relationship (see Hodge 1995). This approach is motivated by a belief that any successful conceptual approach must be built on the common insights of many others, and represents an attempt to apply Rawls's idea of 'overlapping consensus' (1987). Rawls points out that a consensus affirmed by opposing theoretical, religious, philosophical, and moral doctrines is likely to be both just and resilient. Public policy based on overlapping consensus is therefore more likely to thrive over generations.

Drawing from all of the above leads to the following evolution of ideas. Figure 10.1A is a simple schematic showing the ecosystem and the human sub-system within. Figure 10.1B shows a conceptual split, thus enabling illustration of the interaction between the two. Figure 10.1B can be considered a 'free-body diagram,' a technique used in applied mechanics. It is an analytic convenience and does not mean that people are considered as separate from the ecosystem. Figure 10.1B provides a model of the physical system that must be dealt with by any system of reporting on sustainability. This must be conceptually linked to human decision-making in a way that allows practical definition of the elements of a reporting system, a step taken in Figure 10.1C. Figure 10.1 provides the core conceptual framework for this work.

Strategic Reporting Elements
From the framework shown in Figure 10.1, four strategic elements emerge as areas of diagnosis, or indicators domains, in the reporting system. They are:

- *Domain 1: Ecosystem.* Data and information facilitating an assessment of the integrity and health of the ecosystem.
- *Domain 2: Interaction.* Data and information facilitating an assessment of the interaction between people and the ecosystem: how and to what extent human activities contribute to provision of basic human needs and the quality of life; how these activities are valued; how these actions impose stress or contribute to restoring the ecosystem; and how successful we have been at meeting the goals and objectives of policies, regulations, and legislation.
- *Domain 3: People.* Data and information facilitating an assessment of the well-being of people – individuals and their families, communities, and the institutions they create to achieve their goals – including consideration of the range of physical, social, cultural, and economic attributes.
- *Domain 4: Synthesis.* Data and information facilitating recognition of emergent system properties and providing an integrated perspective for decision-making and anticipatory analysis that spans Domains 1, 2, and 3. (Hodge 1995, 80)

Each domain spans a complex set of data and related interpretive information. Together they provide a template to be used in developing a reporting system for different decision-making groups in society: individuals, communities, corporations, regions, provinces or states, nations, and so on. The reporting elements provide an effective organizational template because

- they are directly linked to the goal of achieving progress toward sustainability

Figure 10.1

Conceptual framework

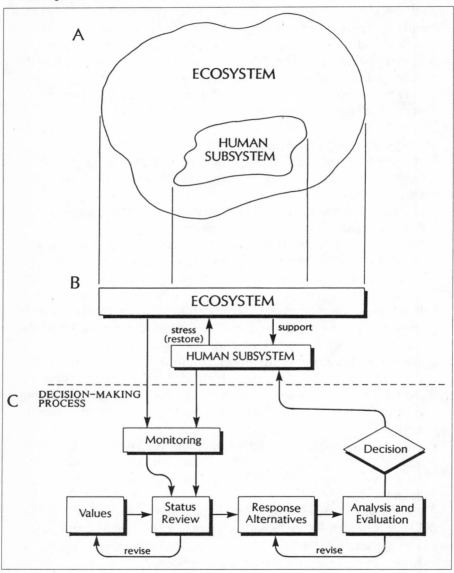

Source: Hodge (1995)

- they are conceptually simple, clear, and understandable
- they reflect the system being considered
- they keep the focus where it needs to be, on people and the ecosystem
- they allow a degree of compartmentalization that is useful for strategic thinking within the concept of a whole system.

Linking the Overall Goal to the Framework

Practical assessment must begin by defining general goals that provide a framework for subsequent identification of specific measurable objectives. The following domain-specific goals are derived from an expression of the overall goal in terms of the four strategic reporting elements. In each case, the goal provides a test to be applied against data compiled in each domain to assess whether or not progress is being achieved:

- Domain 1 goal: to maintain or improve ecosystem health and integrity
- Domain 2 goals: to increase the ability of human activities to support all aspects of human well-being, including economic, physical, social, and cultural attributes; to reduce the physical, chemical, and biological stress imposed on the ecosystem by human activities; and to increase the extent to which human activities restore ecosystem health and integrity
- Domain 3 goal: to maintain or improve human well-being
- Domain 4 goal: to maintain or improve human and ecosystem well-being overall.

The above goals are supported by a large number of specific measurable objectives that apply to each system element.

From Theory to Practice

The Use of Narration

The first step in any process of assessing progress toward sustainability is examination of the long-term social and ecological history of a community or jurisdiction. This provides a natural opportunity to include a broad range of citizens in the assessment process; they are the repository of the collective sense of the history that needs exploring. Telling their story allows us to identify trends that are important to the sustainability question. This approach draws from the practical maxim developed by Richard Neustadt and Ernest May in their analysis of the use of history in policy analysis: if you want to find out what the problem is, 'don't ask "What's the problem?" ask, "What's the story?" – that way you'll find out what the problem really is' (Neustadt and May 1986, 274, 106).

Focus on Decisionmakers

Within any society, different groups of decisionmakers are entrenched in cultures that are characterized in terms of values, motivation, and needs. Thus, corporate culture can be differentiated from, for example, bureaucratic culture, which in turn is different from the culture of academics, and so forth. To be broadly applied, the system of reporting must be sensitive to these different cultures and tailored to the needs of different decision-making groups. The following four groups are probably the most significant in Canadian society:

(1) individuals, families, and households
(2) corporations and corporate groupings
(3) communities and settlements
(4) regional, provincial, territorial, and federal governments

This choice is pragmatic, although it can be seen as an extension of the three components of the conventional model of the market economy: firms, households, and government.

The Boundaries Issue

Ecosystems defined or bounded by *natural* characteristics, such as a drainage basin or forest limit, rarely coincide with political jurisdictions or areas defined in law by ownership. Lack of such concurrence of boundaries often causes discordance between ecosystem functions and human decision-making. From a reporting perspective, this creates the need for 'multiple boundaries,' superimposing the area that is the focus of study (boundary 1) on the 'n' implicated ecosystems or political jurisdictions (boundaries 2 to n). Explicit recognition of multiple boundaries in the reporting system encourages decisionmakers to consider implications beyond their immediate responsibility.

These additional boundaries can be difficult to define. Air emissions can travel hundreds of kilometres a day. 'Particulate life' can be five to ten days, as it is for PCBs, and deposition in water can be followed by revolatization, with the contaminant continuing its global journey (Summers and Young 1987). Migrating wildlife can also traverse vast areas and physical, chemical, or biological stress imposed in one part of the world can significantly affect the food web in another.

The relationship between human activities in one jurisdiction or ecosystem and their implications on environmental and social conditions in other jurisdictions or ecosystems can be complex. These kinds of implications for international trade have only recently been given attention (e.g., WCED [1987], ch. 3). Reporting is pivotal to a large number of related issues, including international regulation of resource use, trade in endangered species, subsidies, environmental requirements in foreign investment, transfer of environmentally friendly technologies, enforcement, and dispute resolution. On a more local but equally crucial scale, Rees's approach to calculating the 'ecological footprint' of urban areas – the extent of ecological carrying capacity of areas beyond urban boundaries that are implicated by urban activities – provides another important perspective (Rees 1992).

Most important is that the differences between the boundaries of decision-making jurisdictions and natural ecosystems be recognized and an attempt made to deal with the implications. With computerized geographic information systems, portrayal of data and related analyses dealing with such boundary problems is now more possible than ever before.

Classifying and Valuing Human Activities

An essential starting point for dealing with human activities is provided by the Standard Industrial Classification (SIC), which is structured by activities, and the valuation of human activities developed through the System of National Accounts (SNA), which uses the SIC as an organizing template. The following three observations are offered in support of this fact. First, the majority of human activities that are currently overstressing the environment are the ones driving the market system, the very activities described in the SIC. Second, the Statistics Canada database, compiled on the basis of the SIC, provides the most complete and long-term data available describing human activity. Third, because of their common use, the SIC categories are linked to current societal decision-making.

Nevertheless, in addition to activities driven by the market and measured in dollars, which the SIC captures, many other human activities both provide for human well-being and in the process stress the supporting ecosystem. These also require treatment. Important examples of activities not adequately described through the SIC include: non-wage household and home operation, maintenance, and improvement; childcare and rearing, most of it carried out by women; voluntary activities; subsistence activities; and illegal and black-market activities of the underground economy. The value of non-wage household activities may be as high as 53 per cent of GNP (Adler and Hawrylyshyn 1978; Waring 1988), although a more common estimate is roughly one-third (Burns 1975). Recent work in Canada suggests a range of 32 to 39 per cent (Jackson 1992). Statistics Canada estimates that for 1986-7, 5.3 million Canadians were involved in volunteer work, which was valued at $12 billion using an average service sector wage (Ross 1990).

The extent and value of subsistence activities is considerably greater in rural areas than in urban. In a country such as Canada their overall contribution to wealth may be small but in rural areas, especially in the North, their significance to the quality of life is large (YTG 1988, 52-3; Usher and Staples 1988; Victor 1990).

In addition to both market and non-market human activities, several 'useful combinations' of activities deserve careful consideration for policy purposes. Obvious examples are energy production, transportation, and use; water use and distribution; tourism and recreation; and generation of waste, accidents, and spills, and so on.

Many human activities not included in the SIC are studied by different groups of professionals, who group and classify data in ways that may or may not be compatible with the SIC. The lack of a common taxonomy is a major impediment to integrating different databases that contribute to current policy and decision-making. The standard activity classification (SAC) shown in Figure 10.2 is offered here to overcome this problem, at least conceptually.

In practice an initial crude assessment of the 'benefit' of human activities can be obtained by combining with 'employment' data the figures for value-added by industry, taken from the National Accounts,

Figure 10.2

General framework for a Standard Activity Classification

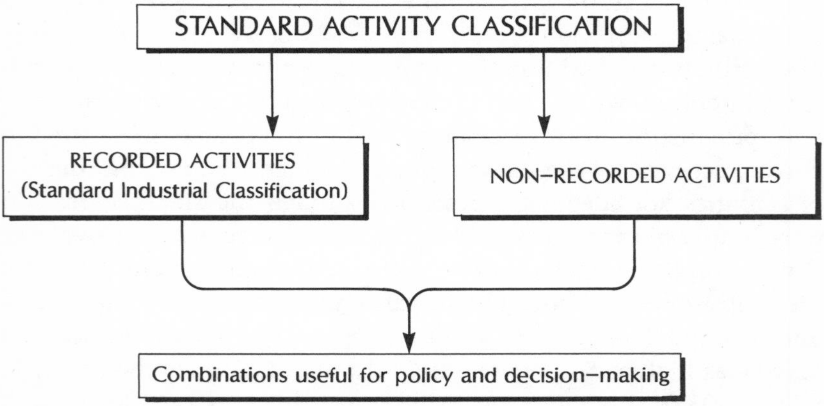

Source: Hodge (1995)

Provincial Accounts, or equivalent. Using such dollar assessments of value-added as a surrogate for value is controversial. In addition to money-based assessments of value-added, time-based (Waring 1988), land-based, (Lands Directorate 1983), and energy-based (S. Holtz, personal communication) valuation approaches have been suggested for human activities.

The rationale for these alternative approaches centres on the need to be more sensitive to issues of ecosystem integrity, equity, and social justice. These concerns are often masked by the values driving contemporary macro-economic analysis. The topic remains unresolved and is a subject of current research. Unfortunately, while there is a vast literature regarding the 'value' of the environment, treatment of the value of human activities, except as it relates to pricing market activities, is sparse.

Stresses Imposed by Human Activities

Historically, we have been preoccupied with pollution, but human-induced stresses on the environment are significantly broader than emissions of chemicals. It is useful to differentiate five families of human-induced stress: (1) addition or loading of substances and heat; (2) physical restructuring and land use change; (3) harvest or extraction of renewable resources; (4) extraction of non-renewable resources; and (5) introduction of non-native species and genetic and other bio-technological manipulation. (See Hodge 1995 for a summary of work from Rapport and Friend 1979; Rapport 1983; Francis et al. 1985; Bird and Rapport 1986; Regier 1988; and Colborn et al. 1990). These stresses are usually imposed simultaneously and in a linked manner, making identification of specific causes and effects almost impossible except in rare cases. The uncertainty must be seen as a characteristic of contemporary decision-making, not as an impediment. The ecosystem itself integrates the effects of many simultaneously induced stresses, and it is to the ecosystem that we must turn for assessing cumulative effects. This emphasizes the usefulness of bio-indicators.

Nevertheless, identifying and assessing specific stresses induced by human activity is relatively straightforward. Management and reduction of those stresses is equally possible through specific action on the part of society. The relationship between stress reduction and explicit societal decision-making is the practical link that lies at the heart of the approach to assessing progress toward sustainability advocated in this chapter.

The five stress families are categorized in terms of physical, chemical, and biological categories in Table 10.1. Assessing individual human activities on the basis of physical, chemical, and biological stresses provides a simple and comprehensive approach to stress assessment. Such assessment is now undertaken as a requirement for development of most new major projects through the process and techniques of environmental impact assessment. Nonetheless, the stresses induced by ongoing, everyday human activities are probably more significant. It is the cumulative effect of these activities that dominates human influence on ecosystem conditions.

Table 10.1

Human activities grouped by physical, chemical, or biological imposed environmental stress

Induced stress type	Human activity
Physical	Physical restructuring
	Land use change
	Erosion and sedimentation
	Discharge of heat
	Noise
	Extraction of non-renewable resources
Chemical	Discharge of chemicals
Biological	Harvest of renewable resources
	Various forms of habitat disruption
	Accidental or planned introduction of non-native species
	Genetic and other biotechnological manipulation

Source: Hodge (1991, 16)

Mapping the Assessment Process

The four domains of the conceptual framework serve to define the content and limits of reporting on sustainability. Each domain consists of a hierarchy of indicator families ranging from the most general at the apex through a progressively finer level of detail to specific measures at the bottom. Sample hierarchies for each of the four domains, without particular measures, are shown in Figures 10.3, 10.4, 10.5, and 10.6 respectively.

An assessment hierarchy is a powerful tool. It provides a map of the assessment process and serves to show explicitly what factors are or are not being considered in the assessment process. Figure 10.3, for example, shows that to undertake a comprehensive assessment of the health

Figure 10.3

Assessment hierarchy domain 1: Ecosystem

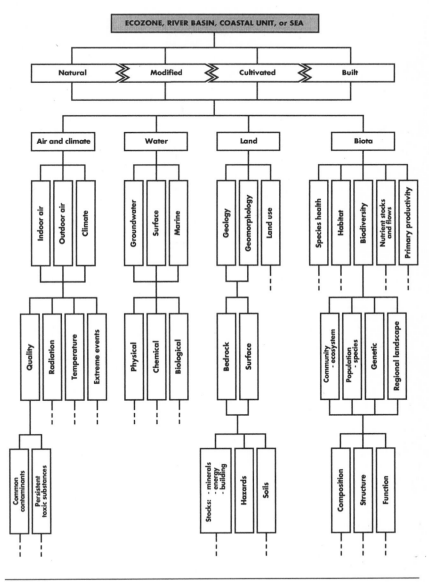

Source: Hodge (1995)

Figure 10.4

Assessment hierarchy domain 2: Interaction

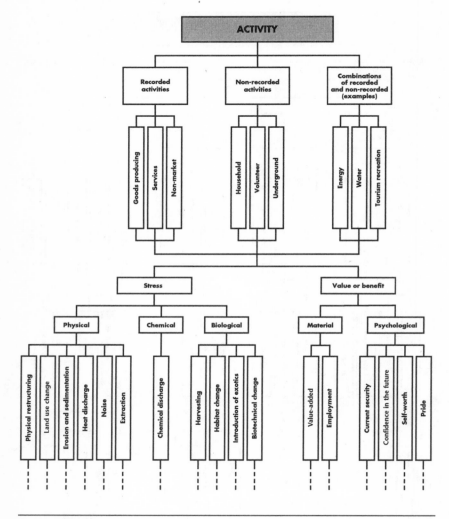

Source: Hodge (1995)

or integrity of a given ecozone or river basin, natural, modified, culti-
vated, and built sub-systems of the ecosystem must be considered.
Within each of these, air and climate, water, land, and biota must be assessed. To assess the water sub-system, groundwater, surface water, and

Figure 10.5

Assessment hierarchy domain 3: People

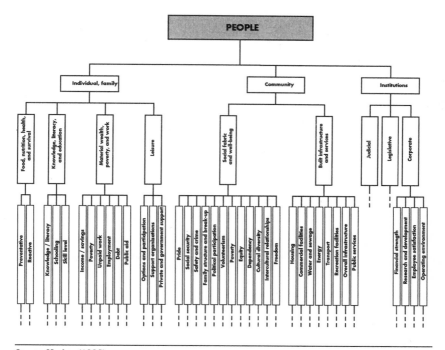

Source: Hodge (1995)

marine water require assessment. For each of these, further down the hierarchy at the more finely detailed level, water quality, quantity, and temperature would be factors. Within each of these, a large range of specific measures can potentially come into play.

Working in the other direction, the concentration of a given contaminant is an indicator of water quality. In turn, water quality is one of several indicators of the overall state of the water sub-system. The state of the water sub-system is an indicator of say, the modified component of the ecosystem that itself is an indicator of the overall health and integrity of the ecozone or river basin. The assessment process builds from specific measures to the apex, drawing on the best available knowledge.

The assessment hierarchies do not attempt to map lateral relationships between cells. They map the assessment process, not the system and are therefore not system models. This point must be emphasized.

Figure 10.6

Assessment hierarchy domain 4: Synthesis

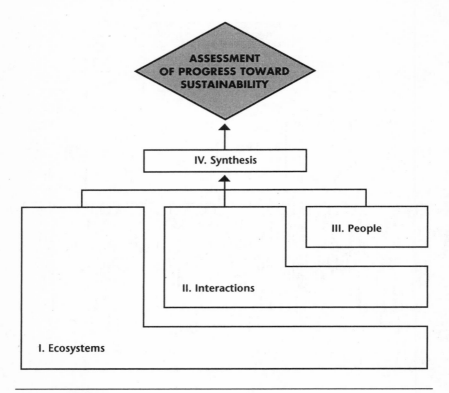

Source: Hodge (1995)

Further, the particular choice of classifications reflected in these assessment hierarchies is not unique. Experts on a given topic might well suggest modifications.

Indicators

An indicator is best described as

> a measurable descriptor, quantitative or qualitative, of normative interest which facilitates assessment of the past, current, or future state or performance of system constituent parts, controls, and feedback loops as well as the system as a whole.

In turn, indicators of sustainability ...
- are motivated by a parallel care and respect for people and the enveloping ecosystem now and in the future (the normative interest);
- facilitate assessment (past, current, future) of the system that spans the ecosystem, interactions, people, and the related decision-making system (Hodge 1995).

Indicators of sustainability should:
- be directly linked to specific objectives, which in turn are nested within general goals motivated by the concept of sustainability
- accurately and unambiguously reflect the degree to which the system component being measured meets the related objective
- be measurable and based on available and reasonably accurate data
- facilitate anticipatory action as well as analysis of past and present trends
- be sensitive to changes over time and space, and in the case of the human sub-system be sensitive to differences between sub-populations
- facilitate comparison of similar system components
- facilitate action to reinforce positive results and correct negative ones (Hodge 1995).

From time to time, a given indicator can be seen to fall into more than one assessment hierarchy. This is usually because it is a *direct* indicator in one and an *indirect* indicator in the other or others. An example is employment, an essential characteristic to monitor when assessing the value of human activity (Domain 2) and when assessing human well-being as well (Domain 3). In fact, employment is a *direct* measure of human activity (how many people are doing what) and only an *indirect* measure of well-being (the result of the job, not the activity itself).

Much care must be taken to recognize underlying assumptions when using indirect indicators. As an example, growth in energy consumption was enthusiastically supported for the first three-quarters of this century. During this period, energy use was often singled out as an indirect indicator of growth in economic activity. This was appropriate as long as a proportional relationship between the two variables existed. In the 1970s, the various energy crises and heightened sensitivity to the financial and environmental costs of energy production led to an uncoupling of the two. Increased energy use is no longer linked to economic growth. In fact, significant effort is now being directed to reduction of energy use. Energy content of economic activity (joules or barrels of oil equivalent per unit of GDP) is sometimes offered as an indirect indicator of energy use efficiency (Indicators Task Force 1991, 87; UNEP 1992, 380). This is only useful if macro-economic structure remains constant.

An additional example to note is the use of economic growth as an indicator of the depletion of natural resources. Through the past several centuries, growth in economic activity has been roughly proportional to the use of natural resources. Thus, extrapolated economic growth has been used as an indicator of future resource depletion, often serving as the basis for an expression of concern given the physical limits of many natural resources. If, however, greater value is assigned to the intellectual properties of human activities than has been historically the case, if the use of natural resources per unit of human activity decreases, if the level of human activities dependent on resources diminishes, or if population growth trends change, this relationship could dissolve, rendering the 'growth-no growth' economic debate obsolete.

Differentiation between direct and indirect indicators provides insight into the debate over the use of 'compound indicators,' or indices that depend on more than one variable. There are thousands of such indices associated with almost every aspect of numerically monitored human endeavour in specialized use. The aggregation process of developing any index must assign weight to the components. This entrenches a particular relationship between variables, setting the significance of each. If the assumed relationship is correct, such indices can be powerful. If the relationship changes, is not valid in the first place, or has important variables missing, indices can be misleading.

A particular problem arises when an index developed for one purpose becomes popularized and misused. The prime example applies to gross domestic product. Gross domestic product was developed as a measure of national income for use in analysis of national and government finances. It was never intended as a means to assess total welfare (Anderson 1991, 18). Yet growth in gross domestic product is popularly misused by politicians and the news media as a general indicator of national welfare. In using any index, care must be taken to ensure that underlying assumptions are valid and that the components of an index respond to the question being posed (Ott 1979; Smith et al. 1993, 161-2).

Standards, Criteria, and Targets
While goals and specific objectives provide the overall framework for assessment, standards and criteria provide the comparative mechanism for assessing any given indicator at the most detailed level. A standard usually enjoys some elevated status: if incorporated within a formal reg-

ulation it can have the weight of law. A standard sets a minimum or maximum value that must be achieved. Criteria are not entrenched in law but can carry significant weight. They are usually expressed as a desirable minimum or maximum. A hierarchy of potential criteria exists: state at a point in time; change of state, or trend; and rate of change of state, or change in trend. The setting of standards and criteria is dynamic. As values change and scientific knowledge increases, assessment standards and criteria inevitably evolve, although there is always some time lag.

Few indicators have set standards or criteria that facilitate assessment. Recourse to an interpreted set of goals and objectives is therefore necessary. Thus, assessments must depend on judgments based on the best available data, experience, and, frequently, intuition. Under these circumstances, one's operating value set determines assessment criteria.

Making Judgments

In coming to a judgment of progress, conflicting signals must be weighed and combined in some way. This is done either with mathematical models that apply weighting factors and aggregate data and information using formal rules or through some other process of judgment. All processes of judgment involve weighting factors although they are not always explicit.

One process is the 'weight-of-evidence' approach used every day in our courts of law. Its use as an approach to environmental assessment has been pioneered by the International Joint Commission in the Great Lakes basin ecosystem (IJC 1990, 1992, 1994). The approach is now being explicitly used in the assessment of priority substances under the Canadian Environmental Protection Act (CEPA Pulp Mill Effluents 1991; CEPA Cadmium 1994). Jerome Nriagu uses the approach in an assessment of heavy metals in the Canadian environment (1995).

Use of the 'weight-of-evidence' approach often causes discomfort for those schooled in reductionist science and technology. In a sense, it is an admission that the situation is imperfectly understood. Rather than rejecting the process, however, a preferred approach is to draw on the experience of our courts of law and instill a degree of rigour that validates it. A key aspect of so doing is to articulate the rationale for assessments clearly and explicitly. In this way, the result can be scrutinized, tested, and modified as new information becomes available.

Designing a Report Card

Much of the recent interest in indicators has been motivated by a desire to identify a small group of key indicators of sustainability that provide a report card for effectively monitoring and communicating progress. This interest is subject to a long-standing debate between government policymakers on the one hand and scientists on the other. The former, faced with a responsibility to account to the public for government activity, argue that a few simple indicators are required to monitor and communicate progress on public policy issues. The latter, understanding the complexity of the systems being monitored, are resistant to building simple indicators on assumed causal relationships that are weak at best. Furthermore, the process of peer review that is engrained in every scientist demands transparency in data measurement and interpretation, which is often side-stepped by the 'nutshell' information sought by policymakers (Bartelmus 1994, 5).

The issue is complicated by the fact that the ecosystem and the human sub-system are dynamic: what is considered a critical sustainability concern today will inevitably be overtaken by other issues and concerns tomorrow. This is the nature of change and growth.

There is no simple, universal right in this matter. Certain key issues may appropriately dominate public policy in any given political jurisdiction and at any given time. It may be entirely possible to capture the essence of progress related to these issues in a few simple measures that aid both monitoring and communicating processes. Such measures fall at or near the bottom of the assessment hierarchies shown in Figures 10.3 to 10.5. Good examples are found in the work of Canada's Indicators Task Force (1991), the Dutch work so well illustrated by Adriaanse (1993), and the Sustainable Seattle initiative (1993). A simple approach is particularly powerful when the relationship of cause and effect that frames a certain issue can be identified, accurately described, and linked to a specific public policy initiative. In such a case, the success of the policy can be tracked and communicated to both the public and decision-makers. Unfortunately, cases in which this approach applies are rare. Further, there is some danger that by locking interest to a specific current concern, the use of such simple indicators can inhibit anticipatory thinking.

A more generally applicable approach, and the one followed by the British Columbia Round Table on the Environment and the Economy in its recent report on Urban Sustainability (1994), is to develop a report card based on aggregated categories that lie at or near the top of the assessment hierarchies. While it might be possible to apply numerical analysis in the aggregation process, it would be difficult and the results would be suspect. Insights are brought to bear not only from *measure-*

ment of state, trends, and changes in trends where possible but also from intuitive knowledge and professional judgment. Further, elements contributing to the aggregation process are rarely compatible in terms of units, and an exact weighting relationship is rarely agreed upon. From a statistical perspective, aggregations involve not only apples and oranges but a large variety of vegetables and soil as well, even though they all contribute to conditions and trends in the garden.

Rather than engaging in rigorous numerical tracking, a report card synthesizes a large number of often conflicting factors. A general application of the weight of evidence assigns trends to particular categories. Only some of the contributing factors enjoy established standards or criteria. Often factors are assessed using a weight-of-evidence rationale and applying the assessor's general sense of progress.

Table 10.2 provides a generic list of aggregated indicators and the associated goal. Each of the indicators is the result of a broad synthesis of signals. In turn, the result of each assessment serves as an indicator contributing to the even more aggregated assessment of progress toward sustainability that is completed in the final Domain 4 synthesis. Together, these seven aggregates are a powerful set of sustainability indicators. Each is complex, occupying a position high up on the assessment hierarchy – at the top of each of Domains 1, 2, and 3 – and supported by often conflicting data sets. They form a useful report card for summarizing progress toward sustainability.

Associated with any one of the seven aggregates listed above, may be a symbolic, simple indicator. Fish returns, an indicator in use by Sustainable Seattle, 1993, might be an example. While it may be useful to signal conditions of the aquatic ecosystem, however, such an indicator says little about terrestrial vegetation and air, and we thus see its limits. It is only through trial and error that symbolic indicators might emerge.

Proposed Table of Contents

Synthesis of the above ideas leads to a seven-part generic table of contents:

(1) Introduction
(2) Telling the story
(3) Assessing ecosystem well-being
(4) Assessing what people do
(5) Assessing human well-being
(6) Toward sustainability: Assessing the balance
(7) A look to the future

Table 10.2

Generic report card listing

		Responds to the question...
	Domain 1: Ecosystem	
1	Ecosystem well-being	Is ecosystem health and integrity being maintained or improved?
	Domain 2: Interaction	
2	Economic success	Is economic success being maintained or improved?
3	Contribution of non-monitored activities	Are other non-recorded activities (e.g., household and volunteer activities) as effective now as historically at contributing to human well-being?
4	Imposed environmental stress	Are the physical, chemical, biological, and combined stresses imposed on the ecosystem by human activity diminishing?
5	Restoration	Are more or fewer resources now directed at ecosystem restoration than previously?
	Domain 3: People	
6	Human well-being	Is human well-being being maintained or improved?
	Domain 4: Synthesis	
7	Synthesis	Taken together, do the responses to the above six questions suggest progress toward sustainability or not, and what are the implications for the future?

The proposed structure is driven not by issues but by systems. It draws on a set of values based on care and respect for people and the ecosystem together and equally. Its strength is its capacity to assume an holistic and anticipatory perspective. The labels are not essential, but the range and content of topics are.

The approach starts with a narration of the story of the community, region, or political jurisdiction being considered. Parts 3 and 5 force a review that spans ecosystem and human conditions. These two sections can be thought of as providing results or effects. They appropriately bracket part 4, which focuses on human activities. The emphasis is crucial because human activity is the motor of both positive and negative change and is controlled or modified by human decision-making through our laws, regulations, and unwritten systems of rules. This point deserves emphasis: we do not manage the ecosystem; we manage human activities that subsequently interact with the ecosystem, causing change. Part 6 then provides an opportunity to stand back and look at the whole system, to identify emergent properties, and to make a judgment about current trends in progress that spans the entire range of topics previously addressed. If long-term progress toward the stated goals is not being achieved as reflected in the responses to each of the seven questions posed in Table 10.2, overall progress toward sustainability cannot be said to be occurring. Lastly, part 7 is a reflection on the future. This discussion can be simple or sophisticated, depending on what kinds of analytical tools are brought to bear.

Three general approaches can be taken. First, over the very short term – a year or two – predictions can be made with some degree of confidence. Second, over the medium term, it is useful to develop a set of reasonable scenarios that attempt to bracket possible future outcomes together. In this way, one can hope for the best while preparing for the worst. Third, the most powerful anticipatory thinking emerges when future desired conditions are identified and the policy steps to get there are 'backcast' to the present. A policy path is thus established that takes society toward a desired future.

The idea that humankind should move toward an 'anticipatory and preventative' stance from one that is 'reactive and curing' is the dominant theme of the report of the World Commission on Environment and Development (WCED 1987). Anticipatory thinking lies at the heart of the sustainability concept that is put into operational terms by the approach to reporting on progress reflected in the generic structures proposed here.

References

Adler, H.J., and O. Hawrylyshyn. 1978. Estimates of the Value of Household Work, Canada, 1961 and 1971. *The Review of Income and Wealth* 24 (December 1978):333-55

Adriaanse, A. 1993. *Environmental Policy Performance Indicators – A Study of Indicators for Environmental Policy in the Netherlands.* The Hague: Sdu Uitgeverij Koninginnegracht

Anderson, V. 1991. *Alternative Economic Indicators.* London: Routledge

Bartelmus, P. 1994. *Towards a Framework for Indicators of Sustainable Development*. Working paper series No. 7. New York: United Nations, Department for Economic and Social Information and Policy Analysis (DESIPA)

British Columbia Round Table on the Environment and the Economy. (BCRTEE). 1994. *State of Sustainability: Urban Sustainability and Containment*. Victoria: BCRTEE

Burns, S. 1975. *The Household Economy*. Boston: Beacon Press

Bird, P.M., and D.J. Rapport. 1986. *State of the Environment Report for Canada*. Ottawa: Environment Canada

Canadian Environmental Protection Act (CEPA) Pulp Mill Effluents. 1991. *Effluent from Pulp Mills Using Bleaching. Assessment Report, Canadian Environmental Protection Act*. Ottawa: Environment Canada

Canadian Environmental Protection Act (CEPA) Cadmium. 1994. *Cadmium and Its Compounds. Assessment Report, Canadian Environmental Protection Act*. Ottawa: Environment Canada

Checkland, P., and J. Scholes. 1990. *Soft Systems Methodology in Action*. Chichester, UK: John Wiley

Colborn, T.E., A. Davidson, S.N. Green, R.A. (Tony) Hodge, C. Ian Jackson, and R.A. Liroff. 1990. *Great Lakes, Great Legacy?* Washington, DC, and Ottawa: The Conservation Foundation and The Institute for Research on Public Policy

Daly, H.E. 1989. Sustainable Development: From Concept and Theory towards Operational Principles. Paper presented at Hoover Institution Conference, Population and Development Review. Also published in H. Daly. 1991. *Steady State Economics*, 2nd ed., 241-60. Washington, DC: Island Press

Francis, G.R., L. Grima, H. Regier, and T.H. Whillans. 1985. *A Prospectus for the Management of the Long Point Ecosystem*. Technical Report no. 43. Ann Arbor: Great Lakes Fishery Commission

Goldberg, M. 1989. *On Systemic Balance – Flexibility and Stability in Social, Economic, and Environmental Systems*. New York: Praeger Press

Hodge, R.A. 1991. Towards a Yukon SOE Reporting Framework. Prepared for Sustainable Development Committee, Yukon Council on Economy and Environment and the Department of Renewable Resources. Government of the Yukon, Whitehorse

–. 1993. *Reporting on Sustainable and Equitable Development – Project Paper no. 1, Conceptual Approach*. Ottawa: Evaluation Unit, Corporate Affairs and Initiatives Division, International Development Research Centre

–. 1994. A Systemic Approach to Assessing Progress toward Sustainability in the Fraser River Basin. Report prepared for the Fraser Basin Management Program, Vancouver, British Columbia

–. 1995. A Systemic Approach to Assessing Progress toward Sustainability. PhD dissertation, School of Urban Planning, Faculty of Engineering, McGill University, Montreal

Indicators Task Force. 1991. *A Report on Canada's Progress towards a National Set of Environmental Indicators*. SOE Report no. 91-1. Ottawa: State of Environment Reporting, Environment Canada

International Joint Commission (IJC). 1990. *Fifth Biennial Report on Great Lakes Water Quality*. Ottawa and Washington, DC: International Joint Commission

–. 1992. *Sixth Biennial Report on Great Lakes Water Quality.* Ottawa and Washington, DC: International Joint Commission

–. 1994. *Seventh Biennial Report on Great Lakes Water Quality.* Ottawa and Washington, DC: International Joint Commission

Jackson, C., 1992. The Value of Household Work in Canada, 1986. In *National Income and Expenditure Accounts.* Catalogue no. 13-001, First quarter, 1992, xxxiii-li. Ottawa: Statistics Canada and Ministry of Industry, Science and Technology

Lands Directorate. 1983. *Land Use Classification for Land Use Monitoring.* Working Paper no. 17, 1983 revision. Ottawa: Lands Directorate, Environment Canada

National Round Table on the Environment and the Economy (NRTEE). 1993. *Toward Reporting Progress on Sustainable Development in Canada – Report to the Prime Minister.* Ottawa: NRTEE

Neustadt, R., and E. May. 1986. *Thinking in Time.* New York: Free Press

Nriagu, Jerome O. 1995. *Origin, Long-Range Transport, Atmospheric Deposition and Associated Effects of Heavy Metals in the Canadian Environment.* Downsview, ON: Atmospheric Environment Services, Environment Canada

Ott, W. 1979. *Environmental Indices: Theory and Practice.* Ann Arbor: Science Publishers

Rapport, D. 1983. The Stress-Response Environmental Statistical System and Its Applicability to the Laurentian Lower Great Lakes. *Statistical Journal of the United Nations,* Economic Commission for Europe 1:377-405

Rapport, D., and A. Friend. 1979. *Towards a Comprehensive Framework for Environmental Statistics: A Stress-Response Approach.* Statistics Canada Catalogue no. 11-510. Ottawa: Supply and Services Canada

Rawls, J. 1987. The Idea of an Overlapping Consensus. *Oxford Journal of Legal Studies* 7 (1):1-25

Rees, W.E. 1992. Ecological Footprints and Appropriated Carrying Capacity – What Urban Economics Leaves Out. *Journal of Environment and Urbanization* 4 (2):121-30

Regier, H. 1988. *Generic Guidelines for the Review of Ecosystem Initiatives in the Great Lakes Basin.* Toronto: Institute of Environmental Studies, University of Toronto

Robinson, J.G., G. Francis, R. Legge, and S. Lerner. 1990. Defining a Sustainable Society: Values, Principles, and Definitions. *Alternatives: Perspectives on Society, Technology and Environment* 17 (2):36-46

Ross, D.P. 1990. *Economic Dimensions of Volunteer Work in Canada.* Ottawa: Supply and Services Canada and Department of the Secretary of State

Smith, K., J. Swisher, R. Kanter, and D.R. Ahuja. 1993. Indices for a Greenhouse Gas Control Regime: Incorporating Both Efficiency and Equity Goals. In *Energy Investments and the Environment – Selected Topics,* edited by C. Siddayao and L. Griffin, 157-238. Washington, DC: Economic Development Institute, World Bank

Summers, P.W., and J.W. Young. 1987. The 'Airshed' or 'Atmospheric Region of Influence' for the Great Lakes Basin. International Joint Commission Symposium, Towards Integrative Monitoring – A Great Lakes Perspective, 18 November, Toledo, Ohio

Sustainable Seattle. 1993. *Sustainable Seattle 1993. Indicators of Sustainable Community: A Report to Citizens on Long-term Trends in Our Community.* Seattle, Washington

United Nations Environment Programme (UNEP). 1992. *The World Environment, 1972-1992.* London and Nairobi: Chapman and Hall and United Nations Environment Programme

Usher, P., and L. Staples. 1988. Subsistence in the Yukon. Economic Development Department, Council for Yukon Indians, Whitehorse

Victor, P. 1990. *Supplementary Economic Accounts for the Yukon Territory.* Whitehorse: Bureau of Statistics Executive Council Office and the Department of Economic Development, Government of Yukon

Waring, M. 1988. *If Women Counted.* San Francisco: Harper Collins

World Commission on Environment and Development (WCED). 1987. *Our Common Future – Report of the World Commission on Environment and Development.* Oxford: Oxford University Press

Yukon Territorial Government (YTG). 1988. *Yukon Economic Strategy – Building the Future.* Whitehorse: Government of the Yukon

Contributors

Ann Dale is a senior associate with the Sustainable Development Research Institute at the University of British Columbia.

Fikret Berkes is a professor and the director of the Natural Resources Institute at the University of Manitoba.

Raymond Côté is an associate professor and the director of the School for Resource and Environmental Studies in the Faculty of Management at Dalhousie University.

Helen Fast is a research associate and PhD candidate at the Natural Resources Institute at the University of Manitoba.

George Francis is a professor in the Department of Environment and Resource Studies at the University of Waterloo.

Stuart B. Hill is chair of Social Ecology at the University of Western Sydney.

R.A. (Tony) Hodge is a consultant in Victoria, British Columbia.

Bonnie Kettel is a professor in the Faculty of Environmental Studies at York University.

Sally Lerner is a professor in the Department of Environment and Resource Studies at the University of Waterloo.

Marilyn MacDonald is a professor in the Department of Women's Studies at Simon Fraser University.

Deanna McLeod has been a research assistant with the Sustainable Development Research Institute at the University of British Columbia.

Thomas Plunkett has been an MBA student and research assistant in the Master of Business Administration Program at Dalhousie University.

John B. Robinson is the director of the Sustainable Development Research Institute and a professor in the Department of Geography, both at the University of British Columbia.

Barry Sadler is a student of the field of sustainable development and the director of the International Study of the Effectiveness of Environmental Assessment.

Ted Schrecker is the associate director of environmental ethics at the Westminster Institute for Ethics and Human Values in London, Ontario.

Caroline Van Bers is a senior associate with Dovetail Consulting in Vancouver, British Columbia.

Index

The Sustainable Development Research Institute at UBC was established in 1991 to initiate and contribute to interdisciplinary research on linkages between the environment, the economy, and social equity. It develops and coordinates sustainable development initiatives through applied, policy-relevant, and interdisciplinary research and encourages interdisciplinary collaboration. It is a regional link with government, the private sector, and other institutions across Canada. This first volume in the SDRI series has been made possible with the support and ongoing collaboration of the International Institute for Sustainable Development.

Sally Lerner, Department of Environment and Resource Studies, University of Waterloo

Stephen Lonergan, Centre for Sustainable Regional Development, University of Victoria

Tom Meredith, Centre for Society, Technology, and Development, McGill University

Paul Painchaud, Groupe d'études et de recherches sur les politiques environnementales (GERPE), Laval University

John T. Pierce, Community and Economic Development Centre, Simon Fraser University

John B. Robinson, Sustainable Development Research Institute, University of British Columbia

Bill Ross, Faculty of Environmental Design, University of Calgary

Rodney White, Institute for Environmental Studies, University of Toronto

Set in ITC Stone by Typeworks

Printed and bound in Canada by Friesens

Copy-editor: Camilla Jenkins

Proofreader: Gail Copeland

Indexer: Dianne Broad

Date Due

OCT 2 3 1998		
NOV 1 0 1998		
NOV		
DEC 1 1 1999		
DEC - 7 1999		
APR 1 3 2000		
APR - 2 2006		
MAR 3 0 2006		